THE LONDON HISTORY STUDIES

GENERAL EDITOR R. BEN JONES

The First Bourbon Century in France

W. E. BROWN M.A.

UNIVERSITY OF LONDON PRESS LTD

ISBN 0 340 07347 0

University of London Press Ltd
St Paul's House, Warwick Lane, London EC4

Printed and bound in Great Britain by
Hazell Watson & Viney Ltd, Aylesbury, Bucks

EDITOR'S INTRODUCTION

THE LONDON HISTORY STUDIES are designed expressly for students. They examine those events and personalities of the last five hundred years which continue to attract the attention of historians and arouse argument among them.

The books in the series are intended to be succinct and concentrated. Short quotations from contemporary sources are used both to enliven the text and to produce evidence to support particular arguments, while differing views of the principal historians are fairly represented. In addition to the facts, students should find a clear statement of the problems involved in each subject, presented in such a way as to ensure understanding and to stimulate thought. Short bibliographies give direction to further research.

The authors are practising teachers who have been asked to write on the subjects in which they are especially interested. They are naturally familiar with the current research in their chosen fields but they can in addition draw on the knowledge and experience of the scholars and leading historians who compose the Advisory Panel. Thus the books contain the fruits of modern scholarship and are written from a close acquaintance with the questions that occur to students and the difficulties that face them.

It is hoped that this series will provide not only vigorous and effective treatment of the topics under discussion, but also an aid to a clear understanding of the methods of the historian.

R. B. J.

PREFACE

The *Grand Siècle* of French history has been under critical examination in recent times, and this book is an attempt to present an account of French government and society based upon the recent research of French and other historians. Foreign affairs cannot be excluded in a century when war so often determined the internal situation, but a full treatment of French foreign policy would involve writing a large part of the history of Europe in the period, and this therefore has not been attempted. In order to avoid language difficulties, suggestions for further reading will be limited to books and articles in English and a relatively small number of French works, usually brief and reasonably easy to read.

An indispensable basic work of this kind is *La Monarchie d'Ancien Régime* by G. Pagès (Paris, 1928). Pagès founded the modern interpretation of French government in this period, and his work has been continued by R. Mousnier, who has written a popular account in the seventeenth-century section of the *Larousse Histoire de France*, Vol. 1, edited by M. Reinhard (Paris, 1954). H. Méthivier has written a volume, giving in concise form an up-to-date survey, *L'Ancien Régime*, in the series '*Que Sais-je*' (Paris, 1961). P. Lough's *Introduction to Seventeenth-Century France* is a valuable interpretation. The most recent book in English is *Seventeenth-Century France*, by G. R. R. Treasure (London, 1966). There are two useful chapters on this period in *France – Government and Society*, edited by J. M. Wallace-Hadrill and J. McManners (London, 1957). The Marxist view is forcibly stated by B. Porshnev in an article 'The Legend of the Seventeenth Century in French History', in *Past and Present*, Vol. 8. Although now in some respects out-of-date, the best text-book treatment of France is probably that of D. Ogg in *Europe in the Seventeenth Century* (London, 7th edition, 1959). Interesting sidelights are presented in a book reprinted from the admirable periodical *Dix-septième Siècle: Comment les Français Voyaient la*

France au XVIIe Siècle, by R. Mousnier and others (Paris, 1955). For comprehensive coverage and reference the monumental *Histoire de France*, edited by E. Lavisse (Parise, 1900–11) is still indispensable.

French economic affairs are dealt with in the *Cambridge Economic History of Europe*, Vol. IV (Cambridge, 1967). P. Goubert has written illuminatingly about 'The French Peasantry in the Seventeenth Century' in *Past and Present*, Vol. 10. J. H. Shennan clears away much confusion in his admirable book on *The Parlement of Paris* (London, 1968). E. G. Léonard covers the Huguenot movement in his *History of Protestantism*, Vol. II (English translation, London, 1967). In recent times the study of society in this period has been dominated by a controversy between Mousnier and Porshnev about the causes of popular risings and the nature of French society, and J. H. M. Salmon deals with this in his article 'Venal Office and Popular Sedition in France' in *Past and Present*, Vol. 37. Many useful articles on French history appear in American historical journals (one of which is *French Historical Studies*). One example must suffice. There is a valuable article, 'The French Crown Versus its Judicial and Financial Officials 1615–1683' by A. L. Moote in the (American) *Journal of Modern History*, Vol. 34.

ACKNOWLEDGMENTS

For permission to quote copyright material the author and publishers wish to thank: the Clarendon Press, Oxford, for extracts from *Richelieu and the Councillors of Louis XIII* (1963) by Orest A. Ranum; and the Universitaire, Leiden, Holland, for permission to translate extracts from *La Fronde* (1954) by E. A. Kossmann. The author is grateful to Mr D. M. Shaw of Bolton School for help with the preparation of the maps.

CONTENTS

MAPS

PART I
Peace after the Civil Wars

[1] THE MORTGAGED MONARCHY OF HENRY IV

When Henry IV became king in 1589, France was in theory almost an absolute monarchy. The medieval maxim still held good: '*Si veut le roi, si veut la loi*'. It was however assumed that there was one fundamental and immutable law, the unwritten Salic Law confining the succession to the throne to the descendants in the male line of Hugh Capet – the Bourbons became kings of France in succession to the House of Valois only because most Frenchmen accepted this law as sacrosanct. A vaguer limitation on royal power was the general assumption that Frenchmen had customary rights and privileges which it was the king's duty to preserve – they had a vague sketch of a constitution in their minds, but no security against a wilful king.

The only constitutional bodies which might check royal power were much weaker than the English Parliament. They were first the Estates General, a body representing in three separate assemblies the clergy, nobility, and bourgeoisie (Third Estate) which met very seldom and had little power – it could pass resolutions but not legislate; and second the Parlements, particularly the venerable Parlement of Paris, co-eval with its English namesake, a supreme law court of over two hundred magistrates, whose consent was necessary for the promulgation of new laws. The Parlement was a very real obstacle to absolutism, the hereditary preserve of certain legal families devoted to the upholding of law; but the king could overcome its opposition by presiding over a formal session called a *lit de justice* and ordering the registration of a decree.

In practice Henry IV had nothing like the power of any modern government. France was in any case too large to be effectively controlled from Paris. A journey to the furthest confines of the state took a fortnight. There was really no conception of a frontier, and the edges of the state were ragged, insecure, and at times indeterminate, with some semi-independent rulers – of whom Henry IV himself, as King of Navarre, had been one. The old domains of the king, built up around Paris, and comprising in the end the northern and central regions under the jurisdiction of the Parlement of Paris, were even in time of peace the only parts of the kingdom to be fairly uniformly governed, and to be kept reasonably free from disorder. After defeating the English in the Hundred Years' War French kings had severe struggles to get control of outlying fiefs, such as Burgundy, Brittany, and the Bourbonnais. The Constable Bourbon, a royal prince deprived of his lands for treachery in 1523, was the last of this breed of overmighty subjects – Henry of Navarre belonged to a younger line of Bourbons. Always the south of France – the Midi – with its own language, Provençal, and its fiercely independent traditions, was only partly subjugated and remained a stronghold of heresies and a centre of constant unrest.

To destroy feudal power and fight the Italian Wars the French monarchy developed systematic taxation very early – the *taille* (tallage, a primitive income tax, from which the nobles were exempt because in theory they fought and the clergy because they prayed), *gabelle* (salt monopoly), and other duties on commodities. Although this system was full of anomalies – internal tariffs persisted, outlying provinces were never properly integrated and paid far less than their share – the revenue enabled France to have a standing army of mercenaries. This in turn gave the monarchy the strength to curb feudalism and to establish a new order of local administration. Governors were appointed to control the former fiefs, now provinces of France. New Parlements were set up to extend the jurisdiction of the king. For local justice and police a *bailli* – usually a noble – was appointed as chief magistrate in each *bailliage* (or *sénéchaussée*, as the area was known in the south), assisted by legal officials, and the responsibility for local finance was given in each *généralité* to other officials known as *trésoriers de France*. The assessment and collection of taille in most parts of France, the *pays d'élections*, was in the hands of appointed officials known as *élus*. Some outlying provinces, which had to be placated by concessions, kept their provincial estates. These were the *pays d'états*, and they controlled their own finances and granted the central government a so-called *don gratuit*.

The establishment of a royal administration throughout France was an amazing success for the monarchy. It was largely the work of Louis XI and Louis XII. Louis XII's successor, Francis I, an extravagant king, greatly increased the scale of an old abuse, the sale of offices, and set up a special revenue department to organize this. In the end nearly every official post had to be bought, either on its creation or from the existing holder, and great efforts were made by the owners of offices to preserve them as family properties. This practice is known as the *vénalité des offices* and in this book will be called venality. The king had sold much of the power won by the suppression of feudal independence. In return the monarchy was burdened with the salaries of officials – often, as creations multiplied, largely redundant – and the loss of revenue due to the fact that all the higher officials gained exemption from taille. As these officials were constantly buying land, they already had the makings of a new nobility rising alongside the old. As Pagès puts it: 'In making venality more widespread, in preparing for the inheritance of office, the kings themselves, at the moment when royal power triumphed over the last resistance to absolute monarchy, set up a new obstacle, which they never succeeded in suppressing entirely'.

During the French civil wars from 1562 to 1596, the monarchy itself was under heavy threats, from embattled Huguenots but also from Catholic Leaguers who put the Pope before the King. Huguenot opposition to absolute monarchy died when in 1585 Henry of Navarre the Huguenot leader became heir to the throne. But this revived the fanatical League, led by the over-powerful

family of Guise. Henry III, the last Valois king, in the end
supported divine hereditary right even though it meant that his
successor was the Protestant Henry IV. But when Henry III was
assassinated by a Catholic fanatic in 1589, Henry IV had a long
struggle to capture the chief centres of monarchical power, and
did not win Paris until 1594. He had shown great military
ability, but he bought rather than conquered the monarchy. The
Parlement of Paris had split over the issue of Catholic League
against Protestant King. All over the country the official order
was divided. Henry won over the officials by becoming a Catholic
and taking them all back into his employment, and then won
over the grandees who led the League by enormous bribes and
offers of governorships. The menace of Spanish rule – at one time
a League Estates General seemed about to offer the French
throne to Philip of Spain – had swung the official class behind
the divinely appointed and consecrated King. By the time that
the Spanish danger had been overcome, Henry's inheritance,
already mortgaged to the venal office-holders, was still further
encumbered by the concessions necessary to bring about peace.

[2] HENRY IV AND HIS GOVERNMENT

Henry IV brought peace to France in 1598 after nearly forty
years of civil conflict and nine of war with Spain. Like our
Henry VII he ended the civil wars, restored strong monarchy,
and established a new and great dynasty on the throne. He was
one of the outstanding conciliators in history, and unlike our
James I he could make conciliation appear a strong policy. By
1598 he had made four settlements which form his main achievement. First, with the Catholic League, a vast movement of
reconciliation not brought about by force. Second, as a necessary
corollary to the first, with the Pope, who had absolved him in
1596, and whose friendship he sought more keenly than any of
his predecessors for centuries. Third, with his old followers the

French Protestants, in the Edict of Nantes of 1598, forced upon him by their desertion of his cause and republican threats, but thanks to his style and temper made into an instrument of toleration beyond anything known in the Europe of that time. Fourth, with Spain in the Treaty of Vervins in 1598, which restored the status quo of 1559. (Savoy refused to give back Saluzzo, and after a short victorious war in 1600 Henry abandoned this claim to please the Pope, and so lost his power to intervene in Italy, but in return gained Savoyard territory near Lyon and rounded off his frontier.)

So France enjoyed twelve years of peace, and her recovery was almost entirely due to the natural energy of the people. A graph of wheat prices in a large number of European centres between 1440 and 1760 is published in the *Cambridge Economic History of Europe* (Vol. IV, p. 470). The highest recorded anywhere is the price in Paris during the decade 1580–90. By 1610 the price had dropped to a normal one; in terms of money this was partly disguised by a devaluation in 1602. No doubt Henry wanted every peasant to have a chicken in his pot, even if he never made the famous statement, but he did little that was positive to achieve it except to give peace. His economic policy was partly good and partly bad, and largely ineffectual. No fundamental reforms were carried out either in government or finance. But Henry eliminated conflicts. No marauding soldiers wandered through the countryside. Even the endemic revolts of the peasants (usually against tax-collectors) ceased during these years. The government and the country recovered confidence under a king whose personal style of ruling was impressive.

Henry was a short ugly man with an enormous nose and an aggressive beard. He was always on the move, quick in speech and action, totally informal and nonchalant, always the soldier, preferring the hunting field to the Court. He said himself: 'I am fitter in the country than in the town . . . getting much more pleasure from wearing armour, spurring on a horse, and giving a sword-thrust, than from making laws . . . sitting down all the time in a council to sign decrees'.

At the centre of the gay outlandish Court was the royal harem.

Henry had an unabated passion for women; fifty-six known mistresses, all of whose favours were bought. His first marriage to Marguerite de Valois was soon in ruins, but he had to wait until 1599 for its annulment by the Pope. He then proposed, against the advice of all his ministers, to marry his long-standing but unfaithful mistress Gabrielle d'Estrées, an amiable but designing woman, and to legitimize their eldest son César de Vendôme, a five-year-old boy. This could well have been disastrous to the monarchy, but Gabrielle's sudden death in 1599 removed the danger. Henry immediately involved himself with a young girl, Henriette d'Entragues, who first secured not only a large grant of money but a written promise of marriage if she bore a son. He broke this promise when in the next year he married Marie de Medici, but Henriette, an untamable shrew, and her family became a major menace to his rule. Her father was a fierce Auvergnat noble, her mother had been the mistress of Charles IX, and her half-brother the Comte d'Auvergne was an illegitimate Valois. Even after Henriette and her family had intrigued with Spain and helped to instigate a revolt Henry could not escape from her, though she too was unfaithful to him. The mutual jealousies of Henriette and his wife tormented him, and he was henpecked by both.

The Florentine Marie de Medici was a majestic Rubens woman, sullen and not very clever but strong-willed. She quite held her own with her fiery little husband. Henry's legitimate family of two sons and three daughters ensured the Bourbon succession and opened the way to future alliances through marriages. These and eight of his illegitimate children were all brought up together in the royal nursery at St Germain. Henry loved playing with them; once he gave an interview to the Spanish ambassador while he went about on all fours with Louis the Dauphin on his back.

Here was a very unusual king, impetuous, amiable, and often ridiculous, who had a rare gift of ruling. He was an earthy cynic who believed in authoritarian rule, but who understood people, preferred persuasion to command, and cared for public welfare: *'Si nous n'avons tous compassion du peuple il faudra qu'il succombe et que nous périssions tous avec lui*'. He forgot his friends as easily as he forgave his enemies.

Nearly the whole business of government was transacted verbally as Henry strode about the gardens of the Tuileries or the gallery of the Louvre. His inner council had no name and seldom sat round a table; in fact its members, five or six in number, were usually consulted in ones or twos. The final decision was always Henry's own. A favourite expression was '*Je veux être obéi*'. But he often forgot his verbal orders, and in the difficult conditions of France at that time many were only pious aspirations. Henry adapted himself well to the semi-independence of the French provinces, avoided head-on collisions and asserted his authority more as the reign went on. One of his most difficult subjects was D'Épernon, formerly a favourite of Henry III, later a thorn in Richelieu's side, a very ambitious and dangerous intriguer who dabbled in treason. On one occasion when D'Épernon had been particularly troublesome Henry wrote: 'Come and seek me out with your mind made up to do what I want, for the servant who wishes to be loved by his master shows his obedience. Your letter is that of an angry man. I am no longer angry. I beg you not to make me so.' That letter conveys as well as anything the personal style of Henry's rule. He could always find the right words, pithy and effective, to move his auditors or readers. D'Épernon avoided treason, remained a governor of a province, and was Henry's companion in the carriage when he was stabbed to death in 1610.

This method of government suited the times, but it had defects. Henry lived by expedients and was completely conservative at a time when administrative reforms might at least have been begun. (Henry VIII and Thomas Cromwell had reconstructed English government, and it was unfortunate for France that no systematic reformer of government held power until the time of Louis XIV.) Henry inherited, and bequeathed to his son, a muddled administration by venal officials, made worse by civil war. Méthivier says: 'The country administered itself'. Because the governors, who were mainly ex-Leaguers, were not to be trusted, Henry tried to confine them to military activity, and especially in the later years often sent out a commissary or *intendant*, usually a *maître des requêtes* from his Council of State, to oversee the local government and report back.

Henry disliked all formal checks on his power. He interfered arbitrarily in municipal elections; their suppression in Limoges in 1602 even caused a riot. He hated the idea of an Estates General. He himself said that this was due to his experience when as King of Navarre he ruled in Béarn, where the Estates were always dominated by the loudest-mouthed fool. The nearest he got to calling a representative assembly was the hand-picked Assembly of Notables in 1597 when he was desperate for funds to fight Spain, and this experiment was not repeated. He did not venture to destroy the provincial Estates where they still met, but he once told the Burgundian Estates that their best privilege was '*Les bonnes grâces de leur roi*'. He found the power of the Parlements very irksome, and tried to make them register edicts before they held debates and made remonstrances.

In all this Henry had the support of Rosny (made Duc de Sully in 1608 and usually known by that name), a rough Huguenot soldier who had been given charge of the finances by 1598, and who became his chief minister in the latter part of the reign.

The real political struggle of this reign concerned the problems of arbitrary rule. Henry's triumph had been very much that of the rich official bourgeoisie, who had a fairly secure hold on their purchased offices, paid no direct taxes, were now usually landowners as well, and in fact if not yet in name a new nobility. For the first time the King's inner council was mainly bourgeois. The Chancellor Bellièvre, the chief minister, was a pious Catholic descended from a line of *parlementaires*, and the sole noble in the inner council was Sully. Bellièvre wished the King to be held in check by strong Parlements imposing on him a respect for the customs and fundamental laws of the kingdom, whose chiefs would form a council with real power. Henry found the arbitrary methods of Sully much more to his taste, but he liked to hear a variety of opinions, and in the end he did much as he pleased.

The climax of the struggle in the royal council occurred over

Sully's plan to introduce the *droit annuel* (called the *paulette* after Paulet its first collector) in 1604. This was apparently regarded by the King and Sully purely as a means of raising money, but it had very important political implications. The holder of a venal office had been able to sell it to any qualified person, and could hand it on to his son, with one restriction; if he died within forty days of a transfer it reverted to the crown. Now it was proposed to remove this restriction and so make the offices completely hereditary, in return for an annual tax of a sixtieth of their value. Bellièvre opposed this, especially as concerned the Parlements, because he saw the dangers of an irremovable class of officials. In the Council of State and Finances, the body of councillors responsible for the administration, Sully won a victory over Bellièvre on this issue by eight votes to six. Henry was encouraged to impose the paulette by the strong support of parlementaires, including those in his inner council, Villeroy and Jeannin. He dismissed Bellièvre and appointed Sillery in his place, but Sully now became the leading minister.

The paulette was a major act of policy, even if unintentionally so. Its defenders at the Estates General of 1614 argued that without it 'the grandees would put their creatures into the towns and the official bodies to serve against the King', whereas now the officials depended only on their income from their office and hence remained faithful in times of trouble. Mousnier, the chief authority on this subject, thinks that the monarchy had been a limited one owing to the power of the venal office-holders, but that the paulette provided a basis for absolute monarchy by giving the officials such an interest in their offices as property that they lost all interest in politics. But was a monarchy absolute when it had to tolerate an independent judiciary and inefficiency in its finances, without the power to remove the stiff-necked or the peculators? Mousnier's last word on Henry is that he was 'the great consolidator of positions gained, the great protector of wealth'.

Opposition to Henry was mainly feudal and conspiratorial. The crisis of the reign occupied the years 1602–4. Among his old associates in arms no one was more important than Marshal

Biron, his best general, whom he had made a duke-and-peer and governor of Burgundy. Discontented and over-ambitious, he formed a treasonable plot with the support of the King of Spain and the Duke of Savoy to overthrow Henry and put the son of Henry and Henriette d'Entragues on the throne. Aristocrats who resented Henry's neglect of them and his authoritarian style formed a faction around Biron containing very diverse elements: the Entragues family, the Constable Montmorency, and malcontent Protestants such as La Trémoille and Bouillon Prince de Sedan. The south-west of France threatened to rise. But Henry was warned by a double agent, and arrested and executed Biron in 1602. Eventually he forced Bouillon to hand over Sedan to French rule, but restored him as a vassal.

Henriette d'Entragues was still very bitter about Henry's broken promise, and stirred her father and half-brother Auvergne to continue their plotting after Henry had pardoned them for her sake. They tried to draw in James I of England, but he let Henry know, and in the end the males of the Entragues family were seized. The father was released after a short imprisonment, but Auvergne was kept in detention until the end of the reign.

Henry now feared war with Spain, and became more distrustful and autocratic. Sully had a freer hand and became more arbitrary. The council was reduced to a cypher, and the King browbeat the Paris merchants and quarrelled more with the Parlement. Financial expedients multiplied and more use was made of commissaries to enforce new taxes in the provinces. Sully's influence was seen in the lessening of interest in the economic plans outlined in the next section. But Henry never gave full power to Sully. He used Villeroy, an ex-Leaguer, to conduct his foreign policy with a cautious concern for Catholic interests. At home he fostered the Catholic Revival. He took more interest in displaying his leadership in building and in patronage of the arts. These points will be developed in ensuing chapters of the book (see p. 27).

Henry had taken advantage of a flowing tide in favour of monarchy in France after the anarchy and misery of the civil wars. The writings of that period against monarchy had served a temporary purpose, and though this kind of thinking does not disappear in the seventeenth century it is not very important. By his alliance with the Church Henry ensured that the vigorously revived Catholicism of the age would support '*le Roi Très Chrétien*', and although he was assassinated by a fanatical Ultramontane Catholic, no responsible Ultramontane any longer countenanced disloyalty, let alone tyrannicide. But in dealing with the Church as in dealing with the Parlements and the financiers the King's scope was limited. In many respects English rulers in the seventeenth century were more absolute than French monarchs.

[3] HENRY IV AND THE RECOVERY OF FRANCE

At the end of the war with Spain the King's financial situation was deplorable, but he had found in Sully the man to solve his immediate problems. There was no genuine reform. A 5 per cent tax on goods entering towns recommended by the Assembly of Notables of 1597 was withdrawn in 1602 because of its unpopularity, above all with the nobles and officials who were exempt otherwise from major taxation. The paulette was the one successful new tax.

Sully was one of the few Protestant leaders still enthusiastically loyal to the King, an army comrade indispensable to Henry because he helped him with his love affairs. His memoirs are the only authority for much that happened in Henry's reign, but he was such a braggart that they are very unreliable. Where his figures of the finances can be checked they have been found to have exaggerated his achievements. He invented a non-existent mission to England for his greater glorification. He attributed to Henry a whole foreign policy (the Grand Design) which was the work of his fertile imagination. Yet although the exact facts are unascertainable, his ruthless methods, while providing for the

Court, a large royal building programme, and rearmament, turned a heavy debt into a modest surplus.

Right at the beginning the army was dismissed without payment of its arrears, much of the debt was repudiated, and taxes owing were remitted. By frightening financiers, tax-farmers and tax-collectors Sully secured a bigger proportion of what they collected, though financial pressures towards the end of the reign forced him to deal easily with them, and Paulet for example was able to squeeze a million livres out of the people of Champagne and remit only a quarter of this sum to the Treasury. Sully himself admitted that the greatest offenders escaped him. He could not force exempt nobles and bourgeois to pay taille, but he held an inquiry and did away with 40,000 wrongful exemptions. He then lowered the tailles in various parts of France, but this gain was lost before the end of the reign, and the gabelle was increased. His arbitrary ways hit the rentiers (mainly rich Parisians) most hardly. A great part of the interest due to them was repudiated, and there was serious trouble in Paris in 1605. Sully was a watchdog on expenditure, and was generous to no one but himself; he left a colossal fortune. The Court had to practice austerity by the standards of the time, and Henry, who had grown up a poor prince and still cared little about court pomp, was considered a skinflint.

During the extravagant reign of Francis I and the period of the civil wars much royal land had been sold, with the proviso that it could be redeemed at the purchase price. Now land values had risen greatly because of the price revolution, and Sully's finest financial service to the monarchy, though it had only a long-term effect, was to find intermediaries who would pay the necessary price for sixteen years' use of this repurchased land, so that without spending any money the crown after sixteen years regained the land.

Sully was the one minister who could stand up to Henry IV, but he never became all-powerful. He used his increasing power in favour of aristocracy, against the *robins* (the legal and official class) whom he despised, and for an anti-Spanish foreign policy in alliance with foreign Protestants. He was isolated in the government, and was the only minister to fall from power after Henry's death. Because he disliked merchants and manufacturers he had little to offer but opposition to the King's economic policies. Austerity was his economic recipe; to impose restrictions on extravagant spending on luxuries by sumptuary laws, and prohibit imports of luxuries. He believed in fostering agriculture, but found that little could be done, except in afforestation. Nobles were forbidden to hunt over growing crops, and the distraint of agricultural implements for debt was prohibited, but these measures may well owe more to Henry's humanity than to Sully's zeal for agriculture. One important development was that Henry made Sully *Grand Voyer*, with charge of a department overseeing communications, roads, bridges and navigable rivers. He improved some main roads, and is famous for beginning the planting of avenues of elm trees along the roads; they were called *rosnys* after him. His greatest work in this department was the commencement of the Briare Canal to join the Seine and the Loire, the first canal project in France, not completed until well on in the next reign.

Henry played the part of a stimulating leader in the economic recovery of France. He rarely read a book, but made an exception of Olivier de Serres's great treatise on agriculture. De Serres discussed the qualities of different soils and the method of cultivation of corn, maize, vines, beetroot and mulberries, and the culture of silkworms. Henry did his best to spread this wisdom. He believed in the direct intervention of the state. He himself fetched an engineer from Holland to drain the marshes of Saintonge and create fertile farm land. He had also, when in 1589 he was fighting for his throne, induced William Lee, the Nottingham inventor of the knitting machine, to leave England where he had met only discouragement, and settle in Rouen. A framework-knitting industry was established, but the hostility of the hand-knitters brought about its collapse after Henry's death. Many of the government's interventions were equally well meant and equally unsuccessful.

Henry, usually cautious and conservative, followed an adventurous economic policy. The ideas came mainly from the King's

Huguenot valet, Barthélemy Laffemas, a self-taught dabbler in industry, who had developed for himself a crude and extreme form of mercantilist theory, and who was a tireless producer of projects. In 1600 he was made Controller-General of Commerce, and head of a commission which held 150 meetings in two years.

Laffemas wanted virtually to end foreign trade except for such exports as would be paid for in gold and silver bullion. Between 1599 and 1601 the government prohibited the export of precious metals, raw silk, wool, rags, flax and hemp, and the import of cloth of gold or silver, silk goods, tapestry and lace. This crude policy led to so much trouble that it was modified in later years, and the Commission of Commerce was pushed into the background. The King took the initiative in making commercial treaties with Spain and England which increased the volume of trade as a whole and stimulated the export of corn, cattle and wine.

The crux of the problem was the home manufacture of silk. The new industry centred on Tours, and a vigorous propaganda encouraged landowners to cultivate mulberries and silkworms. But the production of silk lagged, and the restriction on imports antagonized the rich and the merchants.

The Commission of Commerce produced a comprehensive code for industry and social life. Laffemas tried to go far beyond anything attempted by Elizabeth's government in England and, whereas in England J.P.s had been given the task of enforcement, in France the guilds of masters and workmen, dominated by masters and medievally restrictive in outlook, were put in charge. They had to pay for this power, and this won Sully's support for the policy. In every bishopric a bureau of manufactures was established to ensure that every workman and manufacturer was a member of a guild and obeyed the government's regulations imposed through the guild. This attempt to put the clock back was ultimately unenforceable and domestic industry on a capitalist basis revived in the towns and the countryside. But it never flourished in France as well as it did in England, and Laffemas and his successors, including Colbert, must be held partly responsible. His bureaux were also charged with the arbitration of disputes, oversight of charitable works, repression of vagabondage, and care of orphans. Most of this soon became a dead letter.

Lyon was the chief centre of resistance to the silk regulations and to the new code for industry. Here was the Manchester of France, the second city of the country and a great commercial capital in its own right, which flourished on foreign trade and freedom from guild restrictions. To put an end to riotous outbreaks there on the eve of his marriage in the city to Marie de Medici in 1600, Henry found it necessary to permit the resumption of the trade in silk, and before the end of the year he suspended for Lyon the edict concerning guilds. Lyon had struck a blow for industrial freedom which affected the whole country.

One difficulty in the way of establishing new industries in France was that too much merchant wealth was diverted into buying government offices and land. Money was dear, and a well-meant imposition of a maximum of $6\frac{1}{4}$ per cent interest in 1601 (to help indebted landowners) may have reduced the supply. The government then compelled Parisian merchants to contribute to new industrial companies. Royal workshops were set up for making cloth of gold and silver, silk goods, tapestries, fine cloth, morocco leather, Italian glassware, and objects of iron. They were granted monopolies, advances of capital, subsidies, government orders, fiscal exemptions, and freedom from guild restrictions. The workmen in royal manufactures lived in barracks and worked a twelve-to-sixteen-hour day. Throughout industry Henry supported the employers by the prohibition of strikes, the fixing of wages at low levels, and vigorous action against workmen when they formed illegal trade unions.

The results of these rather naïve efforts were disappointing. The attempt to strengthen the guild organization failed except as a fiscal measure. Some new industries flourished on royal patronage, but most of the 260 new concerns died because even with a monopoly they could not pay. Sully's increased power after 1604 was inimical to the working of the Commission of Commerce.

Overseas trade grew during the reign, but owed little to the government except the all-important peace policy and the

commercial treaties. French merchants and seamen, above all in
the ports of Rouen, Dieppe, St Malo and La Rochelle, showed
great vigour, not least in the illegal trade with Spanish America.
The biggest drawback to the growth of seaborne trade was the
failure of the King to provide naval protection. In an age when
sea-power was becoming a major factor Henry had no fleet and
took no steps to create one. For lack of a Mediterranean fleet the
Levant trade languished. The Barbary Corsairs seized the Bastion
of France, a stronghold on the North African coast, and in 1604
they held 3,000 French sailors captive in Algiers. Henry's desire
to please the Pope made difficulties for him in Turkey, but in
1604 he managed to get new capitulations from the Sultan
governing trade and the position of Frenchmen in the Turkish
Empire, and the patronage of the Holy Places by the Most
Christian King was recognized. Diplomacy was always Henry's
strong suit.

The most sensational result of the enterprise of the Atlantic
merchants was the founding of the first overseas colonies of
France, nearly coinciding with the beginnings of English colonization. Du Gua founded Port Royal (Annapolis in the later Nova
Scotia) in 1604, and a Huguenot De Monts followed this up with
another settlement in 1607; religious troubles arose and the
colony was captured and destroyed by the English in 1613.
In 1608 Champlain founded New France by establishing a
settlement at Quebec. The government was indifferent to all this.
Henry appears to have been unaware of the importance of
colonies, and Sully thought that any to the north of the fortieth
parallel were useless. France, although potentially the most
powerful European state, could take no major part in the contest
for overseas trade and empire until she had a fleet.

The most important effects of Henry's economic policy were
to be found in the textile industries. At Lyon, Tours and Paris
the production of luxury silk goods greatly increased, and the
trade in woollen and linen cloth regained prosperity and developed
an export market. Mousnier states that 'France became once
more an economic power, and a redoubtable competitor in the
commercial struggle'.

[4] RELIGION AND THE ARTS IN THE REIGN OF HENRY IV

The Protestants

The Edict of Nantes, granted to the Protestants in 1598, was the foundation of Henry's religious settlement. Many of the clauses were textually reproduced from the Edict of Poitiers issued by Henry III in 1577 and afterwards repudiated. The places where Protestants could worship were almost exactly the same; that is, in all the places where there was a congregation at the time, and in one town in each baillage or sénéchaussée, but not in Paris or a number of other named towns. The civil rights of Protestants were confirmed; they were to be eligible for all offices without discrimination, and for schools, universities and guilds; but, like all legal civil rights, these were difficult to enforce in an intolerant society. The legal safeguards of the Protestants were strengthened by the new provision of a special *Chambre de l'Édit* in the Parlement of Paris, with ten Catholic and six Protestant judges, and the *chambres mi-parties* as before at Bordeaux, Toulouse and Grenoble, with new special courts at Rouen and Rennes. Two separate decrees conceded under pressure a Huguenot state within a state, by the grant for eight years of a hundred places of surety with Protestant garrisons supported by the state (a much larger army than the King himself possessed) and state maintenance for the Protestant clergy. The Huguenots retained the right of assembly. In effect this edict and its codicils introduced in a rather untidy way a federal element into the French state which conflicted with the main trend towards unified monarchy.

This generous settlement was most unpopular. All Henry's eloquence was needed to get it through the Parlement without a lit de justice. In fact the Protestants were socially and politically privileged. Huguenots such as Sully and Laffemas held very high posts. Lesdiguières was governor of Dauphiné, and the austere Duplessis-Mornay, sometimes called the Protestant Pope, governor of Saumur. The King's personal servants were mainly Huguenots. Sully employed forty-eight in the Treasury. Paris swarmed with Protestant officials, and the church at Charenton in the suburbs, built to seat 4,000, was filled to overflowing. But the zeal of these Court Protestants declined, and within a generation most had become Catholics.

The strongholds of Protestantism were in the Midi, in the Cévennes and in the towns of La Rochelle, Montauban and Nîmes, where contrary to the Edict Catholic worship was banned. In these towns the governing bodies of the Protestant churches, the consistories, had great and even oppressive power. The Huguenots prospered and became more moderate; most were tired of being 'pur et dur'. Moreover they had little in common with the declining lesser nobles who formed the violent fringe of the party, or the sometimes disloyal great nobles who were their leaders. Duplessis-Mornay and after him Rohan had the necessary prestige and sincerity to hold together this ill-assorted party. But it stood outside the main stream of French cultural life. Respectability and (a little later) theological doubts about Calvinism undermined it. Conversions to Catholicism were numerous, and the hard core that remained flourished materially but became ossified. Already by 1605 an Assembly of Clergy began the practice of offering pensions and bribes to converts to Catholicism.

Henry IV and the Catholic Church

The loss of Henry had been a fatal blow to the Huguenot cause. He became more closely allied to the Catholic Church than any of the later Valois kings had been, and earned the respect of the popes. Clement VIII stated that 'The Most Christian King professes the Catholic faith boldly and firmly, and at the same time he lays claim to nothing that belongs to the Church and the Holy See'. He had no deep religious feelings, but he worked hard to overcome the suspicions and win the confidence of the Pope and the French clergy. French kings had largely misused the powers they had gained by the Concordat of Bologna of 1516 to appoint the bishops. Henry reduced the abuses and helped to provide a more spiritual leadership, though court and personal considerations were still important; he once made a four-year old duke a bishop, and he gave two abbeys to the Protestant Sully.

One mark of the Gallican independence of the French Church was its rejection of the decrees of the Council of Trent by which the popes of the Counter-Reformation were attacking abuses and tightening discipline. In 1600 Henry began a move to introduce the Tridentine Decrees into France, but gave up when he realized the strength of the opposition in the Parlement of Paris, the stronghold of Gallicanism.

Henry's chief service to the Counter-Reformation was the favour he showed to the Society of Jesus. Jesuits were the extreme supporters of Ultramontanism, that is a belief in the absolute authority of the papacy in all matters of faith and discipline. Some of them had even approved of the killing of anti-papal rulers. When in 1595 a pupil of the Jesuits had attempted to kill Henry he had banished them from the half of France controlled by the Parlement of Paris. In 1603 he readmitted them provided that their colleges were restricted to Frenchmen. This gratified the Pope and the growing party of zealots in France. The Jesuits attained for the first time a central place in French religious life. Henry endowed a Jesuit college and allowed others to be founded. Their colleges were the best schools in Europe, and many of the leading Frenchmen of the century were taught by them. Henry was the first French king to have a Jesuit confessor, and so established a custom. Méthivier considers that 'the Edict of Rouen recalling the Jesuits has at least as much importance for the seventeenth century as the Edict of Nantes'.

The Catholic Revival

The Catholic Revival was the most important movement of Henry's reign, and it took many forms. Above all it made a deep impression on the official bourgeoisie. One of its greatest leaders was St François de Sales, who arrived in Paris from Savoy in 1602. His widely read works of devotion were full of the gentle humanism which pervades this Revival. He inspired a young widow, Mme de Chantal, who became his lifelong friend, to found a teaching order of nuns, the Visitandines, which by the time of her death had set up eighty schools for girls.

The position of women in the Revival is extraordinary. The most remarkable of these was Mme Acarie, of a rich Parisian legal family. A mystic and a religious leader, she continued to perform the duties of a practical housewife, and even saved her feckless husband from financial ruin. At the same time she was the centre of a circle which included François de Sales, Bérulle the later cardinal, Marillac the later minister, and the Jesuit Father Coton, the King's confessor. She introduced into France the Spanish Carmelite order of nuns, and trained Carmelite novices in her own home. Abbesses intent on the reform of their convents visited her to ask her advice. One such was Angélique Arnauld, whom her formerly Protestant family had made abbess of Port Royal when she was eleven years old. Her parents were the real directors of the convent's affairs, until at eighteen she barred the door to them and carried out a drastic reform which prepared the community of nuns for their later leading role in one of the most remarkable offshoots of the revival, the Jansenist movement.

The Jesuits spread Catholic reform widely among all classes, but for many bourgeois intellectuals they were too lax and easygoing. These stricter zealots looked for leadership to Father Bérulle, a follower of St Augustine and a mystic. He founded the Oratory on an Italian model to train a sanctified priesthood. He eventually became a cardinal, an influential figure at court, and the leader of the group known as the *dévots*, who applied Catholic principles to politics.

The Catholic Revival therefore included many diverse elements in a difficult and temporary unity. Some aspects were peculiar to France, such as the importance of the laity and of women. Although on the whole the influence of the Pope on French politics was increased, the movement was by no means entirely Ultramontane. Even the Jesuits in France had a local colouring. The rather arid Gallicanism of the Parlements and the theologians of the Sorbonne became more spiritual. Many abuses remained in the French Church, but for a time it was filled with a new vitality. It is one of the ironies of history that a philandering ex-heretic should have presided over this spiritual renewal. Henry intervened to soften antagonism of Jesuits against Capuchins and of the monastic orders against the secular clergy. In accordance with his will his heart is preserved in the Jesuit college he founded at La Flèche in Anjou (it is now a military academy).

Henry and the arts

As in religion, so too in learning and the arts Henry gave a positive lead. He set up a commission to modernize the studies of the University of Paris. Although he was no reader he established Malherbe as the poet of the court, and so supported a restrained classicism in literature against the luxuriant baroque of other writers of the time. Malherbe believed in clarity and strict rules, and was completely orthodox in his support of monarchy and the Church. The Bourbons conceived it as part of their task to bring order to the arts.

Henry's most important artistic activity was in building and town-planning. Had he lived longer he would have transformed Paris. As it was, he opened up the Seine to the public for the first time, finished the building of the first modern bridge without buildings on it (the Pont Neuf), and designed the *quais* in its neighbourhood and the Place Dauphine. He cleared away some slums and forbade encroachments and overhangs in the narrow streets. In replanning he made broad straight streets and squares. His masterpiece was the Place Royale, now the Place des Vosges, where the design of the buildings for the entire square was laid down by the royal architects, although many of the houses were privately built for rich clients. Henry took a great personal interest in all this activity, and in the construction of parks, gardens and fountains for water supply. He also did much work at the royal châteaux, and boasted of having planted 60,000 trees at Fontainebleau in one year.

The end of the reign

Henry's reign was all too short a blaze of glory in the history of the French monarchy, and it depended entirely on the maintenance of peace and a precarious harmony both abroad and at home. In Europe his diplomacy succeeded but he had few friends. He had continued to help the Dutch and so had exasperated Spain, but talk of annexations in Flanders had raised Dutch disquiet. Henry mediated between Spain and the Dutch Republic, and after tortuous negotiations their long conflict was temporarily ended by the Twelve Years' Truce of 1609. He then made an alliance with the Dutch to guarantee the truce. A plan for an alliance with Spain, based on royal marriages, strongly backed by the Queen and Villeroy, broke down for the time being, and the Spanish government felt humiliated and annoyed with the King.

Events in Germany were moving to a crisis at the same time. Here the success of the Counter-Reformation had led a number of Protestant princes to form an Evangelical Union under the patronage of James I. In 1609 they were drawn into a dispute with the Emperor when he occupied the strategically placed Rhineland territories of Cleves-Julich, in dispute between two Protestant claimants. Sully urged on Henry a Protestant foreign policy, and he began to put diplomatic pressure on the Emperor and to rearm in preparation for a war.

Henry's cautious handling of this crisis lasted until early in 1610, when he suddenly showed what Mousnier calls 'une aggressivité folle'. At last his amours had a fatal effect on his policy. For months he had pursued a young girl of the court, Charlotte de Montmorency, daughter of the Constable of France. He prevented her marriage to a personable young courtier, and arranged instead that she should marry the Prince de Condé, reputedly a homosexual. Charlotte was flirtatious and tantalizing, but Condé surprised the King by carrying her off to Péronne and eventually to the safety of Brussels. Henry made an international crisis of this situation by demanding that the Condés should be sent back to France, and finally making the refusal of Spain a reason for going to war.

War against Spain and the Emperor with only Savoy and the reluctant Evangelical Union as allies, and with an army of only 50,000 and no navy, must surely have undone most of the good that Henry had done in his remarkable reign. His new policy was opposed by the Queen and by all the ministers except Sully. Much of the new life and vigour of France was concentrated in the dévot movement, which was bitterly hostile to the King's policy. The outspoken criticism of his adulterous behaviour is faintly reminiscent of the abuse heaped on Henry III his predecessor, and it had the same effect, the assassination of the King by a fanatic who believed he was serving the Catholic cause.

By May 1610 the King had prepared his campaign. The Queen was crowned and consecrated to give more authority to her regency while Henry was out of the country. Three days before Henry was due to leave Paris the assassin Ravaillac followed the open carriage in which he was driving with d'Épernon, caught up with it in a traffic jam in a narrow street, and stabbed him to death. The crime was almost certainly the work of a solitary half-crazed extremist, though so many people hated the King or his policy that a conspiracy was suspected, and there are historians who still look for one. Sully was so certain of it that he secured himself in the Bastille. Henriette d'Entragues, d'Épernon and even Marie de Medici herself have been suspected. But a good deal is known about Ravaillac and he must surely belong with Oswald and many others to the company of fanatical lone assassins.

Even more than in the case of President Kennedy the assassination of Henry IV created a legend. In the ensuing time of troubles his work looked more and more impressive. Sully's writings embroidered on it. Richelieu and Louis XIII believed that they were continuing the policy of Henry the Great. But he achieved popularity and high fame after his death rather than while he was reigning. He had brought about a difficult balance by his remarkable flair for political compromise, and in the midst of dangers and difficulties he had been generous and had never badly misused his autocratic power. He had founded a line of kings, given France an invaluable breathing-space of peace and order, and revived the style and authority of monarchy. He had regained the support of the Church and the papacy. But he was never fully trusted, and the whole precarious achievement was threatened by his final folly; it was this folly that led to his death.

[5] THE EARLY YEARS OF LOUIS XIII

The period from 1610 to 1624 is an interlude in Bourbon rule, neatly divided into two halves, the first the rule of the lazy, incompetent, power-loving Regent, the Queen Mother Marie de Medici, the second that of the immature, neurotic but zealous young King. One can adapt the saying of Frederick the Great about the emergence of Pitt in England. For fourteen years France was in labour but at last she brought forth a man – Richelieu.

This interlude was dangerous to the future of the monarchy but by no means disastrous. Nothing constructive was achieved, but it was a period of peace abroad and only minor civil conflicts, so that on the whole the natural recovery of France continued, aided by price stability. The Catholic Revival was at its height, making a deep impression on the life of the people. Government was weak and lacked direction and drive, and hence there was a strong aristocratic reaction and the autonomy of the provinces increased, but disloyalty did not lead (as it usually did in the century 1560–1660) to collaboration with foreign powers. The pro-Spanish foreign policy which persisted until 1621 was widely popular as a proper Catholic policy, though it held dangers for the future. The political vicissitudes are tiresome and futile, but the weakness of the government allowed the dominant issues in French politics to come more clearly into view when the powerful controls of Henry IV were removed.

The rule of Marie de Medici

The proclamation of Marie as Regent was itself a blow to absolute monarchy and an assertion of the constitutional authority of the Parlement of Paris, which within two hours of the King's death had declared the regency. The next day the Parlement was augmented to a grand council by the presence of the princes, dukes-and-peers, and high officers of state. In it the nine-year-old King held a lit de justice and himself proclaimed his mother the Regent.

Marie retained in office her husband's ministers known as the *barbons*, but Sully was now a complete misfit, and was dismissed after a few months to facilitate a spending spree. After a short campaign in which Julich was captured, foreign policy was reversed by Villeroy, who revived the Spanish marriage project. Spain and France were allied for ten years; Louis XIII was to marry the eldest daughter of Philip III, the Infanta Anne of Austria; the heir to the Spanish throne, the later Philip IV, was to marry Elisabeth, Marie's eldest daughter. This alliance secured the weak government of the regency from many perils.

Ties of loyalty to the crown had been dissolved by the death of Henry IV. The Italian Regent gave the real power to a camarilla of secret advisers, her confessor Father Coton, the papal nuncio, Leonora Galligai her witch-like foster-sister and principal lady-in-waiting, and Leonora's husband the handsome, foppish adventurer Concini, an intelligent, unscrupulous favourite, whose hold over the Regent through his wife was unbreakable. The Bourbon princes Condé and Soissons deeply resented this foreign rule which excluded them from power, and they led the trouble-makers among the grandees. To quieten them the Regent gave them large bribes, pensions and governorships. They built up private armies and eventually by a show of force compelled her to convoke a meeting of the Estates General, the last before 1789. in 1614. But the elections went against the grandees, and they had little influence on the proceedings. The Estates General had no legislative power, but each of the three estates, Clergy, Nobles and Third Estate, meeting separately, presented a *cahier* of proposals at the end. They agreed on nothing except the need for a special court to try dishonest financiers.

The most important proposal, supported by the Nobles and Clergy, was the abolition of the paulette and with it the inheritance of office. Venal officials were very unpopular and the higher orders resented the wealth, power and pretensions of the developing noblesse de robe. The Third Estate was split on this question. Two-thirds of their members were officials, and they carried a wrecking resolution approving of the abolition of the paulette but not of inheritance, and coupling this with a demand for the abolition of the pensions paid to grandees and the reduction of the taille. The wrangling between the three estates on these and also on religious questions left the government free to do as it pleased, and action on the paulette was postponed because no alternative means of raising money had been found. During the dispute, the nobles displayed their arrogant contempt for the Third Estate: 'We do not want the children of shoemakers and cobblers to call us brothers. . . . There is as much difference between them and us as between the master and his valet.'

The Third Estate drew up a very strong resolution that it should be a fundamental law of the kingdom that the king held his crown only from God, and no outside power had any right to absolve subjects from their allegiance for any cause whatever. The Ultramontane clergy objected strongly to this outspoken attack on papal claims, and Marie rejected it. On the other hand, the demand of the clergy that the decrees of the Council of Trent should be received in France was rejected by the other estates. The last Estates General before the Revolution dissolved in bickering and confusion, and the grandees renewed their defiance of the Crown.

At this meeting Armand du Plessis de Richelieu, the 29-year-old Bishop of Luçon, emerged as an outstanding politician. He had already proved himself a model bishop in a poor and difficult diocese, and had acquired powerful friends, Father Bérulle and Father Joseph du Tremblay, a leading member of the Capuchin Friars. Tall, spare, and delicate, Richelieu had a commanding presence and an eloquence which induced the clergy to make him their spokesman at the concluding session. He won the Queen Mother's heart by his panegyric of her government, his support of the Spanish marriages and her foreign policy, and his advocacy of strongly Catholic measures, including pressure on the Huguenots. He insisted on the value of churchmen as ministers, and demanded a place for an ecclesiastic in the Council of Affairs. Marie made him her secretary and took more and more notice of his advice. The Catholic revivalists forming the political group known as the dévots looked to him for shrewd political action. He was determined to achieve power and greatness, and had few scruples as to the means.

Richelieu's first big opportunity came in 1616. Condé had by a show of force made a place for himself in the government as head of the Council, and Concini (now Marshal d'Ancre) persuaded Marie to change her ministers to meet this threat. The barbons were replaced by a vigorous ministry led by Mangot and Barbin. Barbin arrested Condé and imprisoned him in the Bastille, and Richelieu was then appointed Secretary of State for War and Foreign Affairs. He intimidated the rebellious grandees by a show of vigour not seen since the death of Henry IV. Abroad he achieved little but learned much. He had pinned his faith on Concini, for whom he had a considerable respect, and his career was nearly ruined when Concini was assassinated in April 1617. It is strange that Richelieu's career was sandwiched between those of two Italian adventurers. Concini who initiated him into statecraft, and Mazarin who succeeded him.

Louis XIII destroyed the faint and dubious hope of a better regime. He had been of age since his thirteenth birthday in 1614, but the Queen Mother was too arrogant to realize how precarious was her rule since she was no longer Regent. She felt contempt rather than affection for her son, and left him to his own devices. Ignorant, starved of love, lacking in confidence, and prone to violence, his two ruling passions were hatred of the flamboyant favourite Concini and passionate devotion to his own favourite, his falconer Albert de Luynes, a petty nobleman from Provence. Luynes and the King plotted a coup d'état, had Concini shot, his wife executed for sorcery, and Marie and her principal supporters exiled to the provinces. The feeble barbons were restored to their ministries. Luynes became a duke-and-peer, aggrandized not only himself but his whole family, and aimed, not very successfully, at being the power behind the throne.

Rule of the King

Louis, however immature, asserted himself. He followed the same Catholic policy as his mother at home and abroad. His autocratic temper, seen in the 'execution' of Concini, revealed itself also in severe measures against extravagant dress, against pensions and venality of office, and against duelling. When he ordered the execution of a Breton nobleman for duelling he said, '*Je dois la justice à mes sujets, et en cet endroit je dois préférer la justice à la misericorde*'. But neither the King nor Luynes was capable of firm rule. In an Assembly of Notables the government brought forward a reforming edict of 243 articles, but although approved this was never carried into effect, and the paulette and venality of office had to be restored to keep the officials loyal in the next crisis.

The Queen Mother was determined to regain power. Richelieu mediated between her and the King, and secured for her the governorship of Anjou, but she was unsatisfied, and in 1620, aided by a group of governors who hated the upstart Luynes, she raised a revolt which was quickly crushed. The King enjoyed soldiering, and he and Luynes decided that they would bring to an end the intransigence of the Huguenots in Béarn, a part of the old kingdom of Navarre not yet assimilated into France. Their attack on Béarn brought about a Protestant rising throughout the Midi, led by Rohan. Luynes died while besieging Montauban. Béarn was subdued, but the Protestants emerged with their privileges otherwise intact, except that they lost all their places of surety but three: La Rochelle, Montauban, and Montpellier. Rohan gained a pension and the governorship of three towns. Lesdiguières, governor of Dauphiné, the most powerful of the Huguenot chiefs, had opposed the revolt. He now became a

Catholic and was rewarded with the mainly honorary office of Constable of France, which was abolished after his death.

For a time the strongly Catholic outlook of Louis XIII was reflected in foreign affairs. The Thirty Years' War began in 1618 with a revolt against the Habsburg Emperor Ferdinand II by his Protestant Bohemian subjects. France brought about a settlement between the Catholic League and the Evangelical Union in Germany in the Treaty of Ulm in 1620, which prevented the German Protestants from going to the rescue of their leader, Frederick Elector Palatine, who had been elected King of Bohemia by the rebels. French diplomacy therefore helped to defeat Frederick, who lost Bohemia by his defeat in the battle of the White Mountain in December 1620.

Spain had sent forces to fight for the Emperor. On the death of Philip III in 1621, his son Philip IV appointed as chief minister Count Olivares, who adopted a vigorous and ambitious policy. Spain seized the Catholic Val Tellina in North Italy from its mainly Protestant overlords of the Grisons in order to get a clear line of communications to Austria and the Rhineland; renewed the war against the Dutch Republic; occupied the Elector Palatine's Rhineland territories; and helped to bring about the entire collapse of the Evangelical Union.

The dévots might rejoice in the Catholic triumphs, but the King, however devout, was concerned with the menace to France in these events. He embarked on an anti-Spanish policy, but neither he nor any of the successive groups of ministers he employed after Luynes's death was able to deal with the complexities of the situation. In his perplexity the King admitted his mother to the Council in 1622, and to please her secured a cardinal's hat for Richelieu.

Louis knew his need for a strong minister and a firm policy in the European crisis, but he was much prejudiced against the new Cardinal, whom he and his ministers regarded as an unscrupulous intriguer. They tried to separate the Queen Mother from Richelieu without success, and in the Council of Affairs she put forward his views, against futile warlike gestures but in favour of building up anti-Spanish alliances. Unsuccessful efforts to cooperate with

Savoy and Venice in restoring the status quo in the Val Tellina underlined the incompetence of ministers.

A new political group had arisen, the *bons français*, who inherited the policy of the *politiques* of the period of religious wars. They were Gallican Catholics and very anti-Spanish and were strongly represented in the Parlements, among the merchants, and even among the theologians of the Sorbonne. Father Joseph gave them some support, although he was no Gallican, and used the international resources and information of the Capuchin Order to further their political aims. Their leading publicist was a priest, Fancan, who in 1623 issued a powerful pamphlet, *La France Mourante*, attacking the existing ministry of the Brûlarts and demanding the appointment of Richelieu as chief minister. He above all wanted effective action against Spain in the Val Tellina.

Strangely enough the dévots were equally enthusiastic about the claims of Cardinal Richelieu, because of his strong orthodoxy and moderation. The Brûlarts, vocally but ineffectively hostile to Spain, were overthrown in February 1624. La Vieuville, the new chief minister, refused to admit Richelieu to the Council, and the Queen Mother was so much annoyed that she sulked and stayed away for two months. Her power, backed by that of the dévots was sufficient to force the King and the minister, in the critical state of foreign affairs, very reluctantly to admit Richelieu to the Council as a consultant only. It was the thin end of the wedge. Once the King was exposed to the personal influence of Richelieu there could be only one outcome.

Meanwhile La Vieuville pursued the anti-Spanish policy with more vigour than discretion. He made an offensive and defensive alliance with the Dutch Republic. He arranged the marriage of Henrietta Maria, Marie's youngest daughter, with Charles Prince of Wales without bothering about the concessions to English Catholics which Richelieu tried to make a condition of the match. England was about to go to war with Spain, and could be a useful if difficult ally. La Vieuville seemed also on the point of war with Spain and to be heading for a direct confrontation with the Pope in the Val Tellina. The dévots, very powerful in the official class, were appalled, and the King began to share their fears. A more subtle direction was needed. La Vieuville played into their hands. He behaved very high-handedly, acting on his own initiative without consulting the Council. At a time when all ministers lined their own pockets he was conspicuously corrupt. Above all he was in the spider's web of the master politician of the age. Richelieu inspired Fancan to write a pamphlet which was a blistering attack on La Vieuville and a demand for Richelieu to be allowed to save the country. The King at last was convinced, and in August 1624 ordered the arrest and imprisonment of La Vieuville and the appointment of Richelieu as chief minister. It was over a hundred years since a churchman had held such a position in France. It was a triumph for the Catholic Revival, and for Marie de Medici whose influence in the state had been miraculously restored. Both the dévots and the Queen Mother were to be rudely disillusioned.

Principal Events, 1598—1624

FRANCE AND COLONIES		EUROPE AND OVERSEAS
Edict of Nantes. Sully Superintendent of Finance	1598	Philip III King of Spain. Peace with Spain: Treaty of Vervins
Henry IV marries Marie de Medici	1600	English East India Co.
	1601	Peace with Savoy
Biron conspiracy. Jesuits readmitted	1602	Dutch East India Co.
	1603	James I King of England
Sully chief minister. *Paulette* instituted	1604	Charles IX King of Sweden
Place des Vosges begun	1605	Time of Troubles in Russia
François de Sales: *Vie Dévote*	1607	Virginia colony founded
Champlain founds Quebec	1608	German Evangelical Union
	1609	Spanish-Dutch 12 Years' Truce. Cleves-Julich crisis
Henry IV assassinated. Louis XIII King of France. Regency of Marie de Medici	1610	
Dismissal of Sully. Rise of Concini	1611	Gustavus Adolphus King of Sweden
	1612	Matthias Emperor. Michael Romanoff Tsar of Russia
Meeting of Estates General	1614	Dutch establish New Amsterdam
Louis XIII marries Anne of Austria. Concini supreme. Richelieu a minister	1616	Shakespeare dies
Louis XIII's coup d'état Luynes favourite	1617	
	1618	Bohemian Revolt. Outbreak of Thirty Years' War
Revolts on behalf of Marie	1619	Ferdinand II Emperor. Frederick King of Bohemia
Agreement of Marie and King	1620	Battle of White Mountain

FRANCE AND COLONIES		EUROPE AND OVERSEAS
Huguenot Revolt. Luynes dies	1621	Spanish-Dutch war resumed. Philip IV King of Spain
Richelieu a councillor and cardinal	1622	Olivares chief minister in Spain. Palatinate conquered by Catholics
Fancan: *La France Mourante*	1623	
Richelieu chief minister	1624	

PART II
Louis XIII and Cardinal Richelieu

[6] RICHELIEU'S STRUGGLE FOR POWER

By 1624 it was quite clear to all serious observers and to the King himself that Louis XIII needed a pilot. He had a strong sense of duty and was anxious to be a worthy son of Henry IV, but he lacked confidence even more than ability, and was moody and irresolute. A chronic invalid – he was worn out by the age of forty – and without a son until 1638, his regime could only be precarious.

The King soon felt that he had found the guidance and the firm will he needed to buttress his own weaknesses. Richelieu was outwardly subservient. Often he clearly outlined alternative policies for the King, who could always feel that the final decision was left to him. The trust and affection between them grew with the crises they faced together. Until 1630 the inner circle of government included opponents of many of Richelieu's views, but Louis usually took the Cardinal's advice, and in return was served with unswerving fidelity. Richelieu described himself as the King's '*créature*', and this in the end infuriated his first patroness Marie de Medici, who thought that as her pensioner he should put her service even before that of the King.

Richelieu was at first in no position to dictate a policy. He was determined this time to maintain and improve his hold on power, with all the wealth and advantages for himself and his family which would accrue. Necessarily he was an opportunist. The

King's support seemed at times too frail a prop against the hatred of the courtiers and grandees, from Queen Anne and the King's brother Gaston downwards. He could not survive without the support of the Queen Mother and the dévot party with which he had always associated and to which she became more and more attached. At every step he had to carry with him a King who was inconsistent and ruthless – Louis had already brought about the assassination of one minister and the disgrace of several others.

Had Richelieu a long-term consistent policy for which he worked from the start of his ministry? This was the popular theory of his career until fairly recently, but it is difficult to hold if one accepts as genuine his *Testament Politique*, a comprehensive statement of his views and defence of his policies, apparently written near the end of his life. Sir Richard Lodge, his Victorian biographer, believed in Richelieu's omniscience, and felt it necessary as a result to maintain that the *Testament* was a forgery. Today it is generally accepted by historians as a genuine expression of Richelieu's views, even if much of it was compiled by clerks. If this is accepted the case is strengthened for regarding Richelieu as a minister who trimmed his policies to circumstances and did not always see where he was going.

There was one imponderable backstairs influence on the Cardinal. Father Joseph du Tremblay, an eccentric genius who was head of the Capuchin friars in France, may have largely inspired the somewhat erratic policy which Richelieu followed, but it is impossible to be certain of this. He was a great man in his own right, saintly but filled with political ambition, a leader in the Catholic Revival in France, and through his friendship with popes and his control of missions overseas a figure of world importance. An early friend of Richelieu, he preferred to wield political power as his unofficial adviser. Father Joseph wanted the Catholic states of Europe to join in a crusade against the Turks, whom he loathed and feared, and about whom he wrote an epic poem 'La Turciade'. He believed that Spain was the chief obstacle to this project, and hence, although in other respects he was a dévot, he supported the anti-Spanish policy advocated by the bons français.

At a time when the official order and the upper bourgeoisie

were bitterly divided over foreign policy, and when it was impossible to disentangle foreign affairs from home affairs, Richelieu, who felt he needed to keep the support of both the dévots and the bons français, did some difficult tightrope walking. At first he maintained the existing policy of resistance to Spanish control of the Val Tellina, and the consolidation of an alliance with England on the basis of the marriage of Charles I and Henrietta Maria. But he had to face more trouble from the Huguenot chiefs, Rohan and Soubise his brother, who had seized positions near La Rochelle. The dévots, including the Queen Mother, wanted a settlement with Spain, no alliance with Protestant England, and the repression of the Huguenots. The French ambassador in Madrid was induced by them to negotiate a peace by the Treaty of Monzon, which Richelieu disliked but was not strong enough to prevent. This treaty gave France the illusion of having won the day for the Protestant Grisons, overlords of the Catholic Val Tellina, but in fact left the Spaniards in a position to use the road through the valley and the passes leading from it.

The year 1626 was critical for Richelieu. A group of courtiers and grandees became alarmed at his firm government and strong hold on the King. They centred round the frivolous heir to the throne, Gaston Duc d'Anjou, a young man of some charm, but dissipated and foolish, who was his mother's favourite. At this time she and Richelieu were trying to force Gaston into a marriage with Mlle de Montpensier, which he and his friends were determined to prevent. This faction had nothing constructive to offer. It stood in part for high aristocratic independence of the monarchy and provincial separatism; opposition to any strong rule and to any reform which threatened its privileges was its mainspring of action. A major achievement of Richelieu was to detach Condé, its former leader, from this cabal and to keep him loyal to Louis throughout the reign.

Gaston's faction now conspired to assassinate Richelieu and possibly depose Louis in favour of Gaston. The plot was revealed; Gaston appeared to repent very humbly, and the King gave Richelieu a military guard. He replied to the Cardinal's offer to resign; 'All my affairs, thanks to God, have succeeded well since you were in office. I have every confidence in you, and it is true that I have never found anyone who has served me so much to my taste as you. The Queen Mother makes you a similar promise. Whoever attacks you, you will have me for your second'. The King struck hard. His old playmates the Duc de Vendôme (Governor of Brittany) and the Grand Prior his brother, both sons of Gabrielle d'Estrées, were suddenly seized and imprisoned. The Duchesse de Chevreuse was exiled – she was the most active intriguer of her day and her involvement threw grave doubts on Anne of Austria, her closest friend, who, according to malicious rumours, would have been glad to marry Gaston if the King were removed from the scene. Chalais, lover of the Duchesse de Chevreuse, had been chosen as the assassin of Richelieu, and the King saw to it that he was condemned to death and himself arranged the details of the execution. Gaston was forced into the marriage he disliked, but escaped punishment and was even granted new royal estates with the title of Duc d'Orléans.

Dévot reforms

The survival of Richelieu in this hurly-burly was convincing proof of his hold on the King, but he needed the backing of the dévots who had stood by him, and for the next two years he worked closely with them. Together they attempted widespread reforms at home and embarked on a policy of war with England, friendship with Spain, and the suppression of the Huguenots. Fancan, Richelieu's bon français agent and publicist, was imprisoned in the Bastille in 1627 for opposing this line too bitterly. The ministry was remodelled. D'Effiat, a reliable client of Richelieu, became Superintendent of Finance. Michel de Marillac, made Keeper of the Seals, was one of two brothers, the other being a high officer in the army, who had befriended Richelieu during the crisis of 1617, and now had become virtually his clients. Marillac was a deeply religious man of saintly life who was also an ambitious politician. He was gradually transferring his attachment to Cardinal Bérulle, the leader of the dévots. Marillac was

very active in office, meticulous and hard-working, and a convinced reformer.

One reform which appealed very much to the dévots was the
abolition of duelling. This mainly bourgeois party had strong
religious objections to the absurd lengths the nobles went to in
defence of their honour. The King hated duelling. Richelieu as a
noble had more sympathy, but his own brother had been killed
in a duel; as a cleric he must condemn such wanton killing, and
as a statesman he deplored the loss of valuable young lives. An
edict against duelling was registered in 1624. The Comte de
Montmorency-Bouteville had been exiled for repeated and excessive duelling. He defied the King by returning to Paris in 1627
and fighting outside the Palais Cardinal a duel in which – as was
then usual – the seconds also fought and the Count's second
killed his opponent. Montmorency-Bouteville and his second
were condemned to death. He belonged to one of the greatest
French families. The Princesse de Condé, three duchesses, and
the pregnant wife of the Count, all fell on their knees before the
King, but he was adamant. (The unborn child became a great
general of Louis XIV's reign, the deformed Marshal Luxembourg.) Richelieu rejected an appeal to intervene, but to attribute
the execution to him is straining credulity – it assumes that the
King was a mere puppet, and that the puppet-master was
incredibly skilful in concealing the strings. In the *Testament*
Richelieu doubted whether duelling could be eradicated, and
disapproved of extreme severity against it.

At the outset Richelieu hoped to reform abuses, but was soon
forced to compromise. At a special council held at Fontainebleau
in 1625, he proposed the abolition of the sale and inheritance of
offices – the end of the paulette. He drew back in face of over-
powering opposition from the officials. In the *Testament* years
later he defended inaction: 'Venality of office would be a crime in
a newly-established republic, but prudence does not allow us to
act in the same way in a monarchy, whose imperfections have
passed into habit, and whose disorder is part of the order of the
state'. Richelieu's argument was that at least the venal office-
holders would want to protect their hereditary hold on office by

loyalty to the state, whereas the alternative was probably that
they would become the clients of disloyal grandees. (They were
in fact rather like the holders of government stock in Hanoverian
England who had every incentive not to turn Jacobite, because
a successful revolt would destroy the value of the stock.) Basic
reforms here and in the realm of finance were renounced. Richelieu
never had any clear views on taxation, and showed singularly
little interest in a juster system. Among all the ruthless acts of
Louis XIII's reign there does not appear to be a single case of the
punishment of a rapacious tax-farmer, except by the lynch law
of starving mobs.

To give the dévots and loyal grandees a feeling of participation
in the government an Assembly of Notables was called in 1626
– it was the last such consultation, except during the Fronde,
until the eve of the Revolution. Here Richelieu talked vaguely
of fiscal reforms which were never begun, and of the economic
policy which he intended very seriously, and which will be
considered in the next chapter. He also proposed to overhaul the
administration, and Marillac, who as Keeper of the Seals was
head of the legal system and had general oversight of internal
affairs, drew up many rules and regulations. Finally in 1629
Marillac issued a comprehensive code – known from his nickname
as the *Code Michaud* – to regularize the councils, the central
administration, the organization of the army, and the control
of the economy. It was impossible to act so vigorously in France
without arousing the most intense opposition of the established
vested interests. In this case the Parlement of Paris, although
forced to register the code by a lit de justice, kept up a ceaseless
opposition. Richelieu had no heart for this kind of dispute – he
was not vitally interested in administrative reform – and after
the fall of Marillac he allowed the code to become a dead letter.
Such was the fate of the chief legislative measure of the reign.

The English and the Huguenots

It pleased the dévots when in 1627 Richelieu negotiated an alliance with Spain, and France made war on England. He recognized

that England's geographical position enabled her to choke French trade, and he also resented England's claim to the salute in the narrow seas. He had carried to a conclusion the English marriage project, but he was very dissatisfied with the consequences. Henrietta Maria was neglected by Charles I, her French household was dispersed. The crews of seven English ships borrowed for the containment of La Rochelle mutinied rather than act against the Huguenots, and Charles, refusing to attempt a revocation of the penal laws against English Catholics, constituted himself the champion of the French Protestants. Buckingham on a diplomatic mission offended everyone by his arrogance and made extravagant love to the Queen of France.

War was very near. On the French side, the dévots looked forward to an attempt to crush the Huguenots at home and to overcome the leading Protestant state. England resented Richelieu's new naval and commercial policy, and Buckingham saw the prospect of military glory and popularity with the English Protestants. La Rochelle was at this time the biggest French port, and its merchants, bitterly opposed to Richelieu's new companies for foreign trade (see next chapter), sent Soubise to London to persuade Buckingham to lead an expedition to aid a revolt.

The Huguenots were divided. In the Midi, where Richelieu had been tolerant and restrained Marillac from persecuting, they were unwilling to renew their revolt, though Rohan was among those urging them to fight. Even in La Rochelle the office-holders were loyal, but Soubise, the merchants and the pastors carried the day. Buckingham arrived in July 1627 with over 60 vessels and 8,000 men on the island of Ré, just offshore from the city. Meanwhile Richelieu had obtained a promise of naval help from Spain, but the 40 ships tardily sent were so ill-equipped and the crews so ill-found as to be useless. The King and Richelieu took charge of the siege of La Rochelle and the operations against the English army on Ré. Louis XIII was at his best as a soldier. He was brave and action made him less morose, and he was good at military detail. On campaign away from court influences Richelieu found him much more manageable, and military comradeship

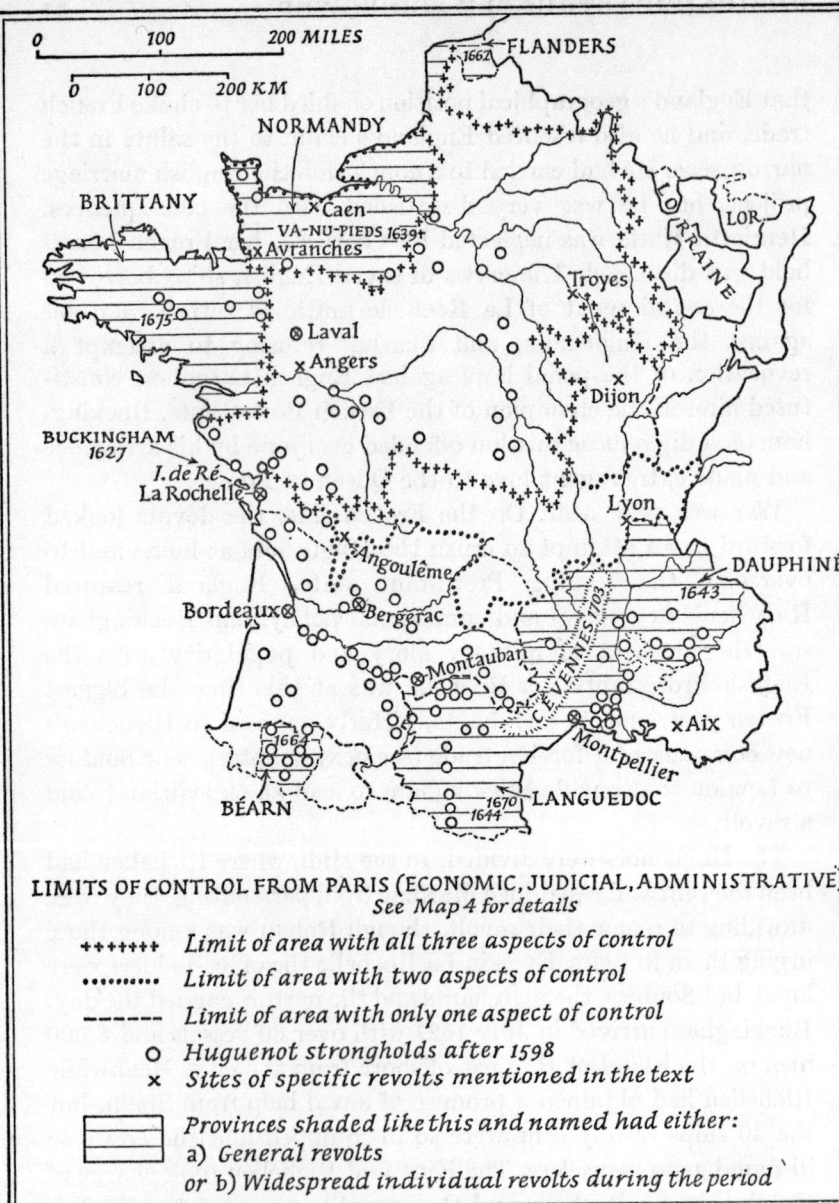

LIMITS OF CONTROL FROM PARIS (ECONOMIC, JUDICIAL, ADMINISTRATIVE)
See Map 4 for details

+++++++ *Limit of area with all three aspects of control*

•••••••••• *Limit of area with two aspects of control*

------- *Limit of area with only one aspect of control*

○ *Huguenot strongholds after 1598*

× *Sites of specific revolts mentioned in the text*

Provinces shaded like this and named had either:
a) *General revolts*
or b) *Widespread individual revolts during the period*

1 FRANCE (BOUNDARIES OF 1715): CHIEF CENTRES OF TROUBLE IN
THE SEVENTEENTH CENTURY (EXCLUDING THE FRONDE)

strengthened the affection between them. Richelieu proved an admirable military commander. The army was even well organized, properly paid, fed and equipped. Buckingham was ignominiously bundled out of Ré, and a mole across the harbour prevented later English relief expeditions from achieving anything. By the time of the last English attempt in September 1628 the French fleet was the stronger. When most of its people had died of starvation – the population was reduced from nearly 30,000 to under 6,000 – La Rochelle surrendered. Peace with England came the next year in the Treaty of Susa.

Too late the Protestants of the Midi now rose against the triumphant royal forces. The next year, while Richelieu was in Italy, the King and Condé crushed all resistance, and Richelieu returned to prepare the Grace of Alès, a general settlement made in June 1629. The codicils of the Edict of Nantes granting the Protestants the rights of political assembly and garrison towns were cancelled, but the religious privileges and legal protection granted in the Edict were confirmed. Once and for all the menace of a Huguenot state within a state was removed, but this was a reasonable and generous settlement. Rohan eventually served in the French army against Spain, as did many other Huguenot nobles. When troubles occurred in the future, above all during the Fronde, the Protestants remained loyal, and their thrift and industrial skill were a strength to the state. The dévots were bitterly hostile to the settlement. Richelieu had broken with them for the first time, and on this issue jeopardized his political future for the sake of a principle.

[7] THE DAY OF DUPES

By 1629 Richelieu and the dévots were parting company. The Grace of Alès offended them and they taunted Richelieu with the title of Cardinal of La Rochelle. Marillac wanted to intensify the movement for conversion of Protestants, and even proposed offering rewards and persecuting those who were not compliant, a foreshadowing of the policy of Louis XIV. On this issue the King, sensitive about his pledged word and that of his father, stood by Richelieu. The Queen Mother was regent north of the Loire during the King's absence at La Rochelle, and for the whole kingdom when he went to Italy. This new taste of power sharpened her appetite to be in fact the second sovereign of France. She took all her advice from Cardinal Bérulle and Marillac, and resented Richelieu's increasing disregard of her. When Bérulle died, Marillac, full of political ambition, began to savour real independent power as Marie de Medici's chief adviser. He drew up the Code Michaud and struck at the corruption and wealth of the highest officials. He introduced a major plan to convert the privileged pays d'états, which paid less than a quarter of their rightful share of taille, into pays d'élections like the mass of French provinces. This caused serious trouble to the government in just those provinces which were already the least under control, particularly Burgundy, Provence and Languedoc. Richelieu disliked and feared the struggle with entrenched provincialism and officialdom that followed and probably regarded Marillac as an old pedant and busybody, though as the Queen Mother's protégé he would be very difficult to dislodge. In truth Marillac was beginning the task of modernization of the ancien régime which Richelieu avoided.

Richelieu's position was now very difficult. Marillac felt strong enough to oppose him openly, and if the Queen Mother finally broke with him, he doubted whether he could keep his hold on the moody King. It was the renewal of the struggle with Spain that brought about the final breach, and regained for the Cardinal the support of the bons français. While the French were engaged in war with England and civil war the House of Habsburg appeared to be on the point of triumph in the Thirty Years' War. The German Calvinists had been crushed and their champion the King of Denmark forced to make peace. The Emperor's overpoweringly successful commander Wallenstein had reached the Baltic. The Catholic success was much too good to last. In 1629 the fanatical Emperor Ferdinand II promulgated the Edict of Restitution, which was a crushing blow at the neutral Lutherans as well as the defeated Calvinists. Gustavus Adolphus of Sweden, probably the ablest European monarch of the seventeenth century, was already helping Stralsund on the Baltic to resist successfully Wallenstein's onslaught. French diplomacy, wonderfully improved by Richelieu, was already at work to take full advantage of every rift in the Catholic forces. Father Joseph's greatest service to Richelieu was his conduct of German affairs, and he was at the Diet of Ratisbon in 1630 to attempt to divide Maximilian of Bavaria from the Emperor by playing on his fear of Wallenstein, who was planning to make the Habsburgs the real rulers of Germany. When Ferdinand had to choose between the Catholic League of princes and his general he dismissed Wallenstein. France and Bavaria had for the first of many times in their history drawn together. At the same time another diplomat, Charnacé, was arranging peace between Sweden and Poland to allow Gustavus more freedom of action in German affairs.

Richelieu was now thoroughly alarmed by the threat of Habsburg domination and encirclement by Spain. When Spain intervened to prevent a French grandee, the Duc de Nevers, no friend of the Cardinal's, from taking his rightful inheritance of the Duchy of Mantua-Montferrat in North Italy, Richelieu persuaded the King to fight. In 1629 he went with Louis across the Alps and they relieved Casale in Montferrat, which the Spaniards were besieging. The next year Richelieu without the King led the army in Italy, while the Imperialists from Germany invaded and besieged Mantua and Spinola himself attacked Montferrat. In March 1630 Richelieu took Pinerolo, a historic moment, for he here met the papal envoy Giulio Mazzarini, later known as Jules Mazarin. At this point Richelieu faced the King with the most crucial decision of the reign, for war or peace. French historians believe almost unanimously that the decision for war was the only sane one. Hauser, in *La Préponderance Espagnole*, writes of Casale and Mantua, 'on these two places hung the destiny of Europe, not only of Italy, but of Germany, of Sweden, of the Netherlands, of the world'. Tapié, in his excellent book, *La France de Louis XIII et Richelieu*, goes so far as to

claim that 'to be or not to be, that was the question for our
country. Louis XIII and Richelieu chose existence.' These judgments appear to need reconsideration, but it will be best to
postpone the discussion of this question to the summing up of
Richelieu's foreign policy.

No doubt Richelieu in his memorandum to the King made out
a strong case for going to war against the encircling Spaniards,
but one has to remember that he had other unexpressed motives
for preferring war. His own power was much more secure when
he and the King were together on campaign, with Louis playing
his favourite role of soldier king. Moreover with France at war
Richelieu was more than ever indispensable. Only he could
possibly handle the complications of European diplomacy in the
new situation now developing.

Richelieu's memorandum to the King after Pinerolo seemed to
be balanced. He pointed out that *'si le roi se résolvait à la guerre,
il fallait quitter toute pensée de repos, d'épargne et de règlement du
dédans du royaume'*. The King decided on war and joined
Richelieu in North Italy. Casale was held but Mantua fell, and
the King, taken ill, returned to Lyon. Meanwhile Marillac,
speaking for the whole dévot party and the Queen Mother,
opposed the decision. His request to be allowed to resign was
rejected by Richelieu, who still felt the need for the Queen
Mother's favour as it became more and more unattainable. Even
the King could not reconcile them much longer. In a letter to
Richelieu Marillac made his position clear: 'It seems to me that
it is the chief glory of good government to think of the relief of its
subjects and of good statutory measures for the state, which
can only be carried out if we are at peace', and at a meeting with
Marie and Richelieu he spoke of 'the miseries and afflictions of the
French people languishing in a great and incredible poverty'. The
social sympathies revealed in such a comment, which might
have come from Vincent de Paul himself, roused Richelieu's fear
that the softer and more pious side of the King's nature might
respond. Louis mixed with his people far more than his son did,
though not so much as his father, and he knew their miseries.
For years a series of peasant outbreaks in many parts of

France had shown the desperation of the poor. Marillac had a case.

For a time it appeared that the dévot cause would triumph. In September at Lyon the King's life was despaired of. The Queen Mother had become reconciled to the Orléans faction, and all was set for the reign of Gaston with no doubt Marillac as chief minister. The apparently dying King asked the great Duc de Montmorency, virtual ruler of Languedoc, to protect Richelieu, who had made ready for flight. Then an intestinal abscess burst and the King rapidly recovered. Richelieu tried desperately to win back the Queen Mother's confidence, but all was useless. The convalescent King fell more than ever under the influence of his wife, his mother, and his confessor, and all were hostile to Richelieu. At last at Paris in November Marie felt ready for a show-down with the Cardinal. Father Joseph in Germany, and Mazarin in Italy, appeared to have secured peace, and therefore Richelieu was less necessary to the King. She dismissed, with much abuse, the Cardinal's favourite niece Mme de Combalet from her service. In council she secured the appointment of Marshal de Marillac (Louis, Michel's brother) to the command of the army of Italy. Then behind locked doors in her own palace of the Luxembourg she passionately begged the King to dismiss his prime minister; either Richelieu must go or she would. Richelieu kept himself well informed. He knew of this interview, and found his way by a tortuous route to a door which Marie had omitted to lock. So he burst in upon them and pleaded with the King for considera-tion, while Marie went beyond all permitted bounds of behaviour in the King's presence, even for his mother. Louis retired to his quarters to consider what to do, but everyone assumed that the Queen Mother had won and all was over with Richelieu, and his enemies came out into the open. But Louis could not bear the thought of ruling without his great minister. He went to his hunting lodge at Versailles, sent for Richelieu, and confirmed him in office. It was the Day of Dupes, not a conspiracy but a confrontation.

The struggle for power did not end but was intensified, with Richelieu now in a very strong position. He at once had Michel de Marillac arrested and sent to Châteaudun, where he died two years later. Orders for the arrest of his brother the Marshal were sent to Italy, and he was held as a hostage for the good behaviour of Marie and Gaston. Richelieu secured from the King a renewed promise: 'Stay near me and I will protect you against all your enemies'. At last the King was weaned from his imperious and stupid mother, but it took time. Ten days after the Day of Dupes Richelieu could still write very humbly to her: 'I would prefer to expiate my misfortune by my death; there is nothing in the world which I would not do to avoid the continuance of your disfavour, I do not say in order to gain your good graces, for which I cannot hope, but only to be free from your anger'. This crawling attitude in the proudest minister France ever had throws a flood of light on the strength of the bond of clientage in the seventeenth century. But without the guidance of Marillac and subject to the foolish whims of Gaston the Queen Mother revealed her essential silliness. She could do nothing effective against the King's firmness and in the end she chose exile rather than humiliation. When she fled to Brussels she lost all influence on the course of events. For the rest of the reign the dévots lacked cohesion and force. Marshal de Marillac was the most distinguished victim of their challenge for power. His trial by a special tribunal went badly, for he could not be proved guilty of treason, and even a charge of peculation was difficult to substantiate. The King wanted a conviction, Richelieu arranged a new trial with a new tribunal at his own country house at Rueil, and Louis de Marillac was found guilty of peculation and executed. He had done nothing beyond the ordinary run of official dishonesty. This was Richelieu's most vindictive action, against an old friend and benefactor; perhaps the old tie rankled, perhaps it was to warn other clients, perhaps simply to intimidate the Queen Mother and Gaston.

Gaston as heir to the throne was a perpetual menace. A widower, he secretly married a Lorraine princess and then organized an invasion with promised help from Lorraine and from the Duc de Bouillon, a semi-independent Protestant grandee. To support this he persuaded his close friend Montmorency to start a revolt in Languedoc. The joint forces of Gaston and Montmorency were crushed by Marshal Schomberg at Castelnaudary in August 1632, and the King refused all appeals for mercy and had Montmorency tried by the Parlement of Toulouse, and when he was condemned had him executed in Toulouse. He was the greatest duke-and-peer in France apart from princes of the blood royal. Gaston made his peace but escaped into exile later, still a grave embarrassment to the King.

By 1632 Richelieu was not only principal minister and a duke-and-peer of France, he was virtually sole minister. The other leading ministers were his nominees and clients. His relatives became more and more prominent in state and church. He arranged useful and splendid marriages for his nieces and so made new clients. His income became enormous. Yet he was still at the mercy of the King's moods, and all his skill was needed to ensure his place and power.

[8] RICHELIEU AND THE ECONOMY

In his early years as a minister Richelieu took a great interest in economic questions, and had a freer hand in this department than in any other. Historians have often neglected this side of his activity. The *Testament* contains a lucid statement of his economic policy. Hauser in *La Pensée et l' Action Économique du Cardinal de Richelieu* stated his belief that Colbert had access to this writing and was inspired by it, but emphasized that Richelieu's economic outlook was more generous and statesmanlike than Colbert's, for he realized that 'commerce is the creator of new values, the generator of wealth for all peoples'. Like Colbert he admired the Dutch economy: 'The wealth of the Dutch, who properly speaking are only a handful of people confined to a corner of the earth where there is only water and meadow land, is an example and a proof of the usefulness of trade. Although this nation derives from its soil only butter and cheese, it supplies nearly the whole of Europe with the greater part of its needs.'

Although his main interest was in foreign trade, Richelieu made some efforts to improve home industry and communications. He revived some of Henry IV's projects. The Briare Canal was completed and a postal service organized. The government set up new glass manufactures in Picardy and a mirror manufacture in Paris, Richelieu took a special interest in building up the silk industry in Tours, near his birthplace. In the Louvre itself and open to public view dévot piety established the carpet manufacture known as the Savonnerie as a charitable work to employ orphans.

In 1626 Richelieu obtained from the King his appointment to a new post, Superintendent of Commerce and Navigation, and to ensure control of the navy he bought out the existing admirals of the Atlantic and the Mediterranean. He made Father Joseph his economic consultant. Vast conceptions appealed to Joseph and he was idealistic rather than practical. Through him Richelieu came into contact with Isaac de Razilly, a clear-headed expert on maritime and colonial problems, who believed 250 years before the American Admiral Mahan that the country which ruled the sea would rule the world. Richelieu spoke to the Assembly of Notables about the loss of 300 French ships at sea in the last four years, about the bullying of the French by Spaniards and Englishmen, and about the maritime domination of Holland. He would create a French navy – it was non-existent – and build up French commerce and colonies overseas. He said that he needed a fleet to prevent English insults, to cut off Spain's American trade, and to deal with the Barbary Corsairs.

The ports were reorganized after an inspection had revealed their shocking condition. At some Mediterranean ports pirates landed daily and plundered; Toulon was without a garrison. The defences were improved and royal dockyards were set up in many ports. When Richelieu became governor of Brittany he virtually created the port of Brest. By 1636 the French navy had 39 ocean-going vessels, and by 1642 there were 63. The galley fleet in the Mediterranean was hampered by lack of manpower, although Richelieu ordered the authorities to send criminals to the galleys as *forçats*. A fleet of 22 galleys was eventually established, and piracy was brought under control. There were bad gaps in organization, a lack of stores and arsenals, and the administration in the hands of Richelieu's uncle La Porte was improvised and chaotic. But at least a navy existed, and in the war against Spain it gave a good account of itself.

The rather grandiose plans for companies for overseas trade – copying those of England and Holland – were wrecked by the hostility of the existing ports and the apathy of moneyed Frenchmen to enterprises of this kind – they preferred to buy offices or make easy profits in tax-farming. First came Razilly's company, based on the Breton port of Morbihan, for trade with America, whose associates were to have noble privileges. All the vested interests, including the Parlement of Rennes, combined to kill it. Then Father Joseph inspired a wider and vaguer scheme, a company called *La Nacelle de Saint Pierre Fleurdelysée*, which took in eastern and western trade and industrial projects of all kinds, foreshadowing the universal scope of John Law's Mississippi Company. But this 'little bark' foundered almost as soon as it was launched.

Above all Richelieu was interested in eastern trade. France was steadily losing ground in the Levant, and it was difficult to regain this trade in face of English and Dutch competition. Father Joseph's Capuchins made contacts with the ruler of Abyssinia and the Shah of Persia. It was hoped to reach Russia by way of the Baltic port of Narva; a commercial treaty with Denmark enabled this to be attempted. But the results were disappointing – the English Muscovy Company influenced the Tsar against the French, their Russian trade remained small, and they were not allowed to make transit to Persia and the markets of the East. The only remaining hope was the oceanic passage to the Far East. A beginning was made in West Africa, and at the time of his death Richelieu was launching a company to settle Madagascar.

In Canada Champlain, the founder of Quebec, was still struggling to make a going concern. It did not help that the English captured Quebec and Acadia and took Champlain a prisoner to London, but when all was restored in 1632 the colony still did not flourish. The dévots had considerable influence on policy in Canada. The religious orders established themselves, especially the Ursulines at Quebec, and successful Sulpician and Jesuit missions began to convert the Indians and explore the hinterland. Champlain was a high-minded governor who wrote: '*Les véritables richesses coloniales sont la culture du sol et la sympathie des indigènes, et non les mines d'or et une odieuse fiscalité*'. It was very difficult to attract settlers. Razilly formed a Company of New France, with a monopoly of trade for fifteen years, the right to twelve titles of nobility, and the duty of sending 300 colonists a year. Yet in 1635 there were still only 200 people in New France, and even so Protestants were banned. By way of contrast the rival English colonies of Virginia, Maryland, and New England now numbered their settlers in thousands and religious dissidents were welcomed; new communities with self-government were vigorously alive, but the Indians were driven out of their hunting grounds.

The one colonial success of the French was in the West Indies. Richelieu had a financial stake in the first enterprise, the settlement on St Christopher, shared with the English, in 1625. A rapid expansion gave France Guadeloupe, Martinique, and other islands, and a population of 7,000 French colonists by 1642. The principal director of this successful enterprise was a Breton merchant's son, Nicolas Fouquet, of whom more will be heard.

Richelieu's economic policy lost its impetus in the distractions of war. His companies failed and only in the West Indies did colonization succeed. But he deserves to be remembered for the breadth of his vision of world greatness, lost sight of in a European struggle. The failure was partly due to excessive supervision by the government, but partly because there was no strong body of merchants in the capital, as there was in London and Amsterdam, where merchant companies were successful at this time.

[9] PERSONAL GOVERNMENT OF KING AND CARDINAL

The kings of the seventeenth century 'can do what they will, but they need to will it strongly'. (Mariéjol in *Lavisse*, Vol. VI, No. 2.) The amazing strength of the joint wills of Louis XIII and Richelieu, guided by Richelieu's intelligence and drawing fully on the loyalty and ability of his clients, gave to France a wartime dictatorial régime of remarkable force in the years between the Day of Dupes and the deaths of the two chronic invalids. They overcame disastrous handicaps by bold improvisations. Again to quote Mariéjol, writing of the navy but stating a general truth about the conduct of the war: 'On seeing these improvisations and these violent acts of will making up for the lack of the resources of a regular administration, one thinks involuntarily of the methods and men of the Convention'. As in 1793, representatives of the central government were sent to all the centres of disorder with plenary powers, and they rode roughshod over the local authorities. They imposed the fear of the King on all classes of disobedient subjects. The Chancellor Séguier in Normandy after the revolt of the Va-nu-pieds in 1639 ruled by terror. So even more did the brutal peripatetic intendant Laffemas wherever he was sent. The King had less regard even than Richelieu for reforming institutions, and few new permanent organizations emerged from the turmoil of these years. Evils that true revolutionaries would have eradicated grew worse as a direct result of the financial chaos. But against a background of misery and revolt the half-famished French army, which had been ravaging the French countryside, triumphed, five days after the death of the King, on the battlefield of Rocroi, and within a few months the peace negotiations began which in the Peace of Westphalia made France the leading power of Europe.

As the government became more absolute it became even more personal. When Richelieu first achieved power in 1624 he asked the King to make decisions in Council and not to give ear to one minister. There had been arguments and an articulate opposition, and even an Assembly of Notables. After the Day of Dupes the dévots lacked leadership and it was impossible to build on the shifting sands of Gaston's frivolity. Government was precarious because the King was so often ill and could hardly live long. Gaston was the heir until 1638, and his tiresome adventures and plots occupied far too much of Richelieu's time and energy. Then, almost miraculously it seemed, the King had a son, and the Queen, Anne of Austria, apparently frivolous, a partisan of Spain who was known to be actively disloyal, always a hater of Richelieu, became much more the centre of political speculations.

But none of these hostile influences reached the Council of Affairs. After the exclusion of the Queen Mother only ministers sat in it. Châteauneuf, given Marillac's post of Keeper of the Seals because he had stood by Richelieu on the Day of Dupes, was disgraced for opposing him in 1632. Henceforth the ministers all said to the King whatever Richelieu instructed them to say. They called themselves his creatures. He was often separated from the King by business of state or the illness of one or the other, but one or two ministers were always with the King, and Richelieu's letters to them were much concerned with the management of Louis. Formal meetings of the Council of Affairs became less frequent, and obviously much business was settled in informal conversation. For every important act of government however it was necessary to get the King's authorization, as a rule in writing. All business had of course to be put before him. Very often instead of writing direct to the King, Richelieu sent his letters through a minister, and on occasion asked the minister in so many words to watch the King's moods and give him the letter when he was amiable. The young Secretary for Foreign Affairs, Chavigny, was the usual go-between, and he was also deputed to manage Gaston, who regarded him as a friend.

Infinite care had to be taken over personal relationships. The King, whose marriage was a failure, was emotionally starved and very vulnerable. Fortunately Louis's friendship for Richelieu was a warm one, but he had a succession of passionate, though chaste, attachments which were a constant source of anxiety to the minister. In early life Louis was devoted to older men, then at a later time to young girls, and at last to a charming young man. Soon after the Day of Dupes Louis fell in love with Mlle de Hautefort, one of the Queen's ladies-in-waiting, and she used her satirical tongue to do all the harm she could to Richelieu. Then he was captivated by a saintly young girl, Mlle de La Fayette, and this was more serious because she and the King's confessor, the Jesuit Father Caussin, tried to win the King over to a dévot policy of peace, and worked on his deeply religious nature and feelings of compassion for the poor and miserable. She entered a convent in 1637, but the King still had long conversations with her through the convent grille. Father Caussin nearly persuaded Louis that he endangered his immortal soul by fighting a war with Protestant allies, but Richelieu counter-attacked so vigorously that the confessor was dismissed for meddling in politics.

Then Richelieu made one of his worst errors. Mlle de Hautefort began to resume her influence over the King in 1638, and Richelieu deliberately introduced a client of his own, the Marquis de Cinq-Mars, son of the former Superintendent of Finance D'Effiat, a spoilt and charming boy of eighteen, as a rival for the King's affections. Louis was infatuated. He made Cinq-Mars Grand Equerry. When the ailing moody King and the arrogant boy quarrelled Richelieu brought them together again, until at last Cinq-Mars resented his patronage and aspired to his power, so that the Cardinal during his last illness in 1642 was fighting a life-and-death struggle against a worthless young protégé of his own.

The ministers and clients of Richelieu

The cohesion of the ministers, after the unity of King and Prime Minister, was the great strength of this ministry. There were five who really counted, Séguier the Chancellor, Bullion and Bout-hillier the joint Superintendents of Finance. Bouthillier's son Chavigny the Secretary for Foreign Affairs, and Servien a second Secretary, who began to create a war department. (There were four Secretaries all told, but the others were mere clerks.) Only two changes took place in ten years. In 1636 Servien was replaced by an able intendant from the army, Sublet de Noyers. When Bullion died in 1641 Bouthillier held the superintendency alone. The Bouthilliers were among Richelieu's oldest family friends, and their family's wealth and greatness was entirely bound up with his. They were intelligent interpreters of his wishes and little more. For independent initiative in foreign affairs Richelieu looked not to Chavigny but to Father Joseph, his diplomatic expert and intended successor. Séguier was a powerful Chancellor, thrusting his way into the administration and the judicial system, asserting the government's authority in difficult times. He controlled the intendants and commissaries sent into the provinces, and he dealt with the governors and the Parlements. He was as much concerned with police as with justice.

In many ways Bullion, so beautifully named, was the most interesting of these ministers, and there is a good account of him in O. A. Ranum's fascinating book, *Richelieu and the Councillors of Louis XIII*. By holding the purse-strings he could exercise some independent power, and this he enjoyed. His task of raising money for this spreading war was nearly an impossible one, and he was constantly robbing Peter to pay Paul, breaking promises to pay, and throwing a smoke-screen of confusion around his activities which Richelieu was incapable of penetrating. Ranum states that 'Louis never asked if money was available, he simply requested it', sometimes through Richelieu, who did not often worry the King with financial problems. On the other hand, Richelieu could sometimes get money only by using the King, and according to Ranum 'only the Cardinal's favour with the King enabled him to impose on the superintendents what was essentially a ruinous policy for France'. Bullion 'knew well that the Cardinal's wealth was increasing rapidly out of the confusion between the King's and Richelieu's personal wealth', and he is said to have burst out once with the demand: 'Close two mouths for me, His Eminence's household and the artillery; after that I will answer for the rest'. He was evidently rapacious on his own account. His annual income was reputed to be $1\frac{1}{2}$ million livres, and Richelieu, after accusing him of making illicit profits,

demanded that he should 'take up the King's affairs with the
same passion and ardour that he demonstrates in his own'.
Within these usual seventeenth-century limits he appears to have
done his best in an intolerable situation. He dared to make
himself enormously unpopular, so that he had to be buried at
night. He directly influenced the war by allocating good or bad
funds to the generals; Rohan, a hard fighter, had to give up the
struggle in the Val Tellina in 1637 for lack of the funds that
Bullion, who disliked both him and his campaign, denied him.
But in the last resort he was loyal to his taskmasters, and Louis
wrote him a piquant epitaph in a letter to Richelieu: 'The more
I think of him the more I miss him for his firmness. Tell M.
Bouthillier that he should be a little more firm and strict than
he is, otherwise he will grant us everything we ask and there will
be no money for the second half of the year'. Nevertheless the
King confiscated part of Bullion's fortune.

Richelieu was on the whole a good master to his clients. Most
of them, apart from the ministers, were relatives either by blood
or marriage. He made his brother Archbishop of Lyon, his
mother's brother was intendant of the navy, and a good proportion of the high commands in the army and the navy at the time
of his death were held by his dependants. Two young nephews,
Pontcourlay and Brézé, won brilliant naval victories. A cousin,
La Meilleraye, inherited the control of the navy from the Cardinal,
with his Richelieu dukedom and the revived title of admiral.
Some were inadequate but all, with two exceptions, were reliable.
Condé's own eldest son, the Duc d'Enghien (the Great Condé of
the next reign) married one of the nieces, a brilliant match which
set the seal on Richelieu's social position. Enghien, the most
highborn, was also the most successful of Richelieu's relatives,
for he was the victor of Rocroi. Even this royal prince had to
pay court to his patron. On one occasion he passed through
Lyon without calling on Richelieu's brother. A peremptory
letter from the Cardinal compelled him to return from Dijon
to Lyon simply to make good this lack of respect.

Richelieu himself wrote: 'While disorder flourishes and it is
impossible to rectify it, reason wills that one should draw order

out of it; which I have tried to do by granting offices to those whom I can most strongly compel to follow my instructions'. His biographers Hanotaux and La Force agree that his administration, 'by the necessities of the time, and somewhat against his own idea, so strongly methodical, was above all fragmentary, pragmatic, inspired by times and circumstances, by places and people; scarcely planned, by no means organized, it rested only on direct order and immediate obedience'. The fact is that his indomitable will enabled him, with the King's firm backing, to make a going concern of an inefficient system, but by overstraining it he added to the evils he found and recognized but would not attack. Innovations were few and generally unsystematic.

One great exception was the administration of the army, which in the hands of Sublet de Noyers began to take shape before the end of the reign. He had a natural gift for orderly work, much more usual in the age of Louis XIV, and his work stood. For though he was dismissed very soon after Richelieu's death, one of his army intendants Michel Le Tellier succeeded him and built up over the next twenty-five years the most advanced military organization in Europe. Colbert served his apprenticeship in that department. But Sublet de Noyers is the exception. Richelieu was not in general a constructive administrator.

The Parlement of Paris

In dealing with existing institutions Richelieu mixed caution with boldness. The most powerful lay bodies were the Parlements. His use of special tribunals, always including some parlementaires, to try great offenders suited the King's idea of prerogative, but aroused the opposition of the Parlement of Paris. A more regular body which annoyed them was the Chambre de l'Arsenal, a special court outside their control orginally for the trial of forgers and counterfeiters. When they humbly protested against this interference with their jurisdiction, they were summoned to Metz because the royal court was there, and told by the keeper of the seals Châteauneuf: 'This state is monarchical; everything in it depends on the will of the prince who establishes the judges as he wishes'. Not content with this, the angry King himself spoke to them: 'I intend . . . that the things which I command should not be questioned, but that everyone should obey me . . . you are instituted only to judge between *maître Pierre et maître Jean.*' It is clear that Richelieu at times restrained the King when he became too autocratic, and once Louis wrote indignantly protesting to the Cardinal that the counsellors of the Parlement defied him with impunity.

Finance directly or indirectly caused most of the disputes between the government and the Parlement. Its refusals to register edicts imposing new and increased taxes and the sale of new offices led to lits de justice, fresh remonstrances, and the frequent exiling or imprisonment of resisting counsellors. Naturally the biggest clash of all occurred when the Council in its desperate search for new offices to sell, proposed to dilute the Parlement itself. The long wrangle produced two compromises. Seventeen new counsellors were appointed instead of the twenty-four originally proposed. An edict of 1641 regulated the Parlements for the future. They must register royal decrees without discussion, but they were then permitted to remonstrate. At the height of the dispute the President and eight members of the Chambre d'Enquêtes, a junior section of the Parlement of Paris and the most troublesome, had been removed from their inherited and inheritable offices and they were not restored. But the Parlement lived to fight another day.

Finance

Everything comes back to finance and taxation. Bullion's efforts were at times heroic, but his only known constructive suggestion, that the clergy should be made to pay taille, was rejected. The government was far too dependent on the moneylenders and tax-farmers to put the squeeze on them as Sully had done. Richelieu admitted in his Testament that of 19 million livres collected from the gabelle only $5\frac{1}{2}$ million reached the Treasury. The revenue from this salt monopoly, which caused so much misery and so many outbreaks of revolt, did almost nothing to meet the demands of the Treasury, which amounted to over 170 million by the end of the reign. The variations in the gabelle were bizarre. Some places in Brittany were exempt, and there were differences of the order of sixteen to one in its incidence in other provinces. The main tax, the taille, was also very unequally levied. Not only were the nobles, the clergy, and the officials paying the paullette exempt, but in the pays d'états, where the tax was levied on land, the nobles were adept at evading taxation, and the total of the taille came to only about a quarter of what it was in the rest of the country, the pays d'élections. (It is notable that from 1631 Richelieu himself was the governor of the most privileged province, Brittany, and that he made no excessive demands there, kept on good terms with the provincial Estates, and avoided outbreaks of revolt.) The most heavily taxed province, Normandy, is said by Mariéjol to have paid one-sixth of the whole taille of France.

The yield from all these taxes was utterly inadequate. Richelieu was driven in 1637 to invite an alchemist, a protégé of Father Joseph, to demonstrate before the King in the Louvre his power to transmute metals. Alas, he failed to change lead into gold, but played some fraudulent tricks for which he was executed. Naturally the government borrowed money when and where it could, but its credit was poor, and France had no banking system. Great men whose fortunes came from the state lent money; Turenne pawned his plate for the army in Germany; Richelieu was a big creditor himself. In general, the rate of interest ranged from $13\frac{1}{2}$ per cent to 20 per cent. Once again the tax-farmers, lending the government its own money, were the main beneficiaries.

So for lack of a state system of finance France was on the verge of bankruptcy. It may be noted for comparison that the English Commonwealth in the 1650s was able to support, not without strain but without disastrous chaos, armed forces considerably larger in proportion to the population than the most that Richelieu could achieve. All the evidence suggests that it would have been impossible at that time to impose on the French a unified state financial system such as England already had, and

Richelieu was certainly not the man to attempt it; but this does raise some doubts about the claims of Louis XIII to be an absolute monarch.

Expedients saved France from bankruptcy, although towards the end of the reign expenditure was outrunning income by over 50 million livres. First of course came the creation of new offices; 42 edicts were issued after 1635. There was a never-ending supply of candidates for what came to be known later as the noblesse de robe; as Richelieu wrote in the *Testament*, the King's subjects drew rank 'from a variety of offices whose only use is to occupy their leisure and flatter their wives'. Moneylenders preferred to lend a private individual the money to buy an office, rather than lend direct to the government; the security was better. Unfortunately each new office-holder meant one more rich man exempt from taille, and when in 1641 Richelieu suggested exempting postmasters from taille, Bouthillier made a heartfelt protest: if he did, 'all the rich men in the parishes will become postmasters'. The bad effects of the duplication of offices are obvious. The state, already handicapped by anomalies of every kind, was saddled with additional nearly useless officials. Those who held office already could legitimately argue that duplication was a breach of faith with them. Extra stipends had to be found, and the state was more and more heavily mortgaged to the bourgeoisie.

While rogues and swindlers of every kind preserved their property and privileges the innocent *rentiers*, who had lent money to the government on long term, the nearest equivalent at that time to the holders of national debt, suffered in 1639 a reduction of their income by a quarter and again in 1642 by another eighth.

What finally enabled the government to go on with the war was a new gold coinage. The existing gold coins were in a very bad state. It had been forbidden to weigh them, but this only increased the evil. At last in 1640 they were called in and a fine new coinage issued, the louis d'or of 10 livres, a half louis, and a double louis. By debasing the quality of the gold in these coins the government made a profit of 80 million livres. Mazarin inherited a going concern, however embarrassed. The fact is that

France was so rich and populous that there were always large
untapped resources which could be called upon in the last resort
to save the state. Had all paid equally, the burden of Richelieu's
war would have been quite tolerable. The inequalities created
untold misery.

[10] THE PROVINCES—DISTURBANCES AND REMEDIES

Provincial risings

In nearly every year of the reign of Louis XIII there was a rising
against the government; in many years more than one. Besides
the Huguenot revolts in the 1620s purely economic disturbances
were common. The peasants rose in the neighbourhood of Rouen
in 1623, before Richelieu's ministry; and there were similar risings
in Poitou and in Guyenne in 1624. The anger of the rebels was
directed mainly against the élus who assessed the taille. In the
next few years disturbances became more frequent and more
serious as taxation rose. At Troyes rioters pillaged granaries and
a tax official's house was sacked, at Amiens a new tax official was
attacked, at Laval on the border of Brittany a mob crossed the
border, seized and carried back a quantity of tax-free salt, and
gave it away. In 1630 peasants rose and attacked Dijon, Caen,
Lyon, and Angers. Marillac noted with alarm in this period that
although the towns did not join the revolts the local authorities
took little action to protect tax officials, and even Parlements
could be indifferent. His own policies helped to provoke this
bourgeois reaction, and certainly gave rise to the troubles in the
pays d'états in 1629–31 (Provence, Burgundy, Languedoc)
where all classes resisted the attempt to impose on them the
heavier taxation by élus which was the general rule in France.
Richelieu accepted the compromise that in return for an increase

in their grant the provincial Estates should retain their old control of taxation.

When war with Spain intensified the misery, revolts on a much larger scale occurred. Between April 1636 and the summer of 1637 risings in the south-west covered a quarter of all French territory. Blaizac was captured by 400 armed peasants led by their curés and marching to music, with the cry of 'death to the gabelous.' Ten thousand peasants attacked Angoulême. Troops watching the Spanish border had to be used to suppress them. In Périgord a noble, La Motte de la Forêt, led the rebels, occupied Bergerac, and maintained good order while a tax strike was enforced. These sporadic risings proved, as Tapié who records them says, that 'the provincials were not capable of very much and that everything ended in submission to the authority of the King', for which, like the rebels in Tudor England, they had no substitute. They were surprisingly restrained and orderly. Few besides tax collectors were killed. After each rising a batch of rebels was hanged or sentenced to the galleys.

The Va-nu-pieds

The climax of these movements was the revolt of the Va-nu-pieds in Normandy in 1639. In Avranches the local people had the privilege of manufacturing sea-salt for themselves free of gabelle, and on the rumour that they were to lose this privilege thousands rose in arms, lynched an officer of justice, and raised the whole of Lower Normandy. They acted in the name of a mythical leader, Jean Va-nu-pieds, but among their real leaders were gentlemen and priests, and they formed an orderly disciplined body of 20,000 men. They even issued pamphlets with references to Brutus and Catiline. There are many similarities with the Vendéan revolt of 1793. Some of the leaders went as far as to suggest an attack on Paris, but actually the peasants could not leave their fields for long, and were only capable of guerrilla warfare. Meanwhile a new tax on dyed cloth stirred up the people of Rouen to fury, and they killed the first official who attempted to collect it, and pillaged and sacked the homes of tax-farmers and gabelous. The Parlement of Rouen had its own special grievances, and although it showed courage in stopping the violent outbreaks and arresting the leader of the rioters, it refused to take any action beyond the protection of property.

The government nearly despaired. Richelieu said it was 'impossible to find what the soldiers required', and unfairly reproached Bouthillier and the Council of Finance for having brought about an almost 'incurable evil'. Bouthillier wrote to his son: *'Nous sommes maintenant au fond du pot'*. In the end the government managed to send in some foreign mercenaries who ravaged the countryside and hanged and pillaged in Avranches, behaving much worse than the rebels had done. The Chancellor Séguier was given a sort of vice-regal authority in Normandy and the right to punish all seditious persons without trial. He entered a silent and conquered Rouen, interdicted the Parlement and the municipality, and tried rebels by a special commission. The town had to pay for a garrison billeted on the citizens, to compensate the tax-farmers, and to pay an indemnity of over a million livres. Throughout the province Séguier was brutally severe, but in spite of this a revolt broke out the next year at Moulins.

Richelieu's own attitude to the common people appeared to become harder and sterner as misery grew and troubles spread. In the *Testament* he wrote that 'if the people are too comfortable it becomes impossible to keep them within the limits of their duty. It is necessary to compare them with mules, which, being used to a load, are spoiled by a long rest more than by work.'

Local administration: governors

Against this background of disorder, with unpaid famished troops ravaging the countryside and peasant 'mules' kicking their drivers in desperation, Louis XIII and Richelieu were in fact carrying out a work of centralization which had a permanent effect on the French state. Its nature had, however, often been misconceived. Richelieu made no systematic alteration in the

position of the governors of provinces, nor did he institute the
rule of intendants, but the ruthless style of the government left
its mark on both and produced a more unified country, all parts
of which felt its heavy hand.

Mousnier, the chief modern authority on French administration
in this period, says it is impossible to generalize about the position
of the governors or their relations with the intendants. If the
governor was trusted by the regime he might still exercise great
administrative powers. Very few of the grandees holding office in
1624 were capable of ruling or to be trusted. As one by one they
died or made trouble Richelieu brought in more reliable men, so
that in 1642 all there faithful and a number were very competent.
Certainly Richelieu objected to these offices being regarded as
inheritable. Members of the greatest families in France received
cavalier treatment, and in all this we must remember that Louis
XIII was a very active partner with the Cardinal. The Duc de
Guise, governor of Provence, quarrelled with the government in
1629 and was permitted to go into exile instead of reporting in
Paris. Vitry, the assassin of Concini, was the next governor, but
he allowed the Spaniards to win a major success in seizing the
Lérins Islands and was sent to the Bastille; during each crisis
intendants took over control. Bellegarde, governor of Burgundy,
an old crony of Henry IV, dabbled in treason with Gaston and
fled abroad, but his successor was even more a grandee, the
Prince de Condé. After the Duc de Vendôme was removed from
the governorship of Brittany, Richelieu, because the province
was very important to his naval programme and dangerously
independent, secured the appointment for himself.

D'Épernon, governor of Guyenne, was one of the most difficult
to deal with. The old favourite of Henry III and companion of
Henry IV showed no deference whatever for Richelieu or any of
his subordinates; indeed he made a violent physical assault on
Henri de Sourdis, Archbishop of Bordeaux, Richelieu's representative. The King eventually forced him to kneel for pardon
to the Archbishop, but he kept his governorship until his son the
Duc de La Valette was condemned as a traitor in 1640 and he
himself was exiled for the short remainder of his life.

The new governors did not conform to any one pattern. In fact during this period Gaston d'Orléans, though denied frontier provinces, was allowed, between treasons, nominal control of others. In Languedoc, one of the most difficult provinces to control after Montmorency's execution, Marshal Schomberg was made governor and controlled justice, police, and finance, working very closely and without a hint of rivalry with two intendants. One governor asked for the help of an intendant in the Bourbonnais; on the other hand, in Dauphiné the governor and the intendant were constantly at loggerheads.

Intendants

Richelieu's government made more use of commissaries than its predecessors; they were now more usually called intendants, and became more and more important because of the extent and duration of the crises they had to cope with. Although for this reason many intendants stayed for years in one province they never displaced the local officials, and clearly Richelieu never regarded them as permanent. He had very few direct dealings with them. On one occasion during the siege of La Rochelle, when the Parlement of Bordeaux tried to arrest Servien the intendant there, the King made the President of the Parlement go on his knees 'before your master'. There was never any doubt that they had the monarch's full authority and they showed that they deserved his trust.

They used this power in a wide variety of ways. Laffemas hanged and tortured. Labardement burned witches and sorcerers. D'Argenson pulled down castles and crippled feudalism. Some intervened to save the local poor from unjust taxation and exactions. No doubt as Tapié says, 'their patient work of many kinds slowly instilled obedience into the kingdom. Day after day their work prepared the unity of France. It constructed absolutism' – but not systematically. One must agree with Mariéjol that Richelieu (who left the development of the intendant's office to his Chancellor) was 'indifferent to institutions. Provided that he could bend them to his designs it mattered little to him in what way they functioned. He was neither the founder nor the precursor of the monarchy of Louis XIV (*la monarchie louis-quatorzienne*)'. Mousnier states flatly that he disliked intendants. The intendant of the later period is essentially a new kind of official. That Richelieu had no such official in mind is shown by his comment on intendants in the *Testament*; they are 'not only to perform the function of intendant of justice in the provincial capitals, which serves their vanity better than the public good, but to go everywhere in their provinces investigating the ways of the officials, learning how the nobles behave, putting a stop to all kinds of disorder and especially the acts of those who being powerful and rich oppress the feeble and poor subjects of the King'. This is not hypocritical. As Bishop of Luçon the young Richelieu had concerned himself in just this way and was an admirable local administrator. It is a contradiction in his career that he took little interest in orderly national administration, and even as a churchman was more concerned with the high politics of religion than with the spiritual welfare of the people

[11] THE CHALLENGE TO THE HABSBURGS

The decision for war

Whatever aspect of government or society is considered the war dominates the scene. Richelieu's statement in 1630 had been an exact prediction: 'If the King resolves on war we must give up all thought of rest, of thrift, and of the regulation of home affairs'. The unanswerable question is whether, in spite of the disorder and financial chaos it produced, the decision for war was the best one in the long-run interests of France, or whether Marillac's policy, pursued with the energy that only Richelieu could have given it and accompanied by the maximum overseas development, would have enabled France to take an unchallengeable lead in the struggle for world power. There are too many imponderables here. It is clear that Richelieu over-estimated the Spanish Empire in 1630. Olivares himself appeared a worthy antagonist, but the feeble monarchy, the unsound and declining economy, and the defective structure of the state, imposed severe limitations on a vigorous minister. Neither was Habsburg unity as real a menace as it seemed at the time. There was much scope for French diplomacy short of war behind a defensive shield, as Richelieu proved.

The preliminary struggle

The decision to make a warlike stand in North Italy appeared strategically sound, but in some ways this policy was not much more successful than the previous French interventions in Italy since 1494. It is impossible to agree with Hauser that the future of Europe depended on French retention of Casale and Mantua. Mantua was entirely lost to French influence, and if Casale and Pinerolo were held, they did not enable France to control the policy of Savoy, even though Louis XIII's sister was for a time the Regent, and still less to prevent the Spaniards from using the Val Tellina as a route to Germany. The greatest Habsburg success of the decade, at Nördlingen, followed the march of a Spanish army to Germany by this route. Rohan temporarily closed it later, but the defection of the Grisons to Spain in 1637, the direct result of lack of money, left the Val Tellina open to Spain for the duration of the war. Richelieu failed to build here a stable system of alliances, and the appalling difficulties of the unpaid French armies are shown by a report of Le Tellier, intendant with the army in Piedmont, that in six months the army had had no supplies other than a little powder and a pair of shoes, and that the soldiers were 'naked and miserable'. No wonder the policy failed.

It was in Germany that Richelieu's diplomacy brought great successes, and this was seconded by a major military contribution in the later years. But without a good deal of luck the outcome might have been very different. The uncontrollable allies

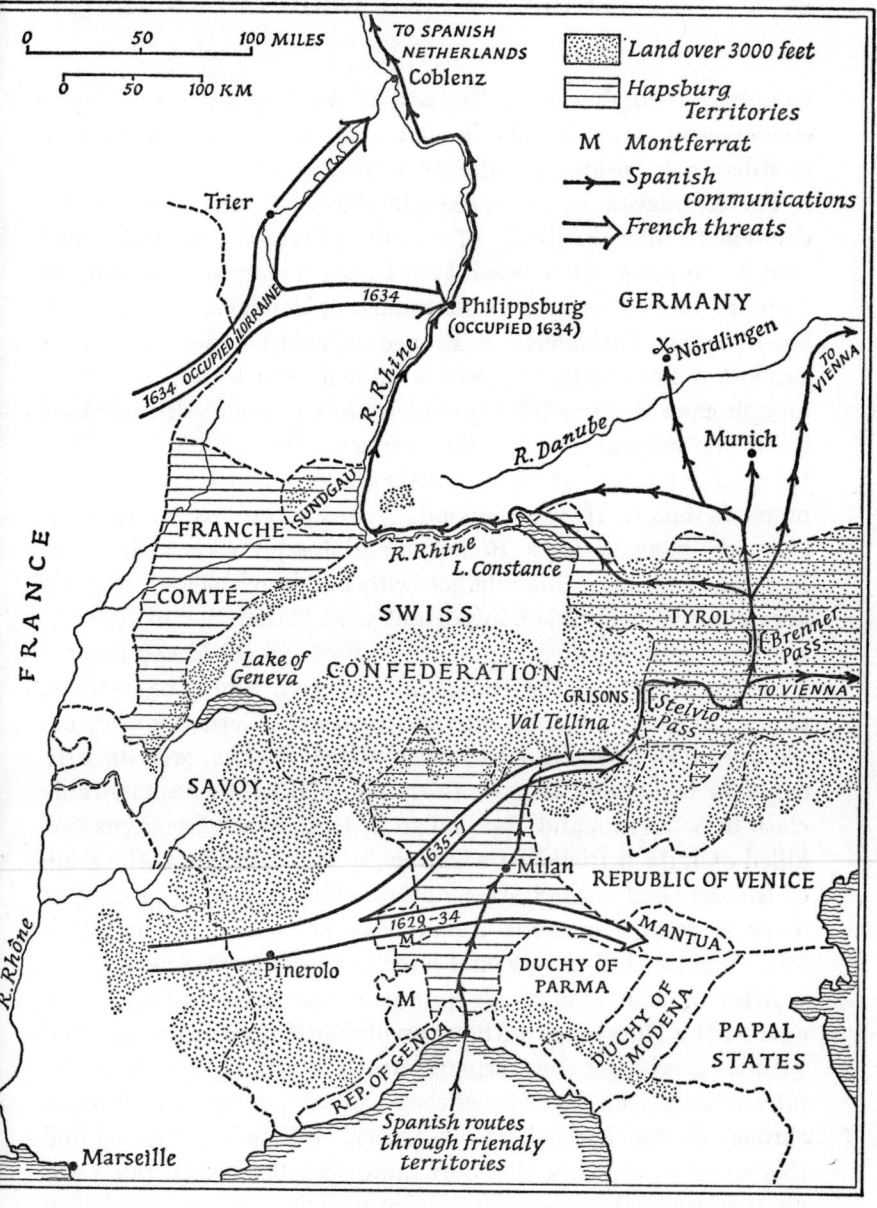

2 FRENCH THREATS TO SPANISH MILITARY COMMUNICATIONS 1629-37

Gustavus Adolphus and Bernard of Saxe-Weimar died very conveniently; the revolts in Portugal and Catalonia against Castilian rule ensured the defeat of Spain.

The foundation of the success in Germany was of course the decision to offer a subsidy of a million livres a year and moral support to the great Swedish king by the Treaty of Bärwalde in January 1631, after he had intervened in North Germany. In an age of ardent Catholicism in France the cold-blooded decision to support a Protestant ally was a difficult one to make. Father Joseph gave it respectability, but there was some self-deception in his attitude expressed in the comment: 'We have to use these things like poisons, of which a little serves as an antidote and too much is fatal'. It was beyond even Father Joseph to take Gustavus in small doses. Richelieu and Joseph never abandoned hope of combining this alliance with one much nearer to their hearts but militarily less important with Maximilian of Bavaria and the Catholic League, and their efforts to shield the League from Gustavus and the Protestants angered him. The decision of Gustavus to advance into south-western Germany after his victory of Breitenfeld, and not to attack Vienna, was directly contrary to French plans in Germany, and led to an inevitable clash between him and Maximilian in 1632. When Gustavus was killed at Lützen Richelieu wrote coolly to the King: 'If the King of Sweden had waited six months before dying it seems that Your Majesty's concerns would have been more secure'. It is fairly certain that they would have been more entangled.

After Lützen Richelieu's problem was to secure Germany against the Habsburgs without involving France in the war and without sacrificing the German Catholics, and to cope with the international complications of the revolt of the heir to the French throne. Gaston had joined the Queen Mother in Brussels, and this seemed for a time the more immediate threat. Lorraine was always involved in Gaston's intrigues against France. Richelieu had been particularly harsh to the princes of the House of Lorraine who had been governors of provinces in France, and he had had many troubles with its influence in the three bishoprics of Metz, Toul, and Verdun. Gaston secretly married a princess of

Lorraine, and then revealed the fact in 1634. The response of France was to occupy Lorraine. It was not only overrun but formally annexed and ruled with extreme harshness as a French province, and the restoration of its Duke became one of the major international issues of the time. Gaston responded to pressure and bribes and returned to France on very favourable terms, with a big increase of income. His marriage, to the annoyance of the Pope, was annulled by the Parlement of Paris. After that he was politically quiet except for a half-hearted plot to assassinate Richelieu in 1637, until the Cinq-Mars conspiracy enabled him to play the traitor once more. Richelieu seems to have regarded him as more a fool than a knave, and until 1638 a fool who as heir to the throne was incalculably important. Disloyalty in the royal family concerned him more than popular risings.

French policy in Germany did not have a smooth passage. Oxenstierna, the new Regent of Sweden, proved a very able and reliable ally, but naturally his policy in Germany was a Protestant one. The League of Heilbronn in 1633 between the Swedes and the German Calvinists worried Richelieu and Father Joseph. To influence Germany more effectively the French were advancing towards the Rhine. They had taken the Archbishop-Elector of Trier under their protection in 1631, and after the occupation of Lorraine they took Philippsburg in the Palatinate and some towns in Alsace, effectively blocking the Rhine as a route for Spanish forces and so helping the Dutch in their struggle. The Spanish and Imperialist victory at Nördlingen in 1634 forced the French into the war, long before they were ready, to maintain their new positions. They took Bernard of Saxe-Weimar, the brilliant Calvinist military leader, into their service, and many of the mercenaries in the French army itself were German Protestants. More and more the outright support of German Protestantism was forced on the unwilling French government, especially by the new treaty of alliance with Sweden in the spring of 1635.

Richelieu protected Catholics when he could, as when in allying with the Dutch he rejected Frederick Henry's suggestion that France and Holland should divide the Catholic Southern

F.B.C.F.—6

Netherlands between them. He preferred an independent Belgian territory.

France in the Thirty Years' War

Before declaring war France began the attack on Spain in 1635. Gradually, in spite of an acute shortage of money and supplies, Sublet de Noyers, appointed to the war department in 1636. produced a modicum of order from chaos. There was at first the gravest risk of outright defeat. When the Spaniards from the Netherlands reached Corbie on the Somme in 1636, and their cavalry raided as far as the Oise, it seemed as if Paris itself might fall. The government put on a bold face and calmed the fears of the Parisians, and Richelieu ordered a stoppage of work to encourage enlistment. Somehow an improvised army of 30,000 men was raised and Louis himself led it to Corbie and defeated the Spaniards. Spain was in no condition to maintain an offensive. The Spanish armies were obsolete and their organizational problems in the long run greater than those of the French. The new tactics, strategy and logistics demonstrated by Gustavus and Wallenstein, were lost on both sides in this contest of tired heavyweights. The French generals dragged on from siege to siege, and very gradually got the upper hand, so that the Spaniards held very little French territory at the time of Richelieu's death. The French army was built up to 150,000 men. The effort was all the more exhausting because unpaid soldiers were constantly deserting; half of the troops were foreign mercenaries. Richelieu made caustic comments on most of the French generals, and in the *Testament* wrote '*Il n'y a point de nation au monde si peu propre à la guerre que la nôtre*'. Guébriant, who took over Bernard's German army after his death and who was killed in 1643, was the first good general of the new French army. Enghien began his military career as a volunteer in Picardy in 1640, and Turenne served under Harcourt, one of the better commanders, in Piedmont.

Sea power was very important in the war because it was vital to Spain's communications with the Netherlands and French contact with Portugal. The decisive event was the great triumph of Tromp and the Dutch over the Spaniards in 1639 in the Battle of the Downs. Richelieu had inspired the French navy with a fighting spirit which went far to overcome its defects in organization, and French successes began in 1638 when Richelieu's nephew Pontcourlay won a victory with a fleet of galleys off Genoa, and Archbishop Sourdis defeated the Spaniards off Fontarabia in the Bay of Biscay. Two more victories had a decisive effect on the revolts in the Spanish peninsula. Another nephew, Brézé, at the age of twenty won a battle off Cadiz in 1640, and this victory led to the proclamation of the Duke of Braganza as King of Portugal. Then after Sourdis had suffered a disgraceful defeat off the Catalan coast Brézé won a victory at Barcelona in August 1642 which enabled the French to take Perpignan and make better contact with the Catalan rebels.

Meanwhile Richelieu's diplomacy and French subsidies helped to keep the German struggle going. Here the Swedish generals Baner and Torstensson were generally victorious, and Bernard won some significant successes, particularly the capture of Breisach on the Rhine in 1638. He then occupied much of Alsace and planned to make himself the duke, but his death in 1639 removed this embarrassing prospect and allowed the French to take over his mercenary army and to stake out their own claim to Alsace.

Before the Spanish crisis of 1640 Richelieu had begun to negotiate with Olivares to end the war that neither could afford, but it was hard to come to terms with a power which would not even abandon its claim to the Dutch territories fifty years after they had been irrevocably lost. When Spain's difficulties suddenly increased and the revolts in Portugal and Catalonia threatened a complete break-up, Richelieu began to stall, but did not abandon the negotiations. Much of the ground had already been prepared for the conferences which eventually met in Westphalia in 1643.

The war which Richelieu had advocated and Louis XIII had waged had brought ascendancy in Europe within the grasp of France (Rocroi was about to be won). This and the creation of the army and navy and a good diplomatic service are Richelieu's immense contributions to France. He had won Lorraine, if only temporarily, and made decisive moves towards the Rhine, and he had laid the foundation for controlling the future of Germany, though doing far more for Protestantism than he had intended. The cost to France in misery and disorganization had been frightful, and greater than it need have been because Richelieu was so little interested in better administration and finance.

[12] RELIGION AND THE ARTS UNDER LOUIS XIII

Progress of the Catholic Revival

The French Catholic Revival deeply affected the society in which Richelieu worked, and had a profound influence on both the King and the Cardinal. We have seen that it produced a political group which aspired to power and had a policy with a religious basis, and Cardinal Bérulle and Marillac, its leaders, were old friends of Richelieu. But the noblest leader of the revival in this period, the dominant figure in the 1630s, St Vincent de Paul, was not political, but primarily concerned with works of charity. His pity for the forçats who rowed the naval galleys led him to persuade Richelieu to found a hospital for them. Vincent organized the Sisters of Charity, and set up hospitals for foundlings, incurables, and the poor – a model for later developments under Louis XIV. The Chancellor Séguier endowed an orphanage, and many other charitable institutions were founded by pious donors of the upper bourgeoisie. Vincent's establishment at St Lazare was a place of retreat for the pious and a centre for good works of all kinds, including the Lazarist mission of priests serving the remote countryside, the galleys and Moslem lands. Another centre for charity and propaganda was the Compagnie du Saint Sacrement, a lay society founded in 1629. This society was full of good works, but it had a sinister side – it was a secret society, intolerant, spying out heresy to inform the authorities and urge severity.

The revival of religion deepened old divisions and brought out new ones. The Jesuits had been placed in a very strong position by Henry IV, and they retained their control of the King's conscience and of higher education, but the zealots of the revival regarded them as lax, and although in France they were only moderate Ultramontanes there was a powerful current of Gallican feeling against them. In the early years of Louis XIII a new divisive Gallican movement had been begun by the Abbé Richer, who had extended his attack on the Pope's pretensions to an attack on the powers of bishops and a demand that priests should have a larger share in the management of the Church. Richelieu forced him to recant in 1629 but Richerism persisted among the curés right down to the French Revolution. In the 1630s Jansenism appeared, bitterly anti-Jesuit, an austere uncompromising offshoot of the Counter-Reformation. Its originator in France, the Abbé de St Cyran, director of Angélique Arnauld's nunnery of Port Royal in 1636, was an old friend of Richelieu, but very much annoyed him by extreme theological views and forthright criticism of his 'Protestant' foreign policy to such an extent that in 1638 Richelieu ordered St Cyran's imprisonment. (Jansenism will be dealt with in Chapter 15.)

The Cardinal and the Church

As the effective head of the French Church Richelieu steered a middle course between Gallicanism and Ultramontanism. He found both the lay Gallicanism of the Parlement and the clerical Gallicanism of the priests a menace to authority. To accept the Pope's claims unreservedly would however prevent an independent foreign policy with Protestant alliances, so that Richelieu could never be an Ultramontane. He commissioned Marca, a former president of the Parlement of Pau, to write a book, *De Concordia Sacerdotii et Imperii*, to show that Gallican liberties were not incompatible with the rights of the Pope.

Richelieu had to take into account the sincere religious feelings of Louis XIII; St Vincent de Paul had considerable influence with him, and even more important was the constant pressure of Father Joseph. The Cardinal insisted on decency and order. He did much for French theological learning by becoming Proviseur of the Sorbonne and rebuilding it. Since the early years of the King when a papal commission was set up for the purpose, there had been unsuccessful attempts to reform French monasteries. Richelieu threw himself into this task, but met a stubborn resistance. To gain more control, but also to enjoy the huge revenues, Richelieu secured his election to the headship of two monastic orders, the Cluniacs and the Cistercians, by becoming Abbot of Cluny and Abbot of Cîteaux, although he had not taken monastic vows. It was a great abuse that the chief reformer was also the chief pluralist with an annual income from the Church of $1\frac{1}{2}$ million livres. Yet he was sincerely concerned about its better management, and in his *Testament* devoted far more attention to the clergy than to any other topic.

In many respects Richelieu was conservative and conventional. He distrusted upstart scholars and preferred nobles as bishops. He and his contemporary Archbishop Laud were the last important advocates of the employment of bishops for political tasks (most of whom were failures). Richelieu's nomination of Father Joseph as his successor showed his faith in the clerical order. On the other hand religion must not encroach. He fell foul of Cardinal Bérulle and the dévots for trying to make it the determining factor in politics, and he got rid of the King's confessor Father Caussin for the same offence.

The main cause of trouble between Richelieu and the clergy was his demand that they should pay some share of the big increase in taxation. It was the custom for the King to summon an Assembly of Clergy every five years, and for the clergy on these occasions to vote a sum of money, a don gratuit, not as voluntary as it sounds, in lieu of tax. They never paid anything like a fair share. Between 1624 and 1639, while taxation in general had greatly increased, their annual contribution had actually diminished from 1,300,000 livres to 1,173,000 livres annually.

In the financial crisis of 1640 the government demanded a sixth of their income, but there was never any hope of obtaining this, and at the Assembly of Mantes in 1641 Richelieu had to expel two successive presidents before they voted 5½ million livres. The Pope condemned the proceedings and the Parlement of Paris forbade the publication of the Pope's Bull. The clergy still possessed an organization capable of confronting the monarchy.

The arts

The reign of Louis XIII was a time of cultural renaissance, fostered by the new education supplied by the Jesuits and Oratorians. The *salon* appeared as a focus of culture – the Hôtel de Rambouillet, already flourishing in the 1620s, was the first. The King was very economical in his patronage of the arts, but Marie de Medici, Gaston, and Richelieu were great builders, and many grandees became patrons of writers and artists. Italian baroque influences on French art became stronger in the later years of the reign, but characteristic of the arts in France in this period was their strong sense of order, a classical severity restraining the exuberance of the baroque.

Richelieu himself contributed to this orderly spirit. His own style of writing was a model of clarity, and he founded the French Academy – a body of literary men with a strictly limited membership and great prestige – to uphold pure French, the classical rules and decent order against the baroque excesses of the age, which in France took the form of préciosité, much admired in the salons, ridiculed later by Molière. Corneille, the pioneer of French drama, was the greatest writer of the age. His heroic tragedy, *Le Cid*, produced in 1636, written in rhyming couplets, set the pattern for classical French drama. Richelieu allowed it to be published with a dedication to Mme de Combalet, his much-loved niece, and himself arranged some special performances.

A lesser art in which Richelieu showed much interest was that of journalism. He employed a host of pamphleteers, beginning with Fancan. He also founded the first journals, the *Mercure*

Français and the official *Gazette*, to convey information and propaganda. Louis cooperated in the production of the *Gazette* and sometimes wrote for it in a dry, neat style. At times he would draw Richelieu's attention to the need to include items of information which justified French actions and put their enemies in the wrong. It was a modern approach to publicity.

A strict censorship upheld Christian order against threats of atheistic and libertine writing, but it drove out of France the greatest thinker of the age, Réné Descartes, the inventor of a new geometry using Cartesian coordinates, a pioneer in astronomic theory, and above all the founder of modern philosophy in his *Discours de la Méthode* published in 1637, a triumph of deductive reasoning. Descartes is the father of rationalism.

Nicolas Poussin, the leading French painter of the age, also lived abroad, attracted to Rome as the centre of the world of art. But he worked there mainly for French patrons, and remained true to the French classical spirit; his ideal landscapes are strict geometrical compositions, his figures poised and grouped with classical grace; he resisted the baroque spirit of his time.

The same is true of the great French architecture of this period. The Luxembourg Palace, built for Marie de Medici, and the beautiful town and château of Richelieu, built by Lemercier for the Cardinal at his birthplace in Poitou, were in the French style of Henry IV and already old-fashioned. The town of Richelieu still exists, complete but for one gate, its geometrically planned streets and squares set in a rectangle of walls, an unspoilt period piece and a fine memorial. A new style, influenced by baroque but restrained by the French feeling for order, is to be seen in the wing of the château of Blois built for Gaston d'Orléans by François Mansart, and in the church of the Sorbonne – one of the domes of Paris – designed by Lemercier for Richelieu.

Mansart, Lemercier, Poussin, Corneille, and Descartes all exemplify the same sense of order, peculiarly French at this time (a little later the English had Hobbes, Wren, and Newton). All were bourgeois, representatives of the new forces shaping French society. Richelieu rather unwillingly fostered these forces. He was noble by birth and sentiment, and in the *Testament* he described as '*la malheur du siècle*' the rise of the officials at the expense of the nobles, 'who are rich only in their courage and who give their lives for the state from which others extract the substance'. His own mother was a member of this rising class – her family were parlementaires. The greatness of France in the seventeenth century depended mainly on the bourgeoisie.

Death of Richelieu – Conclusion

When his last illness was upon him, Richelieu discovered that Cinq-Mars was plotting to kill him and to make Gaston Lieutenant-General of France; in return for a promise of peace Spain agreed to help the conspirators. Once he knew all the facts Louis XIII did not hesitate to sacrifice Cinq-Mars, who was deservedly executed. Gaston fled, repented, and once more obtained forgiveness. Richelieu wore out his last reserves of strength in fighting this conspiracy, and died in November 1642.

Bonfires were lit to celebrate the hated minister's death. He was solely blamed for the arbitrary acts of the reign, the thunderbolts of power. For two centuries his historical reputation was that of the Mephistophelean terrible minister of *The Three Musketeers*. Then in the days of the Third Republic French historians, humiliated by German greatness and faced by the weakness of French politicians, turned with nostaliga to the great figure of the Cardinal who had given France the mastery over Germany. A new legend of the coldbloodedly rational superman took the place of the old. Louis XIII's very considerable share in the government was belittled.

Richelieu's career contained many contradictions. He was not the Olympian figure of the panegyrists, as he appears in the fine portrait by Philippe de Champaigne, but a minister of extraordinary intelligence and will-power whose career and even life depended on the moods of Louis XIII. His self-seeking contrasts with his patriotism. (Thanks to his Huguenot men of business his personal fortune was much better handled than the national finances, and by 1642 his annual income was three million livres, $2\frac{1}{2}$ per cent of the national income.) As a bishop he administered his own diocese admirably, and he had a gift for military organization, yet at the national level he was no administrator, and this powerful regime contributed little except despotic energy to the problem of creating a centralized state in France. Clear bold statements about problems of government and *raison d'état* – a term he contributed to the vocabulary of political thought – contrast with his cautious conservatism in the handling of many domestic problems. Richelieu rightly emphasized that he had tamed the Huguenots and the grandees, but he had allowed new evils to develop – the power of the financiers, for example – by maladministration. Yet, when all these things are allowed for, he remains one of the most remarkable statesmen in European history.

Further Reading, 1598–1643

In addition to the general works mentioned in the preface the following books are useful for this period. It is concisely covered by H. Méthivier's *Le Siècle de Louis XIII* in the *'Que Sais-je'* series (Paris, 1964). There is no modern treatment of Henry IV's reign as a whole in English, though some aspects are dealt with in D. J. Buisseret's *Sully* (London, 1968). There is a biography by G. D. Slocombe, *Henry of Navarre* (London, 1931). V. L. Tapié's *Le Règne de Louis XIII* (Paris, 1952) is a thorough and modern history of the reign. C. V. Wedgwood's *Richelieu and the French Monarchy* (London, 1949) is readable but superficial. There is a new sympathetic biography of *Richelieu*, by D. P. O'Connell (London, 1968). Richelieu's own *Testament Politique* (Paris, 1947) is clear and revealing; an English translation is projected. H. Hauser's work on *La Pensée et l'Action Économique du Cardinal de Richelieu* deals with a neglected aspect of his career, and *Richelieu and the Councillors of Louis XIII*, by O. Ranum (Oxford, 1963) is a lively treatment of the workings of Richelieu's ministry. Aldous Huxley's *Grey Eminence* (London, 1941), a biography of Father Joseph, possibly over-emphasizes the importance of this mysterious figure, but is very readable. For some knowledge of B. Porshnev's *Popular Risings before the Fronde* (now available in German and French translations) one should consult M. Prestwich's long review in the *English Historical Review*, Vol. 81.

Principal Events, 1624—43

FRANCE AND COLONIES		EUROPE AND OVERSEAS
Richelieu chief minister	1624	Anglo-Spanish war
Chalais conspiracy	1625	Denmark in 30 Years' War.
		Charles I King of England.
		Charles marries Henrietta Maria
Marillac a minister.	1626	Wallenstein defeats
Companies for foreign trade		Mansfeld. Danes defeated at Lutter. Treaty of Monzon
War with England.	1627	Mantuan Succession question
Buckingham's Ré campaign.		
Siege of La Rochelle		
Fall of La Rochelle	1628	Wallenstein in N. Germany. Siege of Stralsund
Peace with England.	1629	Peace of Lübeck. German
Protestant rising in Midi.		Edict of Restitution.
Peace with Huguenots – Grace of Alès		French in N. Italy. Massachusetts founded
Day of Dupes.	1630	Diet of Ratisbon.
Fall of Marillac		Gustavus invades Germany
Flights of Gaston and Marie de Medici	1631	Treaties of Bärwalde and Cherasco
		Battle of Breitenfeld
Revolt of Gaston.	1632	Battle of Lützen. Gustavus
Execution of Montmorency		killed. Christina Queen of Sweden. Oxenstierna Regent
Vincent de Paul founds Sisters of Charity	1633	Wentworth in Ireland. Laud Archbishop of Canterbury.
		Protestant League of Heilbronn
Occupation of Lorraine.	1634	Wallenstein assassinated.
French Academy founded		Battle of Nördlingen
	1635	Treaty of Prague.
		France enters 30 Years' War
Spaniards reach Corbie.	1636	Battle of Wittstock
Corneille: *Le Cid*		

FRANCE AND COLONIES		EUROPE AND OVERSEAS
Descartes: *Discours de la Méthode*	1637	Ferdinand III Emperor
	1638	Bernard takes Breisach. French naval victories
Revolt of Va-nu-pieds	1639	Dutch victory in Battle of the Downs. Bernard of Saxe-Weimar dies
Jansen: *Augustinus*. Montreal founded	1640	Catalan and Portuguese revolts. Great Elector becomes ruler of Brandenburg. Short and Long Parliaments in England
	1641	Execution of Strafford. Fall of Olivares
Cinq-Mars conspiracy. Cardinal Richelieu dies	1642	English Civil War. Tasman's voyage to Australia
Louis XIII dies	1643	

PART III
Cardinal Mazarin

[13] BEFORE THE FRONDE

The rise of Mazarin

In the short period of Louis XIII's reign that remained after
Richelieu's death (November 1642–May 1643) a new and strange
figure of outstanding importance appeared in the council, Giulio
Mazzarini, known in France as Mazarin. He was an adventurer of
genius, and his career was one of the most extraordinary in
European history. He began as a humble client of the Colonna
family in Rome, in whose household his father was a steward.
The money to launch his career he won by gambling. He gained
the favour of Pope Urban VIII, whom he served as soldier and
diplomat in North Italy, working for peace between Spain and
France during the Mantuan Succession dispute. He prevented a
battle between their forces at Casale in 1630 by riding bravely
and dramatically between the armies to proclaim a newly agreed
settlement achieved mainly by his own persistent efforts.

Already Mazarin had been in France, had met and greatly
admired Richelieu, and had become a Francophile for life. In
1633, after he had been appointed to a post in Avignon, he became
a nominal cleric, though he was never a priest. His hopes were
realized when Urban VIII sent him to Paris in 1634 to work, as
special nuncio, for peace between France and Spain. Although
in seeking peace he might be regarded as opposing Richelieu's
policy, he succeeded in ingratiating himself with the Cardinal, as
well as with Louis XIII and Father Joseph. His partiality to the

French offended the powerful Spanish party at the Vatican, and in 1636 he was recalled and for three years remained in Rome with no satisfactory papal employment. During all this time he was a secret agent of the French government, smoothing relations with the Pope and conveying valuable information to Paris; this could hardly remain a secret when, on Father Joseph's death in 1638, Mazarin was substituted for him as the nominee of Louis XIII for a cardinal's hat. At last in November 1639 the longed-for invitation arrived. He would be employed at the French court. Some time before this he had written to his friend Walter Montagu: 'It is my consolation that to a gentleman every country is a fatherland'. France was now his second home, and he never returned to Italy.

Mazarin was a man of taste, and as he became able to afford to buy, one of the great art collectors. Already he had charmed his French friends, including the Queen, by the presents he had sent from Rome. One of his functions in Paris was to direct Richelieu's theatre, and he procured from Italy all kinds of objets d'art and paintings for Richelieu's mansions. But it was not for this that he had been sent for. He became the expert on Italian affairs, working to prevent a rupture with the Pope, who at last, in 1641, made him a cardinal. He was sent on a difficult mission to Savoy, where the misgovernment of Louis XIII's sister Christine had created chaos. Here he proved his worth, softening the harsh measures demanded by Richelieu, achieving order by tact, and leaving the duchy a support to France instead of a liability. He was with Richelieu when the Cinq-Mars affair came to light, secured the submission of Bouillon at Sedan, and intervened to save Gaston and possibly the Queen from humiliation and disgrace. Mazarin was looking to the future.

When Richelieu died Mazarin still had no official position in France. Recent research throws doubt on the accepted story that Richelieu passed over all his well-tried councillors by proposing Mazarin as his own successor. It appears that he merely recommended Mazarin's admission to the inner council. See G. Dethan, 'Mazarin avant le Ministère', in *Revue Historique*, Vol. 227.

Louis XIII had a very high opinion of Mazarin's abilities, but

Dethan rejects the general view that he immediately offered him the first place. It seems likely that Louis intended to work through a triumvirate of Sublet de Noyers, Chavigny, and Mazarin. When Louis was on his deathbed Mazarin and Chavigny engineered the fall of Sublet de Noyers, the strong man of the government, by making Louis believe that he was plotting with Anne to secure her full power after the King's death. The King now tried to fix the form of government by a declaration which made Anne Regent after his death, but under the control of a Council of Regency of three royal persons and four ministers, to act by majority vote. Mazarin was now high in favour. When the future Louis XIV was christened, just before his father's death, Mazarin was the godfather.

On 14 May 1643, Louis XIII died. Four days later the Parlement of Paris quashed his declaration on the Council of Regency, and made Anne the Regent with unrestricted authority, and Gaston d'Orléans Lieutenant-General. Anne had great dignity and pride, and was determined to preserve her son's authority. But she had always been rather frivolous, her friends had nearly all been enemies of her husband's regime, and she had neither the knowledge, the ability, nor the industry to rule alone. Chavigny she associated with the hated ministry of Richelieu, but Mazarin had always been her friend, and now she took him as her Prime Minister and guide. On the whole Gaston stood by the new government; his 'good' period lasted for the next five years.

Many of the old intriguers against Richelieu returned from prison or exile, and there was a sense of relaxation and an outburst of pleasure and gaiety in the Court, regardless of the misery outside. The Duchesse de Chevreuse returned to the Court but not to the full favour of Anne which she had enjoyed in the past. She soon found other courtiers who were furious at the success of Mazarin's insinuating ways, and these – les Importants – hatched a plot to destroy him. Beaufort, the younger son of that César de Vendôme whom Henry IV once thought of legitimizing and making his heir, was a swaggering hero of the Parisian populace. He intended to assassinate the hated minister. But

Mazarin, though soft, was alert, and unravelled the plot. Beaufort went to prison and the Duchess into exile.

The plotters had realized that Mazarin was no ordinary minister. For the rest of his life, except during the Fronde, he held a more powerful position than any other subject under the ancien régime. His relationship with the Queen is as enigmatic as the man himself, but it was not that of a client or créature. He advised Anne what to do and how to do it, just as they both told the child King what to say and what to do. And this strange triumvirate ruled France until Mazarin's death. Anne provided the authoritarian spirit, the young King the divine right, the minister the intelligent direction, tenacity, and low cunning, of this peculiar regime. Because Mazarin had not become a priest he was free to marry, even though a cardinal, and on the evidence of the tone of the letters of Anne and Mazarin most historians have assumed a secret marriage, but it is only a surmise. Mazarin at first lived in his own house close to the Palais Royal (Richelieu's mansion to which Anne had moved from the Louvre). Later he had a suite of rooms adjoining the Queen's in the palace.

Foreign affairs

Mazarin now got rid of Chavigny, his chief rival, and took charge of foreign affairs himself, by-passing the Secretaries of State far more than Richelieu ever did. He pushed ahead with peace negotiations, begun at Münster in 1643. The successes in the war, and the need for the prestige of success for himself, led him to make demands beyond anything Richelieu had contemplated. He set the seal on French supremacy, but created the conditions for the interminable conflicts of Louis XIV.

While the diplomats conducted their long-drawn-out negotiations in Westphalia, French and Swedish armies were winning victories. The new Secretary of State for War, Michel Le Tellier, a former intendant, became Mazarin's most confidential adherent. In the midst of financial chaos he built the organization of the French army on the foundations laid by Sublet de Noyers. Efficiency was now the criterion of promotion, and when Gué-

briant was killed Turenne was brought from Italy to command
the French army in Germany. After crushing the Spaniards at
Rocroi at the very beginning of the reign, Enghien cooperated
with Turenne to make the Rhine and its bridgeheads a secure
frontier for French power; the chief French victory was won at
Freiburg-in-Breisgau in 1644. The French and Swedish armies,
living off the wretched German countryside, were now in a
position to put more and more pressure on the Emperor to
compel him to accept their terms of peace. Bavaria was overrun
by the Franco-Swedish forces, and at last in 1648 the road to
Vienna was open to them, and in October the Emperor signed
the Treaties of Münster and Osnabrück.

Mazarin's efforts to bring Spain to terms were unsuccessful.
Things had gone badly for France in Italy, where a pro-Spanish
pope, Innocent X, was elected in 1644, and a revolt in Naples
was mishandled. In Spain lack of resources prevented Enghien
(Prince de Condé after his father's death in 1646) from saving
the rebels in Catalonia. In the Netherlands Gaston conducted a
war of sieges culminating in the capture of Dunkirk. The Dutch
merchants were weary of the war and the war party there was
gravely weakened by the death of the Stadtholder Frederick
Henry in 1647. Then Mazarin made a disastrous error. To secure
peace with Spain he broke his promise not to negotiate without
the Dutch, and offered to exchange Catalonia for the Spanish
Netherlands. The Spaniards refused and revealed the terms to
the Dutch. As a result, the Dutch Republic and Spain made peace
at Münster, and France, with a declining and neglected navy, was
deprived of the support of Dutch sea power. Spain felt equal to
continuing the war. In fact, when the troubles leading to the
Fronde weakened France in 1648, a Spanish army began a fresh
invasion, but was crushed by Condé at Lens. The war was to
continue for eleven more years.

In the Peace of Westphalia France secured full recognition of
her old gains of Metz, Toul, Verdun, and Pinerolo. Very vaguely
parts of Alsace were ceded to her, with claims of sovereignty over
other parts; this section of the treaty, perhaps owing to a final
rush, was so badly drafted that a conflict over its meaning was

almost inevitable. France gained bridgeheads on the Rhine. The
humiliation of the Habsburg Emperor was complete; he lost all
real control of Germany, whose princes were now virtually
sovereigns; he had to recognize Calvinism as a third fully
independent religion in the Empire; and he had to see French
influence in Germany growing through her control of the Rhineland and through the enlarged power of her protégés in the
German Diet, Sweden, Brandenburg, and Bavaria. Mazarin had
been well served by his subordinates, Servien at Münster and
Servien's nephew Lionne as foreign minister. This diplomatic
triumph handsomely completed the work of Richelieu. It was
achieved without much internal support. The French had never
cared greatly about the war, and in the end showed, according to
Kossmann, 'no interest, no trace of enthusiasm'. The struggle to
overthrow the hated minister who had achieved all this absorbed
the political energies of France in 1648.

Domestic discontents

Clearly Mazarin's main interest was diplomacy. A friend of Le
Tellier's considered that in domestic affairs he was feeble, a
foreigner who 'had no sufficient understanding of internal affairs
and the order of the kingdom'. Yet he gave a more definite
organization to the inner council, which acquired its name of
Conseil d'en Haut in 1643; and he set up a new Council of War.
Moreover he had one systematizing subordinate who now had
a freer hand. This was the Chancellor Séguier, the only one of
Richelieu's ministers for whom Mazarin had much use. After
Louis XIII's death new councillors, mainly nobles and courtiers,
had been created recklessly in the reaction from Richelieu.
Séguier found 120 councillors, and reduced the numbers of those
with votes to 22.

We have seen that Séguier had already under Richelieu
controlled the intendants and developed their role in government.
Now instead of merely supervising they entered directly into the
local administration. In 1643 in many provinces the assessment
and collection of taxes was taken from the local officials and given

to the intendants. It was a momentous step towards centralization and produced a violent reaction from the venal officers. In
fact here was one of the main roots of the Fronde. The trésoriers
de France and the élus had set up central organizations in Paris
which campaigned for their rights. One spokesman said in July
1648: 'If these dangerous innovations continue, and are author-
ized, nothing will remain of our offices but the vain name of
magistrate'.

The intendants intensified the discontent in the countryside by
employing tax-farmers to collect the taille, sometimes backed up
by troops. Urban and rural risings, mainly in the Midi, reached
a peak in 1643, a year when prices were unprecedentedly high
owing to bad harvests. Parlements and local officials generally
refused to cooperate with a government whose centralizing
policy they resented. It seemed as if the popular risings were
bound to lead to a general crisis. Porshnev, the Russian historian
of the risings before the Fronde, attempts to show that the Fronde
was the culmination, but against this is the strange and almost
inexplicable fact that there was a lull in the risings between 1645
and 1648. Better harvests brought the price of corn down to
a normal figure. But these were the very years in which a desperate government with a new Superintendent of Finance,
Particelli d'Emery, scraped money together by every wildcat
scheme that could be devised. The quiescence of the peasantry
cannot be accounted for on the evidence at present available.

From the time of Mazarin's assumption of power Particelli
d'Emery gradually took over complete control of the finances
from Bouthillier. In 1643 the revenues as far as 1646 were already
mortgaged and there was a deficit besides of 100 million livres.
Government credit was obtainable only at ruinous rates of interest
(15 per cent was common) from the great capitalists of the day,
who were not merchants or industrialists but tax-farmers
(*traitants* or *partisans*). They found the money to fight the war
and pay for the Court. It was the worst form of public finance
ever devised, and the confusion reached a climax during Mazarin's
rule – for he himself was in secret the chief financier. Mazarin,
the superintendents of finance, great nobles, treasury officials,

and even a few counsellors of the Paris Parlement, participated
through their clerks and bankers. More and more of the government's expenditure was put on the secret list and did not have
to be accounted for, but tax-farmers regularly bribed treasury
officials to falsify such accounts as there were, and in this way
evaded many of their liabilities under the agreements they had
entered into. Courtiers and others without sufficient capital to
advance could share in this bonanza by proposing new ways of
squeezing money out of the public; every projector of a new
source of revenue was allowed at least 10 per cent of its yield.

Richelieu had been concerned to maintain the main structure
of privilege amid the severities of his regime. Mazarin set up a new
plutocracy, and allowed Particelli d'Emery to attack the privileged towns, especially Paris, and the privileged officials. In 1644
a tax imposed on all houses built outside the walls of Paris, the
toisé, caused the first serious riots there. In the end this tax had to be
dropped because of the violent hostility of the poor people who
were its principal victims. Another scheme was to impose special
levies and dues on the wealthy bourgeoisie of Paris. This tax on
the aisés was strongly opposed by the powerful financiers and the
municipal authorities. Eventually the government decided to
rely mainly on a new tariff on goods entering Paris, in spite of the
strong opposition it aroused. When the rentiers (mainly the same
rich Parisians affected by the other measures) were deprived of
nearly half the interest due to them they formed a special
committee to look after their interests. Paris was preparing for
the Fronde.

The Parlement of Paris and the government

In Paris a very great deal depended on the attitude of the
Parlement. It had a large share in the administration of the city,
to the annoyance of the municipal authorities at the Hôtel de
Ville. Its members were now very detached from the rich bourgeoisie. Nearly all owned estates and drew a large part of their
income from land. Their children intermarried with the older
nobility, and they themselves belonged to a fully developed
noblesse de robe. On the whole their views were very conservative,

though there were some radical counsellors. Some were affected by the deeds of the similarly named body in England, but in the end they recoiled in horror from English parliamentary extremism. It was only with the greatest reluctance that they took over the leadership of the discontented in Paris.

There was no sign that they would do so before 1648. Of course there had been constant friction over the registration of financial edicts, and in 1645 a president of one of the chambers of the Parlement, Bouillon, was imprisoned for persistent opposition to the registration of the toisé. In particular the Parlement objected to the practice of holding lits de justice during the minority of the King to compel the registration of edicts. It was at a lit de justice in January 1648 that a serious political opposition began to form. At this meeting the nine-year-old Louis XIV forgot the words he had memorized and cried for shame. The government proposed to create twelve new maîtres des requêtes as a means of raising money, and when the existing maîtres denied the Regent's powers she suspended them from their functions and a long deadlock ensued. Soon afterwards it was time for the paulette to be renewed, and the government proposed that magistrates of three sovereign courts in Paris (the Cour des Aides, the Chambre des Comptes, and the Grand Conseil) and of the provincial Parlements should surrender their salaries for four years instead of paying the usual annual tax of one-sixtieth for the next nine years. At once there was an extremely hostile response from the magistrates. The Parlement, although exempted from this measure, accepted an invitation from the other three courts to send delegates to a united meeting in the Chambre de St Louis. The Queen immediately denounced this move in the strongest terms, accused the magistrates of republicanism, and made a number of arrests. As the dispute developed she wanted to arrest all the magistrates, and wept bitterly when her ministers would not agree.

These magistrates were making a determined stand against the monarchy, but purely on fiscal questions which affected them. What was their political outlook? E. A. Kossmann, a Dutch historian who has made the most profound study of the Fronde, has given much attention to the political theory of the parlementaires. There were no radical thinkers among them. The best of them had social ideals. At the meeting of January 1648 Omer Talon, the Avocat-général and hence one of the King's spokesmen in the Parlement, had dared to make an eloquent plea for the poor peasants, sleeping on straw and living on bran and oats to provide luxuries for the tax-farmers of Paris, and he said: 'It is of importance to your Majesty that we are free men and not slaves; the greatness of your state and the dignity of your crown are measured by the quality of the men who obey you'. Broussel, the leader of the most radical group in the Parlement, justified opposition by an analogy with flying buttresses, which, while appearing to resist the building, actually support it. Kossmann maintains that those who became Frondeurs accepted absolute monarchy as completely as their opponents, but it was never a simple absolutism. Richelieu, it was agreed, had driven it too far towards tyranny. The King ought to keep within the bounds of custom. He should uphold the rights of individuals and of institutions. But in the last resort he must be obeyed. Kossmann concludes that 'the state, for them, was like a baroque church where a great number of different conceptions meet, clash, and are finally absorbed in a magnificent system'.

The Fronde originated in a clash between functionnaires of the state. At first the opposition was concerned only with fiscal issues, but it was soon driven to demand constitutional guarantees. The magistrates were divided among themselves, with no resolute anti-monarchical leaders. They relied on the state for their position in the world and many were bribed by pensions. They could not possibly make a revolution, although their actions unleashed revolutionary forces. The government over-estimated the political danger. The Queen, often weak but at times violently authoritarian, and Mazarin, conscious of his intense unpopularity and lacking Richelieu's instinctive knowledge of the French people, provided a panicky leadership in the crisis. Their own aggressive actions provoked all the main outbreaks of popular violence, forced moderate men into revolutionary positions, and allowed anarchy to spread throughout France.

[14] THE FRONDE

Between the entry of Henry IV into Paris in 1594 and the French
Revolution the Bourbon monarchy was seriously shaken only
once, and that was during the five years of the Fronde. This crisis
was far more than merely a political one. Goubert (in *Past and
Present*, Vol. 10) described it as 'a crisis – economic, social, demo-
graphic, physiological, and moral – of an intensity and duration
hitherto almost unknown'. The Beauvais region (of which he has
made an extraordinarily thorough study) was hardly touched
by the armed conflict. Yet between 1647 and 1653 five consecu-
tive years of bad harvests brought about a rise in deaths and
a catastrophic fall in births. Many peasants were crushed by
debts and lost their lands to their creditors, and ruined nobles
sold their estates to the rising bourgeois. The price of wheat in
Paris, taking that of 1640 as 100, reached 295 in 1649, and 305 in
1652; by 1654 it had dropped to 107. The misery of famine and
disease was much greater wherever the armies went. In the area
around Paris, the scene of the chief military campaign, that of
1652, many villages lost a quarter of their population in that year
alone, and in the worst cases far more.

Was the Fronde an abortive liberal revolution, a rising of the
people against a feudal state, a feudal-aristocratic reaction
against a centralizing monarchy, or a series of anarchical outbreaks provoked by the incompetence of the government and the
self-interest of powerful groups? All these views have been maintained by reputable historians. Hatred of Mazarin was a common
factor in nearly all the outbreaks, but he himself increased this
by his peculiar handling of the crisis. The Parlement's programme
of reforms can hardly be called revolutionary – it was in part
reactionary. But the Parlement was like the sorcerer's apprentice,
and soon drew back from the turbulence it had provoked. This
turbulence, in Paris and still more in Bordeaux, had democratic
overtones, but no one of importance produced a clear democratic
programme. The populace was exploited for the purely selfish

aims of the leaders. The incredible frivolity of the grandees, and
of their ladies who intrigued for power, inspired the naming of
the crisis; a *fronde* is a catapult used by children, They thought
themselves fully entitled to act as independent powers. Mazarin
treated them as such and played off one against the other quite
unscrupulously. The only aim of the leaders was to control the
King. The suggestion of convening the Estates General did come
from an assembly of lesser nobles, but no one took this seriously
and the Queen was allowed to forget her promise to call one.
When the Parisian mob shouted for '*Le Roi seul*' they were
expressing the hopes of France, a king really able to rule. Only
time could dispel the anarchy. When Louis came of age in 1651
the grip of the monarchy on the country was gradually restored.
Although still only a young boy under the control of his mother,
he could repeat the success of Henry IV and enter Paris in
triumph. John Evelyn's comment is relevant: 'The French are
the only people in Europe who idolize their sovereign'.

There were many elements of feudal reaction in the Fronde,
but the old feudal order had decayed. The only effective political
role of the feudal nobility was as clients of the court grandees or
the provincial governors. The armies that fought in the civil war
were largely recruited through such clients. The royal princes
Orléans and Condé had a firm belief in their indefeasible right to
a share in government, and many Frenchmen accepted this as a
constitutional convention; but Condé had little grasp of politics,
and Gaston was timid and uncertain. The other leaders were
bribable. Paul de Gondi, the Coadjutor of his uncle the Archbishop of Paris, and later Cardinal de Retz, was in a position to
become the outstanding leader of the Fronde, but he was a
frivolous intriguer for Mazarin's place, without a constructive
political idea. In the end one is forced to agree with Kossmann
that the Fronde was 'neither a parliamentary revolution nor a
popular revolution, nor a feudal revolution . . . [but] a period of
imprudence and exaggeration lacking sense or aim. It is nothing,
for it is everything at once'.

The Fronde of the Parlement

The Fronde arose out of a serious plan of reform formulated by the Parlement. In face of a direct prohibition from the Regent the Chambre de St Louis adopted on 2 July 1648 a Declaration by which the Parlement was to have complete control of taxation. The taille was to be lessened by a quarter, the intendants and tax-farmers suppressed, taxes assessed and collected by the local officials, and a Chamber of Justice set up to examine the affairs of the financiers. Lettres de cachet were to be abolished, and all arrested persons were to be tried within twenty-four hours. This was a charter more for the officials than for the people, particularly when the habeas corpus clause was whittled down to cover only officials.

The weakness of this scheme was that it ignored the problem of the finances. The immediate prospect was the bankruptcy which had been threatened for years. When, as a sop to the Parlement, Particelli d'Emery was suddenly dismissed in July, the Treasury was said to be empty. The Queen and Mazarin had to pawn jewellery for immediate needs, and some of the great ladies of the court lent the Queen large sums of money. Mazarin gave way the more readily to the demands because for the moment he saw an opportunity to gain from a first-class financial crisis. The rate of interest was lowered from 15 per cent to 6 per cent, to save fifty million livres a year. Mazarin was gleeful that the tax-farmers had themselves agreed, for fear of worse, to the cancellation of their assignments. He wrote: 'The whole of the current year and the two following have already been consumed, and we have found a way of consuming them all over again'. The intendants were removed and the venal officials resumed their less efficient administration. Intendants were not restored until after the Fronde, though the government soon of necessity resumed its borrowing from the financiers.

Mazarin's mood changed when he found that the radical wing of the Parlement was determined not merely to ruin the financiers but to prosecute the most notorious. Then the news of Condé's victory over the Spaniards at Lens encouraged a counter-attack, and the government arrested two members of the Parlement, one of them Broussel, its most outspoken critic, a relatively poor, honest, and austere old man who was a hero to the people of Paris. The turmoil which followed was startling. The people were suffering from food shortages and high prices and were ready for trouble. They threw up barricades throughout the city, the Court was besieged in the Palais Royal, and for three days the Parlement and the town militia tried to control the chaos, until Anne gave way and released Broussel, and order was restored. The Parlement had been moderate and cautious, and the richer bourgeoisie and their leaders the municipal officials supported the monarchy. No liberal revolution could develop without bourgeois leadership.

There was no real settlement after this flare-up. Mazarin, more and more the object of the people's hatred, was deeply disturbed, and determined to get the King out of the reach of the people, restore absolutism by the cancelling of the Declaration of reforms, and subdue Paris. The first attempt to carry this out by a flight to Rueil led to a rather humiliating return when the royal princes mediated. But the mood of the people was worsening, and the news from England of Pride's Purge and the decision to try Charles I intensified the fears of the Queen and Mazarin for monarchy in France. Condé's army was at last available, and Mazarin resolved to launch a civil war. On the night of 5 January 1649, the royal party escaped to the unfurnished palace of St Germain, where they slept on straw. The Declaration was repudiated. Condé wanted to attack Paris, but Mazarin would allow only a blockade, and there were no military events of much importance. There was some excuse for the Parlement's denunciation of the Cardinal as 'notoriously the author of all the disorders of the state and of the present evil'.

In Paris there was much confusion. Few members of the Parlement obeyed the royal order to leave Paris for Montargis. The main body was resolute, supported and intimidated by a populace determined not to surrender; but it was alarmed by the allies it attracted. A swarm of grandees and their hangers-on flocked to Paris. Condé's brother the Prince de Conti was the chief of these, and he was made commander of the Parisian militia. His brother-in-law the Duc de Longueville, governor of Normandy, Bouillon the brother of Turenne, Beaufort who had escaped from prison, and the Duchesse de Chevreuse, all joined the Fronde. Gondi now began to build up a following among the Paris clergy and the common people, and he sat in the Parlement as the representative of the Archbishop. These reckless and selfish leaders cared little for the Parlement or its aims, and they disagreed among themselves. The Parlement wanted peace partly to disembarrass itself of these allies.

Horror at the execution of Charles I weakened the rebellious spirit. The Frondeurs denounced the regicides of England and repudiated republicanism. (The worst abuse that could be hurled at lower-class rebels in Marseilles at this time was the cry 'Fairfax! Anglais!') The decisive event, however, in bringing the first Fronde to an end was the danger from Spain. A Spanish envoy arrived in Paris to treat with the Fronde, Turenne was trying to persuade his army to join the revolt, and the Spanish army was beginning an invasion of Picardy. The government made wholesale concessions and the Treaty of Rueil was signed. Mazarin had achieved virtually nothing and had gravely shaken the stability of the regime. The Regent repeated her previous Declaration with some modifications. Enormous sums were promised to the grandees of the Fronde, and Conti was admitted to the Conseil d'en Haut, where Condé and Gaston already sat to menace the authority of Mazarin.

An anarchic interlude

During the blockade of Paris the Fronde had spread to the provinces. In the Marxist view, set out by Porshnev in his work on *Popular Risings before the Fronde*, the peasantry and urban masses should have risen spontaneously, but this did not happen. Longueville, governor of Normandy, left Paris during the outbreak and stimulated a rising in his province, but this enabled the Parlement of Rouen to make very good terms for itself in the Treaty of Rueil, and the province, which only ten years before had been the scene of the great rising of the Va-nu-pieds, was pacified and gave little more trouble. Other disturbances were due mainly to the breakdown of central government. The intendants who linked the centre with the provinces had disappeared, and the credit of the government was badly shaken. The worst trouble occurred where two authoritarian governors, in Provence and Guyenne, were having disputes with the local Parlements and, freed from the restraints they had previously felt, attempted to solve the problems by force. In each case Mazarin eventually tried to mediate between the parties, and brought about a settlement favourable to the Parlement.

It is strange that the Fronde in the provinces was not more widespread. On the whole the provincial Parlements remained loyal, and where they had no trouble with the governor supported law and order. Even Languedoc, so often in the recent past a storm centre, was kept quiet by the Parlement of Toulouse. The chief disturbance other than those of Provence and Guyenne occurred in Anjou, where the people of Angers, instigated by the Duc de La Trémoille, a Frondeur, rose in revolt and organized a democratic regime; but within a few weeks the rightful governor restored order.

Paris was still under the control of the Parlement, and the Court did not venture back until August. Meanwhile Condé made a bold bid for supreme power. He allied himself with the other princes of his family, Conti and Longueville. His armed followers swaggered about. Mazarin clung to power only through the Queen. The pamphlet attacks on him – the Mazarinades – became more and more violent. He intrigued among the factions at Court to regain his authority, particularly by a plan to marry his niece to Mercoeur, Vendôme's son and Beaufort's brother. Condé forced him to put a stop to this, and to sign a statement that he would make no appointments nor take any major step without Condé's advice. Throughout this time Paul de Gondi was intriguing for a cardinal's hat and real power, and at last Mazarin turned to him as the lesser of two evils. Having won Gondi's support Mazarin grouped together for the moment all those who were hostile to Condé's pretensions, Gaston d'Orléans, Vendôme,

Beaufort, and the leaders of the Parlement. He then provoked the second Fronde by having Condé, Conti, and Longueville arrested in January 1650 and imprisoned at Vincennes.

The Fronde of the princes

Mazarin was unable to profit by his coup d'état, and France continued to disintegrate. The very dangerous party of Gondi had been strengthened by Mazarin himself, and the princesses took the field on behalf of their imprisoned husbands. The Court moved about the country to cope with revolts and to keep clear of seditious Paris. After visiting Normandy and Burgundy it moved south to deal with the crisis in Guyenne. Mme de Longueville had tried to stir up Normandy without success. The Princesse de Condé with 7,000 troops linked up with rebellious Bordeaux. Seditious nobles provoked risings in the south-west, and all these Frondeurs joined the Condéans in Bordeaux. They received an envoy from Spain, were promised a Spanish fleet, and had the support of the populace against the Parlement of Bordeaux, the majority of which was still loyal to the King although it detested the governor d'Épernon (the former Duc de La Valette). To try to pacify Bordeaux and please the Parlement of Paris as well, the Queen very reluctantly dismissed the governor, and the Court was able to return to Paris in November 1650.

Meanwhile Turenne was a constant menace. Seduced by Mme de Longueville, he had made an agreement with the Spaniards, moved his army towards Paris, and prepared a raid for the liberation of the princes, who had to be moved from Vincennes, eventually to Le Havre, as a safeguard. Mazarin and the royal army moved north against Turenne, and du Plessis defeated him at Rethel in December.

Mazarin's very success was fatal to his power. The same coalition as had overthrown Condé – the Parlement of Paris, Gondi, and Beaufort – now turned against Mazarin. They had come to terms with Condé's supporters and were demanding the release of the princes. In this new situation the King, guarded by the town militia, was a virtual prisoner in Paris. Gaston, accorded all power by the Parlement, held the key to the crisis. He joined the anti-Mazarinian coalition, and summoned an Assembly of Nobles to Paris. Mazarin tried to get Anne to agree to a second flight, but she refused, and at last, on 6 February, he fled alone to Le Havre and released the princes. He thought he could make a deal with Condé, but found this to be impossible. He then went into exile with his seven nieces, finally taking refuge at Brühl in the Archbishopric of Cologne. The Queen had issued a decree exiling him and she conceded to the Parlement that henceforth no foreigner should be allowed to sit on the council. It appeared to be the end of Mazarin's career.

The Frondeurs in power

There is much of legend in the usual story of Mazarin in exile dictating Anne's policy by correspondence. Kossmann shows that he was unsure and uneasy. Some of his advice was rejected by the Queen or it was useless because it arrived too late. She refused his main request, that she should get the King out of Paris so that they could all reunite. Yet his absence did show the remarkable tenacity of his hold on power. Anne was determined to recall him. Her loyalty was as stubborn as had been her disloyalty to Louis XIII. A group of ministers, Le Tellier, Lionne, and Servien, were most faithful, and above all Le Tellier, who wrote constantly, was a tower of strength. At the worst time, from May to December 1651, the Queen had to suspend them from office.

The Parlement was now again the forum of the Fronde, with the leaders Condé, Gaston, and Gondi attending important sessions. But there was no unity. The feudal aims of the Assembly of Nobles aroused the bitter hostility of the Parlement, and were of no interest to the grandees or Gondi or the people of Paris. Their project of an Estates General was quietly allowed to lapse after all the preliminary steps for calling one had been taken by the Queen. In the see-saw struggle for Mazarin's place between Condé and Gondi, ministers came and went: old ministers of Richelieu's such as Séguier (who had been dismissed by Mazarin),

Chavigny, and Châteauneuf; at one point La Vieuville, Richelieu's predecessor, came out of his long retirement to be Superintendent of Finance, after paying the exiled Mazarin a bribe of 200,000 livres for his support; Molé the First President of the Parlement was twice Keeper of the Seals.

In the struggle for power Condé, the most serious if the most inept leader of the Fronde, found himself more and more isolated. He had obtained the governorship of Guyenne, and eventually he fled there with Conti and Mme de Longueville, began a civil war, threw off his allegiance, and became the ally of Spain.

The Condéan civil war

Louis XIV came of age in September 1651. It was a turn of the tide. Although his rule could be only nominal at the age of thirteen, both Anne and Mazarin felt much more confident and their opponents were correspondingly dismayed. Mazarin welcomed all-out war with Condé, and prepared for his own return. Anne now felt free to take the initiative and left Paris, moving gradually to Poitiers. Here Turenne, who had rallied to the support of the King, took charge of the royal army against Condé. In Paris Gaston and the Parlement were trying to avoid a complete breach with the rebel, but at last the Queen's commands were obeyed, and the Parlement proclaimed Condé a traitor. Mazarin was able to move, and in December 1651 entered France with a force of mercenaries.

The effect of Mazarin's return was to revive Condé's waning power. Except in Guyenne his support at this time was negligible, but all the Frondeurs were thrown into a fury by the confident intervention of the man they thought they had eliminated. Local risings inspired by great nobles were widespread in the spring of 1652. In Paris the Queen was openly defied. The Parlement put a price on Mazarin's head, and his possessions, including his library, were confiscated and sold by auction. Without yet joining Condé, Paris and its commander Gaston d'Orléans were virtually in revolt. Gondi, who at last became Cardinal de Retz, found little room for manoeuvre in this new situation.

With little help from Spain Condé had small chance of success against a revived monarchy. Even in Bordeaux and Paris many parlementaires and nearly all the upper bourgeoisie were loyal to the King. The military struggle in 1652 moved to the Paris region when Condé left Bordeaux and was allowed by Gaston to take command of the Parisian army. Condé could now count on the active backing of the populace of Paris, famished, revolutionary, and dillusioned about its earlier leaders.

Turenne, with a small force, conducted a masterly campaign around Paris. He fended off the army which the Duke of Lorraine brought to help Condé, drove Condé back to the city, and on 2 July 1652, fought the main battle of the Fronde, in the Faubourg St Antoine. After Turenne had defeated Condé, the latter's army was saved by Gaston's daughter, la Grande Mademoiselle, who was more resolute than her father. She had taken charge of the Bastille, and turned its guns on Turenne's victorious army, while Condé's army took refuge in Paris.

Paris was very excited by these events, and on 4 July a mob stirred up by Condé's ally Beaufort committed the worst outrage of the Fronde there. A large representative meeting of the Paris bourgeoisie with the Parlement was held, to take steps to preserve order in the town. As the meeting broke up, the mob attacked the so-called Mazarinians, set fire to the Hôtel de Ville, and massacred indiscriminately. A hundred people were killed or wounded, and one counsellor of Parlement was stabbed to death. An insurrectional government was set up, with Beaufort as governor and Broussel as the mayor. The Parlement proclaimed Gaston Lieutenant-General of the kingdom.

In an effort to placate the city Louis XIV promised to exile Mazarin. For some time Mazarin had been resisting suggestions that he should go away again, but at last he agreed, departed for Bouillon in August, and recommended an immediate peace with Condé. The King's counsellors were more confident of a victory, and refused the defeatist advice. In fact the news of the second dismissal of Mazarin caused a great revulsion in favour of the

King in Paris. Before the end of September Broussel had been
dismissed, but October was the decisive month. Condé fled to
join the Spaniards, the insurrectional government was dis-
mantled, and the old municipal authorities restored. The King
was able to make a triumphal entry, and in a lit de justice forbade
the Parlement to meddle in politics. He exiled Gaston to Blois.
Mazarin, invited to return, wisely waited until it was clear that
the Fronde was quite over. He entered Paris in February 1653,
and was received with acclamation in that fickle town.

The Ormée in Bordeaux

After Condé left Bordeaux his brother Conti held the town until
the end, and it became the scene of the most radical movement
of the Fronde. Among the supporters of Condé in Bordeaux the
extreme left, made up of petty bourgeois and workers, formed
a group known as the Ormée because at first they met in a grove
of elm-trees. The Ormée may have contained Huguenot members,
and these in particular may have been influenced by English
extremists, but there is little evidence of this. Edward Sexby, an
agitator of the New Model Army, headed a mission from the
Commonwealth to France and spent a good time in Bordeaux at
the height of the troubles, and he produced an adaptation of the
radically democratic 'Agreement of the People' as a model
constitution for France. But this seems to have made no impression on the Bordelais, and Sexby was eventually forced to escape
over the city wall. (His extreme views led him in the end to
serious trouble in England, and he was arrested for conspiring
to assassinate Cromwell, but died in the Tower.)

The Ormée had strong class feeling, but very limited ideas. In
the spring of 1652 it conducted a bitter attack on the royalist
group in the Parlement of Bordeaux, and drove them and a
number of other rich bourgeois out of the town. A veritable class
war broke out in the summer, initiated by the rich but won by the
Ormée, who flew the red flag from a number of buildings. It
obtained a special representation of thirty additional members in
the municipal council, and overawed the upper bourgeoisie by a

show of force. Its main political object was to destroy the power and privileges of the Parlement, and to this end it set up a new tribunal to give free and rapid justice without the intervention of lawyers. The idealism of the Ormée is reminiscent of that of Cromwell's Assembly of Nominees in England. The tribunal could have become the instrument of a reign of terror, but only one man was executed for political reasons.

In the last phase of the resistance to royal authority at Bordeaux the Ormists split into two parties. There was an idealistic vaguely republican group hoping for succour from England – which in 1653 Cromwell refused – and preferring in the last resort to surrender to the King rather than to accept Spanish domination. A small terroristic group followed Condé to the end, and was prepared to ally with Spain; its leader Duretête was the only Ormist executed after the Fronde. Bordeaux held out for months after the collapse of the Fronde everywhere else, and surrendered only when a royal fleet and army blockaded the town in July 1653. The chief Ormists fled. Conti made his peace with Mazarin.

Conclusion

At Bordeaux, as everywhere else, the innate conservatism of the French people had been made clear. The state, riddled with discontent and bedevilled by the private ambitions of the grandees and the privileged, was still unbreakably one. Lavisse writes of 'l'inachèvement de l'état'; and it was undoubtedly badly organized and administered. Mazarin was not the master mind of the crisis, but a gambler whose nerve and judgment sometimes failed. But he stood for the only viable form of government. The country was sick of aimless anarchy. Battles had been few and small in scale. Cruelty to opponents had not been a feature of the troubles, but the incidental suffering in the countryside and among the poor of the towns was immense. Ravaging mercenaries and partisans had brought the horror of the Thirty Years' War to France. The French people longed for peace and quiet and only an unquestioned absolutism could provide them.

Mazarin was a compassionate man. Some of the chiefs of the

Fronde were bribed to submit. Gaston d'Orléans, exiled at first, was soon forgiven. Cardinal de Retz was imprisoned in Vincennes, but escaped. There were few executions.

The loss of Condé, who was generalissimo of the Spanish armies until the peace, was a serious blow to the military power of France. It was extremely fortunate for the French that Spain was too weak to take much advantage of the Fronde. The Spaniards had regained Catalonia and Dunkirk, and taken Casale, but their invasion of France had been on a small scale and ineffective; the country remained intact, with Turenne to defend it.

[15] AFTER THE FRONDE

The King and the Cardinal

Louis XIV had to bear too great a burden and he had to bear it too young, from his coming of age at thirteen. The Fronde had not only failed to produce any results; it had failed to produce any coherent projects for the reform of French government. It had revealed the utter bankruptcy of the moribund feudal aristocracy, the futility of the noblesse de robe, the immaturity of the bourgeoisie. Louis was the only hope of the stricken French society. The reaction to the Fronde was le Roi Soleil.

Until the death of Mazarin in 1661 the King, the Queen Mother, and the Cardinal were an indissoluble trio. Anne was glad to retire into the background when her regency came to an end (though the Conseil d'en Haut usually met in her room), but she still held the regime together by her close ties with Louis and Mazarin. The Cardinal, hiding his unpopularity behind the popularity of Louis, controlled the state through the King. For Louis he was a father-substitute. The Venetian ambassador wrote of their relationship as *'une sympathie occulte, une subordination de l'esprit et de l'intelligence'* of the King to his godfather. Louis himself described Mazarin as *'un ministre qui m'aimait, que j'aimais'*. Mazarin devised the King's education, and predictably it was a practical apprenticeship to kingcraft rather than a cultivation of the intellect. Louis had a mediocre intelligence. In his earlier years he acquired some book-learning, but no doubt the Fronde interfered with regular study, and afterwards he did little reading. Physical activity, gymnastics, fencing, and above all dancing, occupied far more of his time, and he loved hunting, shooting, and military campaigns.

When he was at Court Louis had a strict daily routine. He went to morning mass with his mother and lunched with her. For an hour or two a day he attended on the Cardinal and watched him dealing with affairs of state. Gradually he was introduced to council business and took a larger part in council meetings. The frivolities of the Court were also a routine. The King was reputed to be one of the best dancers at the Court, and played in a number of splendid masques. He was surrounded by a group of frivolous young people and kept away from all dangerous influences, which probably included all the more serious older people who might have encouraged him to think for himself. Cards were the standby for the evenings, and Mazarin introduced him to gambling. The King gambled all his life, but at this stage he had not the resources of the Cardinal for this pastime. Mazarin had always been a devoted gambler, lucky and probably dishonest. He introduced a form of roulette to the French Court. He is reputed to have won 500,000 livres from his banker in one evening's play.

If Louis's intelligence was inadequate to his responsibilities, he had an admirable temperament for a king and a noble appearance. He was an extrovert, always at his ease in society, with perfect manners, gracious, affable, and even-tempered. He would have been spoiled by adulation if he had not at the same time acquired a high sense of duty. In his early years he practised writing by copying 'les rois font ce que leur plaît', but he found this was not so, and that his métier de roi – a phrase he used himself – required regular work and much self-control. Superficially Louis had been well trained, but he was isolated from his people, ignorant of the lessons of history and of political ideas, and complacently conservative. The experience of the Fronde had made him deeply suspicious of all opposition, however reasonable. Mazarin kept Louis very close to himself in these years, a safe policy. He even found time to initiate the King into the art of war. Every year from 1653 to 1658 they spent at least part of the summer with the army of Turenne, who was conducting small-scale and rather desultory campaigns against Condé in the no-man's-land between France and the Netherlands. Louis was fearless and had to be restrained from running excessive personal risks. Turenne gave him an excellent military training. The fighting was so static that he was able to live at ease, and he much enjoyed the active life and acquired a taste for military glory.

Secure of Louis's fidelity and the Queen Mother's love, Mazarin's position in these years was extraordinary. He was avid for wealth, and had acquired from Le Tellier's War Office a secretary, Jean Baptiste Colbert, who brought order out of chaos in his accounts and sought out every conceivable means of raising money. Colbert, working fifteen hours a day without respite, accumulated for the Cardinal a colossal fortune. His Church benefices included the Bishopric of Metz and the Abbey of Cluny, the richest in France. He was governor of three provinces, including the newly acquired Alsace, where Colbert's brother Colbert de Croissy was made intendant. Vast sums of money came to Mazarin as considerations for government appointments. Colbert engaged in trade on Mazarin's account, and while the French navy went to rack and ruin Mazarin's private merchant fleet brought him a fortune. He was one of the chief purveyors of army supplies. Finally, acting under assumed names, he was the greatest of the tax-farming plutocrats who were the power behind the throne during his regime.

While the Court moved from the Palais Royal to the Louvre because it was easier to defend against the people of Paris, Mazarin made his own fortress and palace in the château of Vincennes, just outside the city. Here was his private strongroom for the gold and jewels – he owned a score of the finest diamonds in the world – which might be an unpopular minister's best friend. He built new wings at Vincennes and was often host there to the King, the Queen and the Court. But he had it guarded by hundreds of d'Artagnan's musketeers, and even installed a menagerie of wild animals, lions, tigers and bears, in the ditches as a deterrent to intruders.

Mazarin was no mere miser. His spending, like his revenue, was sumptuous, and as a connoisseur he influenced French taste in the arts. He had introduced Italian opera to the court, and the Commedia dell'Arte – the Italian theatre with stock characters such as Pantaloon, Harlequin, Columbine, and Polichinello. His library, dispersed during the Fronde, was re-established; it contained 40,000 books, properly catalogued, and was the first to be freely opened to the public. It was eventually housed in the Collège de Quatre Nations, a splendid baroque building with an oval dome, designed by Le Vau – now the Institute of France. Mazarin did much to spread baroque influences on French architecture.

Like that other Italian adventurer Napoleon Bonaparte, Mazarin was determined to make his family great. His brother became Archbishop of Aix and a cardinal. His nephew, Philip Mancini, he made Duc de Nevers. His two sisters and their families were brought to the French court, where his seven charming nieces became the centre of attention. One of Louis XIV's earliest flirtations was with Olympe Mancini, and his first serious love affair with her sister Marie. For reasons of state Mazarin vetoed their marriage, on which Louis had set his heart. But the connections he succeeded in making through the marriages of his nieces set the seal on his career. Royal favour and the size of their dowries made up for the lowness of their birth. Three married French nobles of royal blood. The loyalty of the Duc de Mercoeur, son of the Duc de Vendôme, had been secured during the Fronde by his marriage to Laure Mancini, and after the Fronde the Prince de Conti was detached from his brother Condé by a marriage with Anne-Marie Martinozzi. Olympe married Prince Eugène of Savoy-Carignano, also connected with the Condé branch of the royal family. Laure Martinozzi became Duchess of Modena, and so the mother of James II's queen and great-grandmother of Bonnie Prince Charlie. Anne-Marie Mancini married the Duc de Bouillon, brother of Turenne. Marie

Mancini, torn from Louis and banished from the court, was married to Prince Colonna, the grandson of Mazarin's original patron. Hortense Mancini was chosen to carry on the family name as the wife of La Meilleraye, a well endowed grand-nephew of Richelieu, who was made Duc de Mazarin. This couple inherited thirty million livres from the Cardinal, and established one of the leading families in France. The last heiress of this family married into that of the Grimaldi princes of Monaco, and it seems appropriate that the Mazarin family papers should now be deposited in a Franco-Italian principality consecrated to gambling. Of the many famous men descended from the Mazarins it is perhaps sufficient to mention two who were great soldiers on opposite sides in the battle of Oudenarde, Prince Eugène of Savoy and Marshal Vendôme.

Administration and finance

Mazarin restored the administrative system after the Fronde, but far too little is known about this. In 1932 Pagès apologized for the brevity of his chapter on Mazarin's government, and gave the lack of information as the reason. On the period after the Fronde not much has since then appeared in print to clear up the difficulties. The enigma remains that Mazarin was apparently not an administrator and yet by 1661 France had a more systematic administration than ever before. The only name clearly connected with this is that of the Chancellor Séguier. Two articles by E. Esmonin have thrown some light on the restoration of the intendants. The government quickly found during the Fronde that the local financial officials were inefficient, and sent out maîtres des requêtes on missions to various provinces to take the place of the defunct intendants and get in the taxes. In the Midi at any rate this move failed because the local officials boycotted the royal representative and he was in some physical danger. After the Fronde, in 1653, a decisive step was taken. By that time maîtres des requêtes were going systematically on tour and the venal financial officials of the Paris region made a strong protest. Séguier presided over a meeting of the Council of Finance where the officials had to appear and face a stern inquiry; they were suspended from their functions and deprived of their salaries, and their central committee in Paris was abolished. The right of the King to use such methods of administration was asserted once for all, in spite of the edict against intendants of 1648, which was never repealed. Soon the old name was resumed, and intendants without being considered as permanently settled, remained long periods in one province or généralité. Colbert himself may well have had some influence on this developing organization. He was a Councillor of State from 1649, and regularly mixed state affairs with those of his master. But this subject, and much else concerning Mazarin's ministériat, is still obscure.

The financiers flourished as never before. In 1653 Nicholas Fouquet, an intendant of long standing who had been conspicuously faithful to Mazarin, was made joint Superintendent of Finance with Servien. Servien did his best to control expenditure and imposed many economies, while Fouquet was the wizard who constantly staved off bankruptcy by new borrowings. When Servien died in 1659 Fouquet was left in sole charge by Mazarin, although Colbert tried hard to get a share of the office.

Next to Mazarin Fouquet was the chief profiteer from this tax-farming regime. He owed much to the skill of German financiers; Jabach, a banker who financed huge deals, and who bought paintings for Mazarin; Herwart, a Protestant who became Controller-General of Finance and introduced a large number of Huguenots into the Treasury. Fouquet made a deplorable system work with remarkable success. He sold offices, alienated crown lands, and played all kinds of unscrupulous monetary tricks. His own funds were inextricably entangled with those of the state. He was a man of great charm, fine taste, and princely ways, who employed Le Vau to build the most magnificent château of the period, at Vaux-le-Vîcomte, where Le Nôtre laid out the grounds and Le Brun had charge of the decorations – the prototype of Versailles. He was a very generous patron of men of letters, including Corneille and La Fontaine.

The Parlement of Paris was thoroughly cowed by the violence of the populace in the last stages of the Fronde. It submitted readily to the royal power, and Mazarin gave a bribe of 300,000 livres to its new First President to ensure its docility. There was only one more flare-up of trouble, when Fouquet drew up some unpopular financial edicts and the King held a lit de justice to compel their registration. Louis was hunting at Vincennes when he heard that the Parlement had resumed the debate. He rode to Paris in his hunting dress, interrupted the proceedings and forbade further debate. One much later report alleged that he lost his temper, flourished his riding whip, and declared '*L'état, c'est moi*'. This story is dismissed as apocryphal. Louis never behaved in such a way in his life, but the alleged remark epitomizes his regime.

Beginnings of the Jansenist Movement

As political opposition to the King died down, Jansenism came to the fore as a form of religious resistance. We have seen that in the later years of Richelieu the Abbé de St Cyran had taken up the leadership of the dévot opposition to the Cardinal's purely secular policy. He was an uncompromising follower of St Augustine, and in 1640 his close friend, Cornelius Jansen, a Fleming, brought out his *Augustinus*, setting out the asceticism and pre-predestinarian beliefs of St Augustine in an extreme form.

Jansenism was ultimately condemned as heretical on the ground that it misrepresented St Augustine's teaching, but the Catholic Church found itself in a very embarrassing position with regard to Augustinianism, especially since both Luther and Calvin had claimed that their doctrines were Augustinian. The very difficult attempt to reconcile predestination and human freewill had been made in the Middle Ages by the central body of Catholic theologians, led by Thomas Aquinas. But the Jesuits, reacting strongly against the harsh pessimism of Calvin, had tended towards the optimistic heresy of a belief in the complete freedom of the will. Many people disliked the worldly wisdom of the Jesuits and their laxity in giving absolution on easy terms. Jansenists have been described as people who hated Jesuits. Though their hostility took doctrinal forms, far more than theology was involved.

St Cyran had prepared the ground for Jansenism in France when he became the spiritual director of the convent of Port Royal. This institution of ascetic Cistercian nuns had moved from its original country site to Paris in 1626. Towards 1640 a number of men, believing in the virtue of retreating from the world but not wanting to take monastic vows, went to live as solitaries in the old buildings of Port Royal des Champs. Eventually the nunnery in Paris became overcrowded and in 1648 some of the Jansenist nuns moved back to form a branch institution in the old buildings, and the solitaries moved to a nearby farm. To the Jansenists it became a holy place, superior to Rome itself. They distributed relics of St Cyran among the faithful. They had a clannish spirit, drawn as they were from a narrow highly intellectual order, and they regarded the world outside as a wicked place. The Jesuits hated the Jansenist sectaries even more because they were rival teachers. They collected small groups of pupils, one of whom, influenced for life by their austere teaching, was Racine. He wrote: 'What peace! What silence! What charity! Work without respite, continuous prayer, no ambition except to receive the vilest and most humiliating tasks.'

The Arnauld family played a great part in the Jansenist movement. Mère Angélique and her sister Mère Agnès led the Port Royal nuns. Altogether eleven women of the family were nuns at Port Royal, and six of the men became solitaries. One of these, Antoine Arnauld, became their leader when St Cyran died soon after he emerged from his five-year imprisonment in 1643. In the same year Antoine Arnauld published *De la Fréquente Communion*. This was largely an attack on the Jesuit practice of absolving sinners easily and encouraging them to partake of the mass with inadequate consideration. (A form of penance very common among Jansenists was abstention from communion over quite long periods). By accepting Jansen's extreme interpretations of St Augustine, particularly the proposition that Christ died to save the elect only, not all men, they risked condemnation as heretics.

Eventually in 1653 Pope Innocent X condemned five propositions extracted from Jansen's teachings by a member of the

Sorbonne. Arnauld and his followers admitted that the five propositions were heretical but denied that they were to be found in Jansen's book, and a long wrangle followed. Mazarin, who cared only for the political aspects of the dispute, persuaded an Assembly of Clergy in 1655 to accept the papal bull, and Arnauld was in imminent danger.

At this point one of the ablest thinkers in France came to the rescue of the Jansenists, and brought them broad support and a new status as the only political opposition. This was Blaise Pascal, an outstanding mathematician, physicist, philosopher, and writer. His sister was a nun at Port Royal, and he had just joined the solitaries when the storm broke. He now wrote a series of pamphlets, *Les Lettres Provinciales*, which appeared during 1656 and 1657, addressed to the Jesuits, attacking their casuistry and low moral standards. His beautiful style secured a big reading public. A supposed miraculous cure of his niece at Port Royal in Paris strengthened his case. Jansenists had powerful sympathizers among the upper bourgeoisie and the noblesse de robe. Mazarin was usually ready for compromises, and in face of this opposition he suspended the persecution and allowed the solitaries to return to Port Royal.

The respite was not for long. The fact is that as a focus for political opposition the Jansenists now seemed a danger to the monarchy. They had always been hostile to Mazarin, who was a supreme example of the worldly exploitation of religion. Cardinal de Retz favoured them, and in spite of their strict principles many of them supported his claim to be reinstated as the Archbishop of Paris. A number of the leading ex-Frondeurs dabbled in Jansenism; Mme de Longueville was the most notable of these penitents. With all this, and the bitter hostility of the Jesuit Order, it is hardly surprising that the government acted. The King appointed a commission in 1660 to examine Pascal's *Lettres*. They were condemned to be burned by the common hangman. It was ruled that the five propositions were contained in Jansen's works, and a formulary condemning them was to be signed by all the clergy. The convents of Port Royal were to receive neither novices nor pupils, and the solitaries were dis-

persed. A long struggle followed. The Jansenists were Catholic
Puritans capable of a tough resistance, and their enemies the
Jesuits were widely unpopular.

The devots had been deeply divided over these events. An
important and active body of lay Catholic reformers now
belonged to the Compagnie du Saint Sacrement, the secret society
for improving morals and discipline, of which Séguier was a
leading member. It was very prominent in the attack on the
Jansenists. Vincent de Paul, revered by most dévots as their
spiritual guide, disapproved of Jansenist extremes, but did not
join the persecutors. He was no politician, and found support for
the charitable work which was the main interest of his life from
Anne of Austria and above all from Richelieu's niece the Duchesse
d'Aiguillon. He and most of his followers were hostile to Mazarin,
but he refused to give active support to the Fronde, and concentrated his efforts on relieving its miseries.

The end of the Spanish War

The career of Mazarin ended in a blaze of glory because he brought
the war with Spain to a successful end, and saw the King
married to a Spanish princess as a guarantee of future peace –
or so men believed. The war dragged on in spite of Mazarin's
sincere desire for peace. He preferred to bribe his enemies rather
than to fight them – it cost much less and the results were far
more certain – and he won some success with these methods. He
also made wholesale use of French money to build up a pro-
French party in Germany to obviate any hostile intervention
from the Habsburg Emperor. He was unable to prevent the
election of Leopold I as emperor in 1658 to succeed his father
Ferdinand III, but he created a League of the Rhine to extend
French influence in western Germany. But to defeat Spain with
the debilitated resources of France proved impossible. Ground was
gained slowly in desultory sieges, and no pitched battle of any
consequence was fought for years. Mazarin's last cynical gesture
was to call in the regicide Cromwell, and this move enabled him
to end the war. In 1658 an English fleet blockaded Dunkirk, and

6,000 vigorous infantry from the New Model Army reinforced
Turenne's besieging force. These English soldiers were stout and
well fed; Mazarin was appalled by their requirements of cash and
food. But Condé was forced to attack, and Turenne won a
decisive victory in the Battle of the Dunes.

Mazarin now at last negotiated the Peace of the Pyrenees. His
territorial demands were moderate; Roussillon and Cerdagne in
the south, Artois and a number of border towns in the north.
Lorraine was to go back to its Duke but to be disarmed, and
France gained a road through the territory to Alsace. (The Duke
of Lorraine refused to accept this settlement.) The Rhine was
now the real frontier of France. One heavy sacrifice required for
victory was the grant of Dunkirk to England; it was soon bought
back from Charles II, but this could not have been foreseen.

Above all Mazarin was determined to bring about the marriage
of Louis XIV with Maria Theresa, elder daughter of Philip IV.
The Spaniards made difficulties about this, and insisted that a
clause should be inserted to prevent the succession of Maria
Theresa and her heirs to the Spanish throne, which otherwise
was quite likely. Lionne, the negotiator of the peace, had to
agree to this clause in the end, but inserted the qualification that
the renunciation was on condition that (*moyennant*) the promised
dowry of 500,000 gold crowns was paid. He anticipated rightly
that Spain would be unable to pay, and hence that the clause
would become void.

One clause in the Spanish treaty restored Condé to his lands
and honours. To get the French to agree to this the Spaniards
had to surrender three additional towns in the Netherlands.
Condé was completely loyal after this to Louis XIV, whom he
respected.

Mazarin's diplomacy was so skilful that it created dangers for
the future by winning for France a position that could hardly
be maintained. When he died in 1661 France was possibly nearer
to complete supremacy in Europe than any state had hitherto
been. Spain and the Empire were humbled and neutralized.
England, with Louis's cousin Charles II restored and the army
disbanded, was a client state, and so was the other great naval

power Holland. French influence was dominant in the Baltic, where Mazarin's diplomacy had brought about the Peace of Oliva, and where Sweden, ruled by a Council of Regency, was dependent on France, and Poland had a strong French party among the nobles.

Yet it was an advance on a rather narrow front. The impoverished army was in no state to sustain such a role. The economy was stagnating and neglected; the highly artificial wealthy class of government financiers kept the state going at the expense of a healthy capitalist development. Ruinous government finance increased the misery of the people who were suffering in 1661 from one of the worst famines of the century. Sea-power had gone by the board, and colonies and foreign trade were forgotten. Mazarin had shown none of the breadth of outlook which had distinguished his great predecessors in government, Henry IV and Richelieu. At Mazarin's elbow was the man who might have given the French economy a sounder basis – Colbert – but so far he had been used almost entirely to construct Mazarin's own fortune of some 40 million livres.

The death of Mazarin

It is doubtful whether Mazarin ever loved anyone. In his last days he lingered lovingly among the paintings – a Raphael, a Correggio – which were the pride of his collection, but he rebuffed the loving Queen Mother. He was proud of his royal pupil, and produced for him some advice which Louis copied out; but this is a collection of platitudes worthy of Polonius, in great contrast to the wisdom of Richelieu's *Testament Politique*. The priest whom he called to his deathbed wanted to discuss with him his misuse of public funds, but he dismissed him with the words 'I sent for you only to hear you speak of God'. The dying Cardinal worried lest his fortune should be confiscated, but on Colbert's advice he gave it all to the King, relying on the magnanimity he had inculcated. After an alarming delay Louis gave it all back, and it could now go to the heirs without question. The gambler's last throw had succeeded.

Principal Events, 1643—61

FRANCE AND COLONIES		EUROPE AND OVERSEAS
Louis XIV King.	1643	Battle of Rocroi. Peace
Anne Regent. Mazarin P.M.		negotiations. Galileo dies
Le Tellier Secretary for War		
Conspiracy of *Importants*.	1644	French take Freiburg
Toisé tax		
Dispute with Parlement	1645	Treaty of Bromsebrö
	1646	Parliament victorious in England
Famine and economic crisis	1647	Frederick Henry of Orange dies. Neapolitan revolt
Fronde of the Parlement	1648	Peace of Westphalia. Battle of Lens
Treaty of Rueil. *Mazarinades*	1649	Execution of Charles I. English Commonwealth
Arrest of the princes.	1650	
Fronde of the princes		
First exile of Mazarin.	1651	Battle of Worcester. End of English civil wars
Condéan civil war		
Battle of St Antoine.	1652	First Anglo-Dutch War.
Second exile of Mazarin.		Dutch colonize Cape of Good Hope
King enters Paris		
Return of Mazarin. End of Fronde. Fouquet in charge of finances	1653	Cromwell Lord Protector. De Witt in power in Holland. Pope condemns five propositions of Jansen
	1654	Anglo-Spanish War. Charles X King of Sweden
Assembly of Clergy condemns Jansenism	1655	Northern War. English conquer Jamaica
Pascal: *Les Lettres Provinciales*	1656	First negroes in America
	1657	Anglo-French alliance. Battle of Dunes
Fouquet builds Vaux-le-Vîcomte	1658	Leopold I Emperor. League of the Rhine
Lionne a minister	1659	Peace of the Pyrenees. Oliver Cromwell dies

FRANCE AND COLONIES		EUROPE AND OVERSEAS
Louis XIV marries Maria Theresa. Pascal's *Lettres* condemned. Vincent de Paul dies	1660	Peace of Oliva. Charles II restored in England. Charles XI King of Sweden: Regency
Cardinal Mazarin dies	1661	

PART IV
The Brilliant Years
of Louis XIV

[16] THE KING AND THE TRIAD

Louis XIV became the actual ruler of France immediately after Cardinal Mazarin's death in May 1661.

At a stroke he abolished the ministériat which had become the settled form of French government. In future all the business previously referred to the Cardinal was to be referred to him. He took real power at 22, and retained it until his death at the age of 77. It was incomparably the longest spell of personal rule in European history, and throughout the period the King worked unremittingly, harder in his later years, and made all the main decisions. Modern presidents and prime ministers are exhausted after a few years. Louis could not retire but there is no sign that he ever wanted to. In these early years he wrote 'le métier de roi est grand, noble, délicieux', and even in the darkest days of the end of the reign he was uncrushed by the great burden of rule.

Louis had the vitality and excellent health necessary for this long career; even the court doctors were unable to kill him. He had abundance of common sense, shrewd judgment as a rule, courteous manners and imperturbable good temper, and great dignity. No one ever had a more profound belief in authoritarian rule, based on divine right. In his memoirs (not necessarily written by himself, but intended for the use of his son) he claimed that 'kings are absolute lords, and naturally can dispose fully and freely of all property'. Bossuet, the Bishop of Meaux, was the most eloquent exponent of royal absolutism, and he not only equated the king with the state but made him almost a god on earth. When Louis attended mass in the royal chapel the audience faced him, not the priest. Protestants could go further in king-worship than was possible for Catholics. Ruvigny was the Protestant delegate at the Court for many years and an ambassador in England for a time. He went so far as to say to Louis, 'I regard you, Sire, as God on earth, since you are His image, and I accept your wishes with the same resignation that I accept His will'. The use of the sun as an emblem recalls the king-worship of other civilizations such as the Egyptian or the Japanese.

The greatness of Louis XIV consists largely in his ability to present himself as the apotheosis of the absolute monarch in Christian Europe. This was what Frenchmen had seemed to want in the confusions of the Fronde, and when eventually he created at Versailles the perfect setting for such a king, his outstanding place among European monarchs was assured. The strength of will which maintained this incredible façade for over fifty years was possible only to a man who cared far more about his public image than about any private feelings, who was in fact rather insensitive, who was apt to take the show for the reality, and who could turn a blind eye on the evils of the time. The splendour of the King shone on the courtiers, noblesse d'épée, noblesse de robe, ecclesiastics, artists and writers, and on the army, but Louis saw far less of his suffering people than hi father had done. Apart from his journeys on campaign he moved mainly in a narrow circle of royal châteaux around Paris, and never during his period of rule visited the troubled Midi. The Fronde had given him a dislike of living in Paris which finally found expression in the building of the new château of Versailles and, after his final settlement there in 1682, Louis very rarely visited his capital, sometimes not for years at a time.

Louis XIV was undoubtedly a great king, great in failure as well as in success, but what was the reality of the absolute power he claimed and presented so dramatically? There are many qualifications to make. He was very conservative, and it is astonishing how little change he made in the actual structure of French institutions. Parlements and provincial Estates were tamed but continued to exist. The administrative irregularities and internal barriers which made France more a federal than a unitary state were only partly ironed out. Only minor changes were made in the various sections of the royal council, and if bureaucracy sprouted this was because the King could not possibly cope personally with all the business he attempted to control in his later years. As a very orthodox Catholic king he was unable to escape from the Pope's spiritual overlordship. Because he was generally calm and orderly in his style of rule he performed fewer arbitrary actions than Louis XIII and Richelieu had done, and he never went beyond the existing traditions of royal conduct in France. The property of Frenchmen was in fact as secure as it had been before.

Louis XIV's achievements were imperfect and incomplete and a feeling of frustration and disappointment, shared by many modern historians, was felt in France before the end of the reign. He had fallen far short of his early promise, but it should always be remembered that, with all its blemishes, his reign was outstanding in European history not only for its length but for the extent of territory and number of people under the firm rule of a single monarch, the advances in order and administration, and above all for the splendour of French culture.

From the moment he took personal charge of the government Louis revived the Conseil d'en Haut of three or four ministers, as it had been in Richelieu's later years. He excluded his mother and brother from the body, and it was not until his son the Dauphin needed experience of government that any member of the royal family sat in the council. Ecclesiastics and generals were also excluded. The members had no written warrant; they were called minister and attended because they were summoned verbally; no office carried automatically the status of minister. So here was a highly flexible instrument of royal power. It is amazing that in his whole reign Louis appointed only sixteen ministers. The great officials who were the main candidates held offices which could be acquired only by purchase for vast sums, and more and more they were inherited. In fact most of Louis's ministers came from three families, the Le Telliers, the Colberts, and the Phélypeaux.

The first ministers were Le Tellier, Lionne, and Fouquet, but within six months Fouquet had fallen from power and was faced with ruin. No doubt Fouquet expected soon to be chief of the ministry. He was the most brilliant member, apparently indispensable because of his financial wizardry. His superb display of grandeur when he entertained Louis at Vaux-le-Vîcomte may have aroused the King's jealousy; certainly his large clientele, which included many nobles, his immense patronage of artists, and above all his fortification of a personal stronghold on Belle Isle, all made him an overmighty subject, a potential Frondeur, in the eyes of the King. Colbert, taken over by Louis from Mazarin's service, was Fouquet's enemy and was determined to supplant him. As Mazarin's secretary Colbert had been involved in the vast web of dishonest finance and knew Fouquet's secrets. In September 1661 Fouquet was suddenly arrested by d'Artagnan as he left the King's presence, and put on his trial for malversation.

Fouquet had powerful supporters, even including Anne of Austria, but the King was determined to ruin him, and Colbert, his bitter enemy since Fouquet had refused to have him as a collaborator in the finances in 1659, ferreted about in Fouquet's papers to build up the case against him. Fouquet was of course guilty, but he was the scapegoat for a group of high officials who had shared in the bonanza of the Mazarin regime, and his disgrace was the means by which Colbert gained control of the finances. A special tribunal was set up with Lamoignon, the First President of the Parlement of Paris, at its head, but when Lamoignon showed that he intended to have a fair trial the King dismissed him and gave his place to the Chancellor Séguier, one of Fouquet's chief enemies. The difficulty was to convict Fouquet without incriminating Mazarin and hence Colbert, and Fouquet alleged that Colbert destroyed 1,500 documents. The case dragged on until the end of 1664. Fouquet was found guilty, but only two judges supported the death sentence which Colbert had demanded and thirteen were for the light sentence of banishment. Public opinion welcomed this as a defeat for Colbert. But the King altered the sentence to life imprisonment, and Fouquet remained in the fortress of Pinerolo until his death sixteen years later. All the judges who had dared to vote for banishment were exiled on various pretexts. Louis was not to be trifled with.

The ministerial group known as the Triad, Le Tellier, Lionne, and Colbert, was fully established by 1665, in which year Colbert probably became a minister; the fact that this is not definitely known shows how personal and informal Louis's government was. For several years this harmonious group of well-seasoned ministers was able to offer firm counsels and strong leadership, and the young King could hardly ignore their advice and may sometimes have followed it unwillingly. In 1667 a foreign ambassador wrote of *'leur belle union . . . leur zèle et . . . leur savoir'*. Outside this group the most important adviser was Turenne, the King's military tutor, but he was fighting a losing battle for authority over the army with Le Tellier and his son Louvois, who became a virtual partner of his father in the war secretaryship in 1664. The King was not prepared to have ministers of Turenne's high noble rank. 'It was not in my interest to take subjects of a higher rank. I must before everything establish my own reputation and make clear to the public, by the very class from which I took them, that it was not my intention to share my authority with them.' Brave words, but these extremely able and hardworking ministers fed the King with the information they wanted him to have and participated in all the decisions, until Louis learned the lesson of divide and rule.

Le Tellier was the leading member of the Triad. He was the only one whom the King addressed as 'monsieur'. When Mazarin died most people expected that he would be made the chief minister. He has been described (by L. André) as 'the greatest civil administrator of military affairs under the ancien régime', whose work only needed retouching until 1789. He had a wider political role than either Lionne or Colbert, frequently acting as a negotiator on special missions from the King. Le Tellier's versatility is shown by the fact that for the last eight years of his life he was Chancellor, and a very active one. His collaboration with his son is one of the most remarkable family partnerships in history.

Lionne's position is a good illustration of the flexibility of French administration and the strength of the venal officiers. He had served his apprenticeship in diplomacy with his uncle Servien, and became the effective head of the diplomatic service in time to play the leading role in the negotiation of the Treaty of the Pyrenees. But the Secretary of State for Foreign Affairs was Loménie de Brienne, a great courtier, and he held the reversion for his son. Lionne's correspondence had to pass through Brienne's hands until in 1663 Brienne agreed to sell the office and the reversion to Lionne for a vast sum. The King could usually circumvent difficulties caused by the venality of offices, but he was not absolute enough to remove them arbitrarily.

It was Colbert who had by far the largest scope for initiative in this ministry, because the King was not interested in the details of finance and the economy, nor even in the navy, but the bias of the King's interest also ensured that foreign policy and war would take priority over the rehabilitation of France. Colbert was the humblest in origin of the three – the others were of the noblesse de robe with some generations of officialdom behind them. Actually the humbleness of Colbert's family connections has been exaggerated. His father was a merchant in Reims, but his uncle was an official in the war office and Le Tellier's brother-in-law, and it was as a protégé of Le Tellier that Colbert rose to the position of Mazarin's secretary. He was however regarded as a servant by Mazarin and afterwards by the King; for example he made the arrangements for the lying-in of the King's mistress and the upbringing of his illegitimate children.

Colbert's empire grew rapidly. He worked unremittingly for fifteen hours a day, and his grasp of administrative detail is almost incredible. The King made him a maid of all work, and he willingly encroached. Officially he was made Controller-General of the Finances in 1665, but already he had taken control of the economy and much of the administration of the country. He dealt with commerce and colonies, and administered the navy long before he became Secretary for the Navy in 1669. In the

same year he bought the secretaryship of the Royal Household.
From 1664 he was in charge of the King's great building programme and administered the royal patronage, especially of
literary men, musicians, and artists. He took over much of the
work of the ageing and decaying Chancellor Séguier. By his over-
powering energy and zeal Colbert nearly became the chief
minister, but the King was determined that this should not
happen, and could use the jealousy aroused in the Le Telliers by
the rise of their former client to curb Colbert's ambitions. Once,
when Colbert quarrelled with Louvois and used angry words to
the King, Louis wrote to him: 'Speak freely, but after I have
given a decision I do not want a word more'. It has been said
that Colbert never rose to the level of a general idea, and it may
well be that his mercantilism and his boldest plans for the
development of France into a world power were inspired by Richelieu's (at that time unpublished) *Testament Politique*, as Hauser
maintains. These ideas and his radical prejudices against the
clergy, the nobility and the venal officials nearly made him a
revolutionary minister, but the determined conservatism of the
King and his own habits of self-interested social climbing and
aggrandizement ensured that he would work within the existing
social, political, and financial framework.

The King very generously rewarded the devoted services of
these ministers, and was excessively willing to meet their
importunate demands for favours. The Le Telliers became
immensely rich; they controlled the war office for three generations, Louvois became a minister in 1672 and a relative, Le
Pelletier, succeeded Colbert as Controller-General on Colbert's
death in 1683. Two of Le Tellier's daughters married dukes and
a son became an archbishop. Even more remarkable was the rise
of Colbert's family. All his three daughters became duchesses
with the help of huge additions to their dowries contributed by
the King. His son Seignelay succeeded him as Secretary for the
Navy and eventually became a minister. His brother Colbert
de Croissy became Secretary for Foreign Affairs and a minister
and was succeeded in these positions by his son Torcy. A son
became an archbishop. A nephew Desmaretz was Louis's last

Controller-General and a minister. One of Colbert's sons-in-law, the Duc de Beauvillier, was the only nobleman to be a minister during Louis XIV's personal rule, and another the Duc de Chevreuse was the King's confidential adviser for many years. Louis's own loyalties went very deep, and he had a strong preference for the families he knew.

[17] THE STRUGGLE FOR ORDER

In 1661 France was in the grip of a famine; there was widespread misery and serious depopulation. Louis makes no mention of this in his memoirs, and he was in fact never sensitive to the suffering of his people. Colbert, however hard, was far more concerned. A large working population was the main source of the prosperity which would solve the financial problem; he offered tax exemptions to men marrying under twenty-one and subsidies to fathers of ten surviving children (not counting any who had become monks or nuns). A series of good harvests and, except for two short military campaigns, a period of peace until 1672, allowed a return of relative prosperity. Even in such a period of recovery and reform violence was never far below the surface. Some of Colbert's interferences with industry provoked serious riots.

The old pattern of revolts by peasants and town workers continued until 1675, after which date a much more efficient army, ruthlessly used, prevented major outbreaks until the Huguenots in the Cévennes rebelled in 1703. As a rule they were risings against innovations in taxation. In the Boulogne district, which had enjoyed special privileges since it was annexed in the sixteenth century, 6,000 rebels rose against a new tax in 1662; several were executed and 400 sent to the galleys. Some Pyrenean districts newly subjected to the gabelle gave trouble for several years after 1664. A false rumour of new taxation started a rising in Languedoc in 1670, which was ended by a massacre of the peasants by a force commanded by d'Artagnan; a hundred rebels were put to death and about six hundred condemned to the galleys.

The last and most serious risings in this period were a consequence of the Dutch War of 1672 – the special war taxes aroused violent opposition in the West. In 1675 Bordeaux and the surrounding countryside rose in revolt against a tax on tin. There was prolonged rioting, a magistrate was murdered, and the government accused the bourgeoisie of condoning the risings. When it was suppressed the Parlement was exiled and thousands of soldiers were billeted in the ruined city – the most dreaded punishment of all. In the same year the greatest rising of all in this period occurred in Brittany, where 20,000 armed peasants rebelled against new taxes, particularly the introduction of the gabelle. They even formulated a programme of reforms, some of which were bizarre – the proceeds of the taille were to be used to buy tobacco to be distributed at mass – but some quite radical, such as the election of magistrates, the abolition of tithe, the payment of salaries to the clergy, the abolition of hunting between March and September, and a free choice of mills for grinding corn. There was a prolonged struggle before sufficient troops could be diverted from the war to crush the rebels. Madame de Sévigné has vividly described the barbarities of the suppression. The governor complained that the soldiers treated Brittany as enemy territory. The King extracted an additional don gratuit of three million livres from the Estates. 10,000 soldiers were quartered on the Bretons, houses were demolished, and the Parlement of Rennes was exiled to Vannes for fifteen years.

Even these greater outbreaks were purely local, all were at a distance from Paris and mainly in the lawless Midi. In an emergency the reorganized army could crush resistance, but the essential thing was to strengthen the royal grip on government. Colbert supplied most of the drive and the greatest contribution to the remarkable achievements in this field, but it has been a common mistake to disregard the share of the King himself, whose fear of a new Fronde and love of order and clarity stimulated ministerial activity. It was the King who checked all independence in the Assembly of Clergy in 1661. He made it more and more difficult for great nobles and ecclesiastics to flourish away from the Court, and so tamed them. He reduced the Parlements to unquestioning obedience until the very last years of the reign. The Parlement of Paris accepted an order in 1661 to recognize decrees of the Council as having the same validity as edicts registered in the Parlement. In 1673 the King ordered the Parlement to make no remonstrances until after an edict had been registered, and no more lits de justice were required during his lifetime. The provincial Estates were also successfully ordered to vote taxes (the so-called dons gratuits) by acclamation and without discussion. The governors of provinces (generally absent at Court) henceforth held their appointments for only three years and had little more than nominal functions. So the forces which had created the Fronde were curbed by the majestic authority of Louis. The Great Condé, loyal and humble, was restored to his military rank by the favour of Le Tellier.

The defence of order meant to the Most Christian King the defence of orthodoxy in religion, as interpreted to him by his Jesuit confessors. The Huguenots immediately felt a cold wave of dislike, but Louis's first concern was with the Jansenists, whom he regarded as past or potential Frondeurs, and he at once instituted a persecution. In 1661 he put on heavy pressure to force them to renounce the Five Propositions of Jansen which had been condemned by the Pope. Novices and pupils were expelled. The chief male leaders fled to avoid imprisonment; more and more Jansenists signed the formula of renunciation, but with the reservation that they denied that the propositions as stated in the papal decree were to be found in Jansen's works. This provided endless material for controversy, but at last a conciliatory pope, Clement IX, assisted in bringing about the so-called Peace of the Church in 1668. The King was tired of the long debate and persuaded by the many friends of the Jansenists that they were no longer a danger. Even Le Tellier gave them some discreet support and helped to bring about a compromise. The Jansenists were able to make the reservation as to fact, and for ten years they enjoyed a tranquil existence. They had the sympathies of the popes, and Arnauld was one of the most important of the French dévots.

Better order depended very much on an improved administrative machine, and Colbert was mainly responsible for the creation of this. First the facts and statistics of the kingdom must be known. Various inquiries paved the way for administrative action. The Chamber of Justice which tried Fouquet dealt also with the tax-farmers, though the greatest offenders could usually escape. Claims to titles of nobility and exemptions from taille came under scrutiny. In the Great Inquiry of 1664 intendants toured the country investigating local government. Most municipalities were found to be hopelessly in debt, and Colbert put them under the tutelage of the intendants in return for the liquidation of their debts. The local financial officials were found to be so inefficient and oppressively corrupt that Colbert proposed that their offices should be abolished without compensation. The King's rejection of this proposal destroyed the hope of a radical cure for French administration under the ancien régime, but he probably took the only line that was politically possible. Colbert bought out a few of the officers, but the government could not afford to solve the problem in this way. Their powers were gradually appropriated by the intendants, and a curious dual system of administration persisted until the Revolution.

The development of this new form of administration by intendants had been long prepared and now proceeded steadily. They participated at every stage in the allocation and collection of the taille. They played a large part in Colbert's attempt to carry out an industrial revolution by government order. He still restricted their numbers seriously, often giving two généralités to one intendant, moved them frequently, and regarded them as primarily inspectors. But his own administrative system forced them to become virtual governors of their provinces, and some began to develop a local bureaucracy by setting up offices and appointing sub-délégués to supervise local districts. This trend persisted in spite of decrees prohibiting sub-délégués in 1674 and 1680. The growth of bureaucracy was inevitable, but it was by no means all consciously planned.

The most disorderly part of France was the Massif Central, particularly the province of Auvergne, where soldiers had to be sent to collect the taille in 1663. A commission of the Parlement of Paris was sent there in 1665 to hold a great assize court known as *Les Grands Jours d'Auvergne*, which revealed extraordinary backwardness, the worst feudal oppression still persisting, and a criminal nobility indulging in brigandage and blackmail. Few of the offenders were brought to justice, however. Royal law had still hardly penetrated this mountain fastness. As with finance, it was necessary for intendants to take over more and more the work of administering justice locally and this they did, with full power to take cases from the local magistrates, or alternatively to sit with magistrates to judge cases. Gradually the new administration underminedfe udal survivals and client age

In the great early days of the rule of Louis XIV it is astonishing how much was accomplished in government by how few people. Goubert estimates that the central government was manned by fewer than 1,000 persons without permanent offices; most of these followed the Court on its travels. There were about thirty intendants in the provinces in 1670, with few offices and few subordinates. The energy and devotion of this body of men (the upper ranks all members of the noblesse de robe) are almost incredible, and in themselves a wonderful tribute to the power of the King in mobilizing support.

To enforce its authority the government was constantly resorting to the use of the army. Special police forces were still rudimentary, though in this respect France was ahead of the rest of Europe; already there were more than 2,000 gendarmes in the French provinces. In 1667 the King accepted a suggestion of Colbert that he should set up a new police organization in Paris, where the Fronde had shown the weakness of royal power; and this force became the model for others in later years. La Reynie, chosen as its head with the title of Lieutenant-General of Police, became almost a minister and had constant private access to the King. He was an admirable administrator, concerned with welfare as well as order, and he and his successor d'Argenson made Paris a relatively orderly and well-run city. It was paved and lit (with

6,500 reflecting candle lanterns), provided with water and given protection against fire. The police supervised the food supply and the markets, exercised a censorship by control of the printers, and attacked the evils of vagabondage and misery by the establishment of a vast workhouse and infirmary known as the hôpital-général.

One of the most ambitious plans of this energetic government was to codify and unify the civil and criminal law. A Council of Justice was set up in 1665. Although Séguier presided, Colbert, his uncle Pussort, and the First President Lamoignon were the leading figures. It achieved much less than was intended. Six new codes were imposed as a result of its work, without any reference to a representative body; this in itself was a new assertion of royal absolutism. The main codes, concerning civil and criminal law, fell far short of the first aims; court procedure was unified, but French law remained a mosaic of separate customs until the time of Napoleon. Useful reforms were made by the ordinance of waters and forests, a maritime ordinance, a commercial ordinance, and a colonial ordinance (Code Noir) concerned with the status of slaves and their protection against their masters – the last not until 1685, two years after Colbert's death.

Before the Dutch War imposed heavy new strains, Louis's government had brought about an amazing recovery, and established a well-balanced regime in which orderly administration had not yet become excessively bureaucratic and the King was admirably served by men of first-class ability. He himself was young and boundlessly energetic, and his egotism and love of glory had reinforced the energy of government without yet causing serious harm. In every sphere, finance, industry, commerce, colonies, the arts and literature, the government gave a vigorous lead, and it had created for the first time in France an efficient military and naval organization. The Triad of ministers remained intact until the death of Lionne in 1671. The harmony within the Conseil d'en Haut was shattered when Louvois was made a minister in 1672, at the same time as Pomponne, the new Secretary for Foreign Affairs. Colbert's dominance in the ministry was at an end.

[18] FINANCE AND THE ECONOMY – COLBERT'S MERCANTILISM

Colbert was not an original thinker. He was perhaps the most thorough mercantilist in history, but he absorbed mercantilism from previous theory and practice; his contribution was a persistent and obstinate determination, backed by the personal authority of a King who, at least in theory, could act as he pleased. Mercantilism was derived from the practice of the Tudors, of Henry IV and of the earlier Richelieu, and from a considerable body of economic writings. It was a theory of the national economy which emphasized the importance of creating a stock of precious metals by stimulating exports and discouraging imports, and so producing a favourable balance of trade. Much of this was just common sense, but it involved a massive interference in the economy by the state, and tended to an overemphasis on foreign trade and monetary wealth; expansion in the luxury trades more urgently than in agriculture or the manufacture of basic necessities. Colbert's own additions were crude; he believed that there was a permanently fixed total of trade requiring a fixed amount of shipping, and hence there must be a ceaseless struggle in which the gains made by one state were necessarily won at the expense of its rivals. He was harsher, narrower and more bureaucratic than Richelieu in his approach, but the resistances of French society at every level were very great, and the projected industrial and commercial revolution had only fragmentary successes.

Finance

It might be argued that what the French monarchy and people most needed at this time was a thorough overhaul of taxation and government finance. Here Colbert was disappointing. He created great resources for the expression of Louis XIV's power and glory, but with all the minor reforms carried out the

financial foundations of France remained rotten, and in the end
bad finance ruined the monarchy. Colbert's financial activity,
and indeed much of his work for the economy, is full of improvisations. He inherited a severe crisis. He was never master of the
King's expenditure; Louis found it all the easier to by-pass
Colbert's controls because he himself was officially Fouquet's
successor as Superintendent. After 1672 military and naval
expenditure on the Dutch War wrecked Colbert's balanced
budgets. In the last years even Colbert was driven to falsify the
financial statements which he regularly presented to the King.
But however imperfect his financial achievements they were
indeed remarkable. They made it possible for Louis XIV to be
the most sumptuous and easily the most powerful monarch in
Europe up to that time. Colbert left a vastly more efficient
financial administration. He made a bad system of taxation work
and so perpetuated it in an age when other countries, England
for example, were forced to modernize their finances to meet the
new demands of the age.

Colbert's first achievement was a penetration of the jungle of
French finance and a great clarification, which enabled him to
present to the King every month a clear account of the financial
situation. His annual statements of income and expenditure and
his estimates of expenditure for the ensuing year were not exactly
budgets because Louis's expenditure was unpredictable and uncontrollable. In 1680 Colbert dared to write to the King: 'I only
beg Your Majesty to allow me to tell you that in war and peace
you have never consulted your finances to decide your out-
goings!' He fought a losing battle for rational economy of
expenditure against the military extravagance of Louvois and
the gorgeous display of Versailles. For Louis glory came before
solvency.

Nevertheless Colbert was able to produce a financial surplus
within ten years of taking office, and the government's credit was
so good that he could borrow at 5 per cent. The biggest single factor
in producing this change was the effective increase in the share
of the revenue which reached the Treasury. The local administration had first call on tax revenue collected locally, and only the

remainder of the revenue was sent to Paris. With the help of his vigorous intendants Colbert attacked the inefficiency and corruption of the venal officials and saved large sums. Tax-farmers were frightened by the trial of Fouquet, and some of them were also tried by the Chamber of Justice. It became much more difficult to make illicit profits. The charges on the revenue were reduced from 52 million livres to 24 million livres.

Colbert recognized that the taille was an evil tax because of the exemption of nearly all the rich and the inequalities of taxation on the remainder. He pruned the exemptions – though as bait for his industrial and commercial schemes he was constantly offering new exemptions. He insisted on very careful surveys by the intendants to allow the fair partitioning of the taille between généralités, elections, and parishes. He lowered the taille in the pays d'élections, where it was heavy, and squeezed a higher don gratuit out of the Estates of the pays d'états, where the taille was light. (Even so Burgundy, a rich pays d'états, paid less than a fifth of the taille paid in Touraine.) The total income from taille was reduced from 42 million livres to 35 million livres.

Colbert believed in shifting the tax burden more on to indirect taxation, payable by all, but still much more burdensome for the poor. The worst of all these taxes, the gabelle, was rigorously enforced, and defaulters were a major source of galley crews; the revenue from this tax was increased by 4 million livres. Colbert reformed the collection of indirect taxes within a large area of central and northern France known as les Cinq Grosses Fermes. He made this region a free trade area by abolishing internal tolls and customs duties, and gave the collection of all indirect taxes to a new syndicate of tax-farmers known as the Farmers-General. The revenue from indirect taxes was raised during Colbert's term of office from 36 million livres to 62 million livres; most of the increases were imposed to meet war expenses.

Industry

Colbert relied on his commercial and industrial policy to expand the French economy and so increase the revenue without overburdening the people. Although he achieved much, there was no significant general expansion. It was an uphill task because the economy began to decline. The inflow of precious metals into Europe from Spanish America was drying up. Prices and incomes in France were beginning to fall, and the most Colbert could do by his methods was to counteract this long-term process. He neglected the creation of new credit by banks, which in Holland and later in England gave a new stimulus to the economy. He had little regard for agriculture as a whole – forestry and industrial crops were his main concern – and French prosperity depended mainly on agricultural output. Naturally a wealthy country, with the finest cornfields in Europe, France was economically backward, still medieval in many ways. No book on agriculture appeared in France in the seventeenth century after that of Olivier de Serres.

Colbert made the economic problem a national one. He made Frenchmen begin to think and write again about economic questions. His restless activity produced remarkable results, mainly in the luxury trades, naval and military supplies, the merchant marine and overseas development. In the last resort the results achieved were sadly disproportionate to the great effort made.

France must produce for herself those manufactured goods she was importing. To achieve this production Colbert would use any method that came to hand – state enterprise, direct subsidies, exemptions from taille and other fiscal privileges, grants of monopolies, imposition of controls by innumerable regulations and by use of the authority of the town guilds. It was necessary to create the skilled working force for these new manufactures. Foreign workmen and organizers of industry were induced, usually in defiance of their own laws, to settle in France and teach their skills to French workmen. Technical inspectors were appointed, and were constantly on tour, supplementing the work of the local authorities in enforcing Colbert's 150 decrees. Protective tariffs were imposed, a moderate one applying only to les Cinq Grosses Fermes in 1664, and a severe one, especially aimed at the Dutch and covering the entire state, in 1667 – in itself this marked a big advance towards a national economy.

Some great enterprises, freed from guild control, were established or developed by Colbert. The Gobelins, existing since the reign of Henry IV as a tapestry manufacture mainly for the Court, he made into a state enterprise directed by Le Brun. A host of Flemish workmen taught the art of tapestry making as practised in Flanders. A corps of artists under Le Brun's close supervision produced the designs. Each master at the Gobelins was semi-independent, acting as a contractor for the tapestries commissioned by the King, and free to work for private customers as well. Le Brun launched out into miscellaneous production for the royal palaces of furniture, furnishings and objets d'art. The creation of Versailles ensured the commercial success of the Gobelins; Le Brun was responsible for the whole of the interior of Versailles, including the painting of the walls and ceilings. He imposed his florid taste on the age of Louis XIV. The Savonnerie carpet manufacture, moribund in 1664, was revived on similar lines, and was successful for the same reason.

A rather different large-scale venture was the establishment by the Dutchman Van Robais of a big enterprise at Abbeville for the manufacture of fine cloth to rival that imported from Holland and England. This was a private enterprise well subsidized by the state, with great privileges and a local monopoly. Here 4,000 workmen were employed under one roof. But this was altogether an exception in the woollen industry, which was almost entirely domestic. In the main the manufacture of fine cloth was stimulated by meticulous regulation of the quality, specifying the widths and lengths of the pieces and the number of threads in the warp, and these regulations were enforced by the guilds. Much domestic industry in the countryside was organized by capitalists outside the guild system, and Colbert felt driven in 1673 to re-impose old laws to force every weaver to enter a guild; but this decree remained largely a dead letter. In fact Goubert has found that in the Beauvaisis Colbert's strenuous efforts to control industry were generally ignored, although that was a region quite near to Paris. By one means or other, however,

Colbert succeeded in making France largely self-sufficient in the production of woollen cloth.

It was still very difficult to induce Frenchmen to invest in industry or commerce. Frequently Colbert attacked the problem of production by persuading financiers who wanted favours from him to invest in large-scale enterprises, as for example the German banker Jabach, who organized the manufacture of buff leather and reorganized the Aubusson tapestries. They were subsidized, but modestly; all told, the subsidies to industry ran at about 500,000 livres a year until the Dutch War forced Colbert to reduce them. Grants of monopolies were a regular practice, but caused outcries and riots when they interfered with existing industry. An example of this was the introduction of the manufacture of Venetian lace by a joint stock company with branch establishments in many scattered towns. In some places it was temporarily successful, especially where there was a vigorous intendant on the spot to enforce the harsh monopoly and drive unwilling workers out of the old style lace-making into the new. Elsewhere it was almost impossible to get any local co-operation. Colbert interested himself particularly in Auxerre in Burgundy because it was near his estate of Seignelay. He dealt with constant complaints from the woman director of the new lace manufacture there, a friend of Mme Colbert. It was nearly impossible to get girl apprentices – he offered exemption from taille to any father who sent three daughters to learn the new trade. The municipal officials, caring nothing about industry, were totally uncooperative, although they were constantly urged and threatened by the minister; in despair he concluded that 'the city of Auxerre is characterized by such prodigious laziness that it will be difficult to change it'. This is a not unfair example of Colbert's extraordinary attention to detail and the severe limits of his power. The municipal officials knew that they were safely entrenched.

Outstanding successes in Colbert's campaign included the manufacture of cannon, which grew by leaps and bounds, and the production of naval stores previously imported – sailcloth, tar, and rope. A soap monopoly, very unpopular and eventually dissolved, brought about considerable progress in manufacture. Sugar refining, firmly based on a developing colonial trade, grew from nothing to a consumption of 17 million pounds of sugar a year. In an industry encouraged by Colbert, Perrot invented a new method of producing flat glass plates, the basis for mirror production on a large scale to surpass the Venetians. This plate glass concern, founded in 1664, still flourishes today. The silk industry developed under Colbert's encouragement; in Lyon the manufacture of silk stockings and cloth of gold was established. These were the patchy results of a colossal effort, and some were of permanent value, but Colbert had not found much willing cooperation, and his bureaucratic mind disdained consultation. His economic dictatorship did not produce the industrial revolution for which he looked.

Commerce

Colbert on the whole did rather less than Sully to facilitate internal trade and communications. He spent rather less on roads, about 600,000 livres a year before the war, and repairs barely kept pace with deterioration. He developed a postal system with 800 post offices. The greatest showpiece was the Canal du Midi, linking Bordeaux with the Mediterranean, a very expensive project which was more grandiose than practical, for it was never much used for avoiding the circuit of Spain, and the local traffic did not begin to repay its cost. Little work was done on river navigation, but the removal of tolls on some rivers encouraged their use. Many internal tariff barriers were allowed to remain, and a great variety of weights and measures continued to hinder internal trade.

Colbert's chief interest was in foreign trade. He was obsessed by the success of the Dutch, whom he admired and hated. He pointed out, and exaggerated, their near-monopoly of merchant shipping, stating in 1661 that they had 16,000 of the 20,000 ships in the world, and the French only 600. (A more realistic modern estimate gives the Dutch about 8,000 ships, half of the world total apart from China.) He rightly believed that the French had unduly neglected the sea and overseas trade.

Colbert never lost sight of the need for building up the French merchant marine. Shipbuilding he encouraged by the usual means – bounties, subsidies, favours of every kind. He offered foreign sailors naturalization after five years. He took a great interest in the maintenance and development of the forests which supplied the wood for ship's timbers. He imposed a tax on foreign ships coming into French ports.

Colbert set about, as Richelieu had done without much success, organizing companies on the Dutch model. Even less than Richelieu did he use the natural drives already present in the seaports of France, and the failure of some of his companies is partly due to this; Paris, unlike London or Amsterdam, was not a natural centre for overseas activity. It was difficult to recruit directors for the new trading companies, and a quarter of these were officials who could not refuse. The vigorous merchants of the Atlantic ports hated and fought regimentation. Above all Marseilles kept up a ceaseless struggle against Colbert's efforts to put her trade into a strait waistcoat. Another obstacle to the success of French trading companies was the fact that industry was not yet in a position to supply enough goods for export. So Colbert schemed and organized with mixed results, and such growth as there was was often a natural one. French trade benefited more from political stability than from Colbert's regulation. Trade with Spain grew most of all, and this was left to private efforts. Ironically, two of Colbert's major creations, the Levant Company and the East India Company, drained France of precious metals and introduced luxury goods into France.

The East India Company, founded in 1664, was the only one of Colbert's companies which survived the reign of Louis XIV. It set up a warehouse at Surat in 1667, and amid the immense difficulties of the Dutch War François Martin founded Pondicherry in 1674. Later French interests were foreshadowed by the establishment of diplomatic contacts with the King of Siam and the Emperor of Annam (the modern Vietnam). Commercially the company was unprofitable and always struggling. Its imports of calicoes, prints, and muslins roused the antagonism of French textile manufacturers. An attempt to settle Madagascar failed, but a settlement was established on the island of Bourbon to challenge the Dutch on Mauritius.

The Levant Company, founded in 1669, was short of capital, burdened with too many officials, and lacked a monopoly. Its Parisian directors tried, from an impossible distance, to dictate to the port of Marseilles, which had for generations controlled the trade with Turkey through its Chamber of Commerce. The great gains in this period were that Colbert created a new efficient fleet of galleys which dealt more effectively with the Barbary Corsairs, and improved the handling of affairs in Turkey itself by the French consulates. His prohibition of the export of coin, though it could not be enforced, made the trade more difficult. The company was dissolved before Colbert's death. Trade with Turkey continued to grow by the defiant enterprise of the merchants of Marseilles.

The Baltic was the source of vitally important masts, tar, hemp, and metals, and to increase French trade there Colbert arranged commercial treaties with Sweden, Denmark, and the Hanseatic League. In 1669 he founded the Northern Company to develop this trade, but it never flourished, and in this case he allowed the Bordeaux merchants for a time (1671) to run a company of their own.

Colonies

A West India Company founded in 1664 proved to be quite unable to cope with the situation in the West Indies, where population was growing fast on the basis of sugar production; by 1697 there were 40,000 inhabitants (27,000 of them negroes) in the French islands. The company could not even feed these colonists, who resented its official monopoly and Colbert's policy of *l'exclusif*, allowing trade only with France. It was impossible to exclude the Dutch and to prevent contraband trade, that with the flourishing English colonies of the mainland for example, who could provide food and wanted raw sugar. In 1674 Colbert dissolved the company. The French share in their own colonial trade grew through the enterprise of merchants, especially in Nantes, rather than through regulation. What Colbert sucessfully provided was orderly administration on the lines of a French province.

This was also his major contribution to the growth of Canada, which became the province of New France in 1663, with a governor and an intendant. Without Colbert's vigorous direction it is doubtful whether this colony, with only about 2,000 population in 1661, would have survived, especially as it had to face the hostile Iroquois, the most powerful Indian tribal confederation. At first Canada was included in the monopoly of the West India Company, but Colbert took the advice of Talon, the excellent intendant he had appointed, and ended the company's control over Canada. A regiment of soldiers was sent out, the Iroquois menace was contained, and the friendly Hurons and Algonquins supported. The King, who was indifferent to overseas enterprise, put difficulties in the way of securing emigrants and forbade Huguenots to enter Canada. But Colbert, with little encouragement, did what he could. He once wrote: 'We are preparing the 150 girls, the mares, stallions and lambs that we have to send to Canada'. He wanted to integrate the Indians with the French population, but the Jesuits, now entrenched in Canada, prevented this – they wished to preserve the Indians in a state of innocence. He encouraged exploration for the sake of the fur trade, and perhaps for vaster designs of a French-dominated North America, and here the Jesuits supported him in their desire to convert the Indians of the interior. From their mission of Michilimackinac Father Marquette and the fur-trader Joliet made the expedition which discovered the Mississippi in 1669–70, and just afterwards Cavelier de La Salle began his journeys, by way of the Ohio, which eventually resulted in the opening up of the entire Mississippi basin as far as the Gulf of Mexico. When La Salle at last sailed down the great river to its mouth he named it the River Colbert in gratitude for the support he had had. By the time Talon left Canada in 1673, and the main burden of developing the colony fell on a remarkable new governor, Frontenac, its future was reasonably assured, and the vision of Louisiana was beginning to open up. The population reached 10,000 by 1680.

The navy

Colbert found the navy totally neglected when he took office. The King was never really interested – only once did Colbert entice him to set foot on a ship, in Dunkirk harbour. With little support Colbert set about creating a French navy which should be second to none, and this was achieved in the later stages of the Dutch War. Expenditure on the navy went up from 300,000 livres in 1660 to 13·4 million livres in 1670. By 1677 it included 116 men-of-war and 83 smaller ships, besides a strong fleet of galleys in the Mediterranean – the biggest fleet in the world. To man this fleet Colbert rejected the press-gang methods of England and attempted an orderly conscription. In 1669, far in advance of his time, he instituted the Inscription Maritime. All sailors had to serve in the navy for six months every third year, an efficient but bitterly unpopular way of coping with the problem. To house the fleet, Colbert resumed the work on ports begun by Richelieu. Toulon was transformed into a good naval base, Brest and Rochefort were built up from nothing, and eventually Vauban improved and fortified the port of Dunkirk. The creation of the navy was the most completely successful of Colbert's achievements.

It is almost inconceivable that one man, even working a fifteen-hour day without holidays, could have controlled all the affairs detailed above, and the cultural activities referred to in the next chapter. Colbert's output of memoranda and letters was enormous. He was frustrated by the King and Louvois, by the wars that he helped to provoke, by the ingrained nature of French society, by lack of physical resources, but he never entirely failed in what he undertook. His defects were those of the born bureaucrat – excessive love of power, over-confidence in his own judgment, a meddlesome attitude, lack of sympathy

and tact. To the end he was the King's domestique, as he had
formerly been Mazarin's, the steward of the biggest and most
complicated estate in Europe. His most permanent achievement
was the building up of administrative machinery which functioned,
however imperfectly, until the Revolution.

[19] THE SUN KING

In 1662 Louis XIV adopted the device of the sun's disk. With
the resources provided by Colbert he intended to make a gorgeous
display of greatness such as Europe had never seen before and was
never to see again. He surrounded himself with a brilliant court in
which he would appear as a demigod. He enslaved the higher
nobility in this dream world; they could not flourish without his
favours, and his favours were given only to those whom he knew
as courtiers. He acted the part of a great king superbly, perform-
ing in public all the acts of his life except his lovemaking; two
hundred of the finest nobles were his personal attendants. The
Duc de Richelieu said: 'I would as soon die as be two or three
months without seeing the King'.

In our minds this vision of splendour is naturally associated
with Versailles, so that it is important to remember that the
Court was not permanently established there until 1683. Until
then the King was constantly on the move, and the Court with
him. Memories of the Fronde must have haunted him in Paris.
Great building works were begun at the Louvre. Bernini, the
supreme baroque architect, was brought to Paris to plan the
extensions, but his design was rejected, and Claude Perrault,
a brilliant amateur architect, designed the superb colonnade of
the east wing. Colbert believed passionately that the King should
live in Paris. But Louis never settled there, and the Louvre was
left unfinished until the time of Napoleon III. Until Versailles
became his permanent home Louis spent much of his time at
St Germain, just outside Paris, but visited Vincennes and particu-

larly Fontainebleau for the hunting. He also paid constant visits to the small château of Versailles, which charmed him more and more. Colbert struggled in vain against the King's growing obsession. Some of the most splendid fêtes of the reign were held at Versailles. Le Nôtre's first plan for the superb gardens was completed in 1668, and the King instructed Le Vau to prepare plans for the enlargement of the château, modelled on Fouquet's château of Vaux, and these first building works were completed in 1674.

This early court of Louis XIV was very gay, with the King the leader of the stately revels. His sense of order and love of punctilio established a routine of pleasure and etiquette which eventually became the norm of civilized behaviour in Europe. The new fashions had a gorgeous dignity, and the periwig, adopted by the King at this time, might be taken as the symbol of the age. The Court hunted, danced and gambled, attended fireworks displays, fêtes and masked balls, watched ballets, plays and operas, and listened to the finest orchestra in Europe.

After a flirtation with Henriette, Charles II's sister and the wife of Louis's brother the Duc d'Orléans, Louis fell in love with one of her maids of honour, a shy, pretty, slightly deformed girl of sixteen, Louise de la Vallière, who became his first mistress. This affair estranged him from his mother for a time – she was devoted to the interests of her niece and daughter-in-law, Queen Maria Theresa. When Anne of Austria died in 1666 Louis acknowledged La Vallière as his official mistress, a title she retained long after she ceased to be first favourite. Her greatest merit was that she genuinely loved the King (though she asked for and gained many favours for her family). When the King went on campaign in 1667 he took with him a mass of courtiers, and at their head the Queen and La Vallière. But already he had fallen in love with La Vallière's companion Mme de Montespan, a florid beauty who belonged to one of the oldest noble families of France, and she became his unacknowledged mistress during this campaign. For ten years Montespan was the uncrowned queen, insolently triumphant and dominant over the King and the Court, although the double adultery strained even Louis's credit with the Church – Bossuet strongly opposed the affair – and she could never be fully acknowledged as the maîtresse en titre. The King's casting off of La Vallière, who at last retired heartbroken to a convent, was characteristically callous. But he believed, and France believed with him, that he was not to be judged as an ordinary mortal; he was one of the supreme egotists of all time. None of the women in his life, until he took refuge finally with Mme de Maintenon, was allowed any political influence.

Louis had a very sure perception of the importance of the arts and sciences. He was a musician of some merit – he played the guitar and the harpsichord and sang quite well – and he took the greatest personal interest in the Court music, directed by Lulli from 1665. His other main artistic interest was in landscape gardening. But he gave strong support to the idea of classical order in the arts, and hence government direction. The arts and sciences were to be subsidized and regimented as were the manufactures, and when Colbert bought the superintendency of buildings he added the direction of the fine arts to his supervision of industry. The King wrote to him: 'I confide to you what is the most precious thing in the world, which is my glory'.

Colbert supervised a huge building programme for the King. He also directed the arts by three methods: Court patronage, pensions, and the taking over or setting up of academies. The importance of Le Brun as a purveyor of art to the Court has already been stressed; his academic solemnity and pomposity exactly suited the King, and stifled originality. His taste was elegant – he once objected to a Caravaggio nativity because such rude images as an ox and an ass appeared in it – and he stressed the decorative elements in art. The finest French painting of the age was non-official and had no support from the King. Claude Lorrain and the brothers Le Nain were the greatest French artists after the death of Poussin in 1665, and like Watteau at the end of the reign they enjoyed no royal favours. The portrait painter Rigaud was the best of the Court artists.

Music and drama in this early period were in a far happier state. The Italian Lulli was a fertile director. He developed the Italian art of opera by introducing ballets and a chorus. With

Quinault as his librettist he wrote the first great French operas, and composed comédies-ballets, of which the most famous is *Le Bourgeois Gentilhomme*, with a text by Molière which is one of the greatest comic dramas in its own right. Molière had settled in Paris, with the Duc d'Orléans as his patron, just before the King established his personal rule. In the next twelve years his comic masterpieces were performed one after the other at the Palais Royal when the Court was in Paris. One, *Tartuffe*, was originally performed at a royal fête at Versailles in 1664. This play antagonized the dévots, and could not be publicly performed until 1669, but the King, to whom the playwright owed his security to write, protected him from the anger of the Church, and when Molière died the King intervened to secure for him a Christian burial. His protection of this outspoken satirist was one of Louis's most enlightened actions.

In general the King and Colbert required panegyrics in return for favours. One of the first objects in patronizing writers was to detach the clienteles of Fouquet and other financiers and attach them to the King, who was ensured their praises and freed from attacks until his last years. Colbert was economical, even cheese-paring, in carrying out this task, with the advice of a minor poet Chapelain – who at once awarded himself, as the greatest poet of the day, the biggest pension of 3,000 livres. On the first list nearly a hundred writers (some of them foreign) were awarded pensions. Molière had 1,000 livres, Racine 600 livres. The total expenditure of 100,000 livres compares badly with Fouquet's munificence, and this was reduced when the Dutch War made economies necessary. On the whole the choice of writers was good, but one who dared to criticize the taille and the gabelle was struck off, and La Fontaine, who hated the official classicism and who had to disguise his criticism by writing fables, was so disliked by Colbert for his independence that he was paid no pension and kept out of the Academy, to which he was at last elected in 1684, to the place made vacant by Colbert' death.

Racine is the supreme tragic dramatist of France. His work followed the heroic tragedy of Corneille – still alive in this period but a spent force – but Racine was introspective, a profound pessimist shaped for life by his early education among the Jansenists of Port Royal. He saw men and women as the helpless victims of their own passions, particularly sexual passions. A strongly romantic outlook is repressed into a severe classical form. In this period he had broken with the Jansenists and lived an irregular life in Paris, but eventually he repented, came under Jansenist influence again, and for a number of years wrote no more plays. The King could have little sympathy with Racine's outlook, but Racine indulged in gross flattery and for many years held the King's favour. When he gave up writing plays he was appointed historiographer-royal and lived at Court.

Of all the fine writers of the time Bossuet, Bishop of Meaux, was nearest to the King. In his sermons and other writings he expressed most eloquently Louis's ideals, the divine right of the monarch, the identity of the monarch and the nation, the sanctity of the existing order – he opposed all change. With sure judgment Louis appointed Bossuet tutor to the hoped-for prodigy, the Dauphin (who has been described as one of the most unpromising pupils any tutor ever had).

The chief enduring glory of Louis XIV's reign is that it was the greatest age of French literature. Besides the writers mentioned already, Mme de Sevigné, encouraged by the new postal service, was sending the most remarkable series of letters ever written to her daughter in Provence, and portraying the life of France. Boileau, the friend of Molière, Racine and La Fontaine, was the arbiter of taste, the author of *L'Art Poétique*; he has been called the Doctor Johnson of his time. The catalogue could be extended.

As far as he could the King canalized all activity in the arts and sciences by means of academies. Richelieu had founded the French Academy, a literary body with a strictly limited membership, and its patron in 1661 was the Chancellor Séguier. When he died in 1671 it was nationalized, the King became its patron, and it met in the Louvre. Its principal specific task, completed in 1691, was the production of an authoritative French dictionary, but it tried to regulate literary taste and enforce classical standards. The Academy of Painting and Sculpture was put under the direction of Le Brun and housed in the Louvre. A Royal Academy of Music, set up in 1672, was confided to Lulli. The members of the Academy of Architecture established in 1671 had to visit Italy. Italian influence on French art was increased by the existence of a French Academy in Rome, fostered by the King, whose members were compelled by Colbert to spend most of their time making copies of Italian works of art for shipment to France.

The Academy of Sciences was set up privately by Colbert, who hoped for practical assistance for industry from scientific discovery. It met in his library, and later, when it had royal recognition, in the King's library. It obtained a grant and was given an observatory. The greatest scientist connected with the Academy was the Dutchman Huygens, attracted by Colbert to France in 1666. He had already improved the telescope, explained the rings of Saturn, invented the pendulum clock and developed the theory of probability, and while he was in France produced the wave theory of light.

For a time the King and Colbert imposed their orderly control on the teeming intellectual life of France. Discipline was sometimes beneficial, and great works of literature and architecture were produced by the imposition of classical rules on the baroque romanticism of the age. It was a precarious balance. Lively thinking was not encouraged, and unorthodox rationalism was expressed mainly in discussion in the salons. The bad effects of excessive regimentation inhibited first-class scientific work. But Louis was an inspiration to the French at this period. The galaxy of talents assembled round the Court owes something at least to a King who took such a large view of his métier de roi.

[20] LA GLOIRE

Louis XIV's motto, *Nec pluribus impar*, was a boast of French ascendancy in Europe which he was determined to maintain. To do so required a much better organized army than the one Richelieu and Mazarin had at their disposal. This army was produced for him by the Le Telliers, father and son, and was made possible by Colbert's finance. Le Tellier himself was the outstanding reformer of the army, though his work is so closely integrated with that of Louvois his son, the great administrator, that it is hard to discriminate between their achievements. Louis needed a big army; a body of 15–20,000 men at the beginning of the reign was raised to 400,000 at the end. By 1667 its numbers were 72,000, and by 1672 120,000. The power of the noble officers was broken and they were completely subordinated to a civil administration. Le Tellier could not abolish the purchase of commissions, but he created a new hierarchy of ranks which were not purchasable. Colonels and captains still bought their commissions, but ensigns, lieutenants, majors, lieutenant-colonels and brigadiers did not, and by leapfrogging the venal ranks it was possible to become a marshal of France without buying a commission, as Vauban did. In any case cadets had to serve for two years before they could buy a commission, and efforts were made to organize instruction for them.

Louis XIV was as interested as his father had been in the details of military organization; he enjoyed planning the movement of troops. Above all he loved parades and military displays, and his desire for smartness and discipline in the army encouraged the reformers. Martinet, the Inspector-General of Infantry, was a harsh disciplinarian – hence the term martinet – who invented marching in step. The use of uniforms spread gradually to all units; by 1672 it was fairly general. It was much harder to discipline the officers, many of them Court nobles; but Louvois attacked absenteeism, and more rigorous controls made fraud much more difficult.

Colbert established arsenals to manufacture weapons for this enlarged army, particularly cannon. Separate artillery units appeared in 1669, but were not common until a good deal later. Specialized engineers were emerging, but were not organized into a separate corps until 1676. Modernization of weapons had to wait until later in the reign – Louvois opposed the introduction of the flintlock musket (*fusil*) instead of the old-fashioned matchlock, and pikemen, though reduced to a third of the whole, were indispensable in the infantry until Vauban invented the ring bayonet in 1687.

The masterpiece of Le Tellier's reforms was the establishment of army magazines, which enabled a greater concentration of troops than had been possible with the foraging rabbles of the past. They saved the French countryside from the worst marauding, facilitated movement, and allowed winter campaigning. The preparations for Louis's first war in 1667 were much more thorough than for any previous war. The King, working through the Le Telliers and their bourgeois administration, was in real command of a powerful instrument of policy. This was not achieved without much strain. Colbert resented the rise of Louvois , 'a young man . . . who believes that his office gives him authority to ruin the kingdom'. Turenne, who had been the real generalissimo since the Fronde, and who had taught the King all he knew of soldiering, had resented his own exclusion from the Conseil d'en Haut and now even more resented the overlordship of civilians. Le Tellier's masterstroke was to bring Condé back as a counterweight to Turenne. Condé was superior to Turenne because of his royal rank. He was so anxious to regain his position that he became almost a client of the Le Telliers. In 1667 he was given the task of conquering Franche Comté, and henceforth he could be played off against Turenne.

More and more the real direction of campaigns passed into the hands of the King, advised by his War Secretary and a virtual chief of staff, who throughout the later years was Chamlay. Above all they decided the disposition of the troops; but they also sent detailed instructions to the commanders in the field which made Turenne complain to the King in 1674: 'I do not believe that it would be in His Majesty's interests to give precise orders from such a distance to the most incompetent man in France'. This was the first modern army, and the problems of relations with the generals posed here were the same as those faced by Lloyd George, Churchill, and Hitler.

This reorganization of the army and Colbert's creation of a navy were two of the outstanding successes of Louis XIV's reign.

The use the King made of them is another matter, and there is
still much controversy about his foreign policy. It involved him
in almost continuous war, with no opportunity to demobilize,
from 1672 to 1713. It is agreed that he was too ready to resort
to war, as he admitted on his deathbed. What is not agreed is
whether he consistently pursued definable aims, such as natural
frontiers or the acquisition of the Spanish succession, and
whether he behaved in a normal and reasonable way by the
standards of the age. Historians have been very divided on these
issues. Voltaire and Lord Acton praised him and excused his
mistakes. Lavisse emphasized the King's arrogance and lack of
judgment on great issues, and considered him perfidious. Zeller
insisted that he tried always to keep his word, but, denied him
any consistent aims except the quest for la gloire, which took the
place of a programme. In this he agreed with Lavisse, who even
called the King's pursuit of glory childish. The King himself may
have made clear his deepest motive when he wrote to Villars in
1688: '*S'agrandir est la plus digne et la plus agréable occupation
des souverains*'.

The foreign policy of the first eleven years of the King's
personal rule was mainly peaceable and it did not overstrain
the government's finances, but it foreshadowed the struggles of
the future. Lionne, no doubt a moderating influence, presented
the young king at the outset as mainly a mediator preserving
peace by a system of client states held together by the best
diplomatic service in Europe. Spain was neutralized by the royal
marriage. Holland signed a treaty of defensive and commercial
alliance in 1662. In England Charles II felt insecure and dependent
on his powerful cousin for support; he sold Dunkirk to France
and married the Portuguese bride chosen for him by Louis.
Portugal was still fighting for independence and looking for
French help, and a contingent of French troops played a decisive
part in the crowning victory of Villaviciosa. The Swedish regency
was bribable and in any case weak and dependent. Brandenburg
and Bavaria were clients in Germany, and a number of princes
were receiving French pensions and belonged to the League of
the Rhine. French ascendancy had been achieved.

Louis XIV made himself the master of this European situation, but he was more concerned with the recognition of his primacy than with strengthening the ties that bound together this fragile alliance, and his diplomatic representatives often misinformed him, telling him what they thought he wanted to hear. Unlike Richelieu and his own later opponent William of Orange he made no use of propaganda in foreign countries, and relied on bribes which were often wasted.

Louis insisted on immediate recognition everywhere as the first monarch in Europe. Diplomatic relations with Spain were broken off for a time because the King of Spain would not accord precedence to the French ambassador. In London the suites of the French and Spanish ambassadors fought for precedence in the street and a number of their servants were killed. In Rome Pope Alexander VII was forced to undergo a humiliating penance for an attack on the French Corsican guards. England's claim to the naval salute in the narrow seas was successfully challenged.

The most important issue raised by Louis in this period was the future of the Spanish Netherlands. Spain had not bought immunity for long from French aggression by the marriage of Maria Theresa. Louis sent a French force to help the Emperor Leopold I to defeat a Turkish threat to Vienna at the battle of St Gotthard in 1664. This put him in a favourable position to split the family alliance of the Habsburgs. Philip IV of Spain died in 1665, leaving a feeble infant son Charles II to inherit the throne. This son by a second wife had balked the claims of Maria Theresa and her younger sister Margarita Theresa the wife of the Emperor. But the new King did not seem likely to live long, and because the Spanish government had never paid Maria Theresa's dowry, which was the condition of her renunciation of the Spanish throne, her claims might become formidable. Louis adopted an extraordinary but a characteristic line of action. By a law of Brabant, private property, in the event of a second marriage, devolved on the children of the first marriage, and Louis claimed sovereignty in the Spanish Netherlands for Maria Theresa on the strength of this. It was a preposterous extension of private rights of inheritance to the field of international law. The Dutch leader De Witt was very much alarmed, but at the time England and Holland were at war, and the Dutch secured Louis as a nominal ally by invoking the alliance of 1662. France took little part in the Anglo-Dutch War, but was able under cover of this to prepare for an attack on the Spanish Netherlands, launched in 1667. It was better organized than any previous French campaign. Turenne was in command and Vauban conducted the sieges; Douai and Lille fell. Condé overran Franche Comté. The chief risk in this War of Devolution was that Louis's arrogance, which had already lost him the goodwill of most of Europe, would provoke an alliance against France. To obviate what he regarded as the chief danger, an attack by the Emperor, Louis in January 1668 signed the secret Treaty of Grémonville with Leopold I, arranging for an eventual partition of the Spanish Empire if and when Charles II of Spain died without heirs; he ensured the neutrality of the Emperor by conceding the throne of Spain to an Austrian claimant. But he had reckoned without England and Holland, who hastily made peace at Breda in 1667, and in January 1668 concluded an alliance, which Sweden also joined to make it the Triple Alliance, to limit the gains which France should make from the War of Devolution. Louis decided to make peace – at Aix-la-Chapelle in April 1668 – on terms acceptable to the Triple Alliance. Spain took the option of recovering Franche Comté in return for the concession to France of the places occupied by the French in the Netherlands.

Two results followed from this settlement. First Vauban, concerned with fortifying the new acquisitions, had to deal with the usual untidy frontiers, made worse by the possession of new enclaves, and he began to press for a strategic frontier. Second, the King, with touchy pride, resented the mild action of the Triple Alliance. He could not bear opposition, and he resolved to break the Dutch. Colbert egged him on because he could see no other way of overcoming the mercantile supremacy of the Dutch – he had already launched a trade war by the tariff of 1667. Louvois had been with the King on campaign during the war and had gained much influence. and he always favoured aggressive policies. During the next four years French diplomatists were at work preparing the way for an attack on the Dutch. Charles II of England had few scruples, had been very half-hearted about the Triple Alliance, and was easily persuaded to sign the secret Treaty of Dover in 1670, promising the alliance of England against Holland in return for a modest pension and help in establishing Catholicism in England. The Swedish nobles who governed the country were bribed handsomely to reverse their policy and support France.

The power of France on land was almost overwhelming, and the English and French fleets together enjoyed a considerable superiority at sea. The Dutch were rich but few in number, and their armies consisted mainly of mercenaries – 6,000 were English. Their very love of freedom had led them to adopt a complex federal structure which deprived them of unified control, and De Witt their leader not only stood for these state rights but was a compromiser who had always been as friendly to France as possible. When the French began their attack in 1672, Louis was confident of a rapid and complete success. He was blind to the subtler risks in his situation.

Louis now seemed to have the overlordship of Europe within his grasp, but even after all Colbert's financial exertions he had nothing like enough financial resources for long struggles against European alliances. He was still very inadequately informed about European opinion. So arrogant a ruler had little comprehension of other people's points of view, and he underrated the forces which might be brought against him in Holland, England, and Germany. La gloire, as a basis for a policy, could only arouse deep-seated and long-lasting hatreds which he would never be able to subdue.

Further Reading, 1643–72

As before H. Méthivier provides concise guides in his books in the series 'Que Sais-je', Le Siècle de Louis XIII (to 1661) and Le Siècle de Louis XIV (Paris, 1962). There is a lack of modern biographies of Mazarin, and that of A. Hassall (London, 1903) is still useful. H. Carré in The Early Life of Louis XIV (English translation, London,

1951) deals with Court and personal aspects. The best English work on the Fronde is P. R. Doolin's *The Fronde* (Cambridge, Mass., 1935), but he treats it too much as a constitutional struggle. E. H. Kossmann's and R. Mousnier's views are most important, and they have commented on the Fronde in a discussion in *Past and Present*, Vol. 18 on H. Trevor-Roper's article on 'The General Crisis of the Seventeenth Century'.

For Louis XIV's reign in general there is a most valuable recent work of manageable length, P. Goubert's *Louis XIV and Twenty Million Frenchmen* (London, 1969), and a new American full biography, J. B. Wolf's *Louis XIV* (London, 1968). D. Ogg's *Louis XIV* in the 'Home University Library' (London, 1933) is still useful. H. G. Judge, *Louis XIV* (London, 1965), has collected and translated documents of the reign, while W. F. Church, in *The Greatness of Louis XIV – Myth or Reality?* (New York, 1959), has collected and translated judgments on Louis's reign by historians from Voltaire to the present day.

There is a short biography of *Colbert* by G. Mongrédien (Paris, 1964), which is good on the personal side, and a massive and authoritative coverage of his economic policy by C. W. Cole, *Colbert and a Century of French Mercantilism* (2 vols., New York, 1939). Two useful articles on aspects of the reign are 'Church and State under Louis XIV', by H. G. Judge, in *History*, Vol. 45, and 'French Society and Popular Uprisings under Louis XIV', by L. Bernard in *French Historical Studies*, Vol. 3 (U.S.A., 1964). The 'New Cambridge Modern History' Vol. V contains chapters by J. Lough on France under Louis XIV, by G. Zeller on French diplomacy and foreign policy (important), and by D. Ogg on French art, thought, and literature during the reign.

Principal Events, 1661–72

FRANCE AND COLONIES		EUROPE AND OVERSEAS
Personal rule of Louis XIV. Fall of Fouquet. Colbert in charge of finances and economy. Famine	1661	French demand precedence in Europe
	1662	French purchase of Dunkirk
Canada organized as New France	1663	Turks attack Hungary
Great Inquiry. Louvois joint Secretary for War. East and West India Cos. Molière: *Tartuffe*. Le Brun Director of Academy of Painting and Sculpture	1664	Battle of St Gotthard. English capture New Amsterdam (New York)
Triad of ministers (Le Tellier, Lionne, Colbert). Poussin dies. Lulli Director of Music. Council of Justice begins reform of law	1665	Charles II King of Spain. Second Anglo-Dutch War. Battle of Villaviciosa
French at Surat. Huygens in France. Perrault's colonnade of the Louvre	1666	Newton invents calculus
Tariff war with Holland. Racine: *Andromaque*	1667	War of Devolution. Peace of Breda. Clement IX Pope
Peace of the Church. Conversion of Turenne. Molière: *Le Misanthrope*	1668	Triple Alliance. Peace of Aix-la-Chapelle. Portugal's independence recognized
Colbert Secretary for Navy.	1669	Turks conquer Crete
Discovery of Mississippi	1670	Secret Treaty of Dover
Lionne dies. Quesnel: *Réflexions*	1671	
Louvois minister	1672	Outbreak of Dutch War

PART V
The Testing Time —
Strains and Conflicts

[21] THE RULE OF THE MATURE KING

The government

From the moment that France entered on the Dutch War the balance of the government shifted decisively. The ministers after 1672 were Le Tellier, Colbert, and the newly-appointed Louvois and Pomponne, the new Secretary for Foreign Affairs. Louvois worked very closely with the King in the conduct of the war at army headquarters during each campaign. The Le Telliers made a strong team in the Conseil d'en Haut, when it could meet; whenever the King was at Court it met three mornings a week for two hours. Colbert had willed the war, but he was now saddled with the intolerable burden of financing it, and was compelled by the shortage of money to curtail his economic plans and lessen his patronage of the arts. Reforming schemes dried up.

In 1679 Colbert was powerful enough to secure the dismissal of Pomponne and the appointment of his brother Colbert de Croissy to the secretaryship of Foreign Affairs. The apparent balance, however, of two Le Telliers and two Colberts in the ministry concealed the real dominance of Louvois, whose ruthless and reckless pursuit of glory appealed far more to the King than the sober caution of Colbert. Le Tellier became Chancellor in 1677 and Louvois was now in sole charge of the war ministry, but he also influenced the King's decisions in foreign policy.

Colbert had to struggle for his political life, and to meet the

imperious demands of war he was compelled to revert to bad
old-fashioned customs such as the sale of offices and domain
lands. A load of new indirect taxes provoked widespread trouble
and serious risings in Bordeaux and Brittany. The growing
deficit, 55 million livres by 1679, gave the financiers and tax-
farmers once more a key position of power, and forced up the
rate of interest. By the end of the war Colbert could not borrow
enough money even at 15 per cent. His problem, and the problem
of government generally, was aggravated by a series of bad
harvests, which kept the price of bread mainly high at a time
when wages were stationary or falling. The shortage of currency
became a worse problem as the reign went on. In spite of his
difficulties Colbert enabled the King to maintain an army of
275,000 men with greater efficiency than had ever been seen in
France.

In his last years Colbert's position was so insecure that he tried
to bolster it up by presenting false accounts to the King. He
opposed unsuccessfully the intensified persecution of the hard-
working Huguenots who contributed so much to the French
economy, and he was unable to prevent the continuance of heavy
military expenditure after peace was made, in the service of an
aggressive foreign policy of which he disapproved. He had lost
the unequal struggle against Louvois. Yet when he was dying
in 1683 Louis realized that he was irreplaceable as a public
servant, and showed a degree of concern very unusual with him.

When Colbert died his empire was broken up. His son Seignelay
inherited only the navy and overseas affairs, and did not become
a minister until 1690. Le Pelletier, the new Controller-General
of Finance, a relative and client of Le Tellier, was a colourless
man in the shadow of Louvois. Louvois himself took over the
superintendency of buildings, a post which involved constant
contacts with Louis concerning the building of Versailles. From
1685, when Le Tellier died, Louvois led the ministry, which
consisted of himself, Le Pelletier, and the feeble Colbert de Croissy.

Louvois was a stern, harsh man, ruthless and even violent,
lacking in originality, more of an administrator than a policy-
maker. He strengthened Louis's natural tendency to become more

arrogant as he grew older, but the weight of opinion among modern historians is that Louis, and not he, bears the chief responsibility for the ruthless policies of the 1680s.

In 1682 Versailles became the official home of the King, the Court, and the government. One wing of the palace was an administrative block. From this time bureaucratic government developed rapidly. The vigour of the ministry declined and the King took more matters into his own hands. Councils, apart from the Conseil d'en Haut, became purely administrative bodies. The King dealt directly with officials and individual ministers; but he was overworked and had many interests and concerns other than the administration, and the result was that officials, entrenched in their growing departments, became more and more their own masters, and at times the initiators of policy.

The same process was of course going on in the provinces. By the time of Colbert's death the intendants were all-powerful in most regions, and in defiance of his regulations had built up their own bureaucracies of sub-délégués and clerks. More and more they tended to remain for years in one généralité.

The King's government had ossified. Louis encouraged hard work, routine, and formalism. Faced with large issues he was apt to plunge in out of his depth without realizing the consequences of his actions. His first great ministry had been a guiding force, but after the deaths of its members and of Louvois the King's ministers were little more than clerks. Louis was almost indomitably complacent, his pride excluded criticism, and he believed in his divine inspiration. He once wrote: 'It is not good counsels nor good counsellors who give prudence to the prince, it is the prudence of the prince which alone forms good ministers and produces all the good counsels which are given to him'. Independence of mind was impossible in this atmosphere.

Literature and the arts

The heavy hand of government was felt by writers, artists, and scientists, as the war brought royal patronage almost to an end. Huygens and some other scientists resigned from the Academy of Sciences as a protest against the barbaric way in which the French army behaved in Holland. The French contribution to science in the great age of Newtonian physics was mediocre, and this is directly connected with the repressive attitude of the regime. Under Jesuit influence the government opposed the spread of Cartesian rationalism – the works of Descartes were put on the Index in 1675. The stronghold of liberal opinions in the French Church, the Oratory, was forced to renounce its Cartesian teachings. One of the Oratorians, Richard Simon, published in 1678 a work of Biblical criticism, *L'Histoire Critique du Vieux Testament*. Bossuet, horrified by its unorthodoxy, demanded and obtained its suppression by the Chancellor Le Tellier. Moliére's *Tartuffe* could no longer be performed because of the hostility of the dévots. Critical authors were silenced or forced into exile, but the spread of rationalism could not be prevented.

Architecture fared rather better than literature, in spite of the draining of the finances by Versailles. During the Dutch War Louvois ordered the building in Paris of the Hôtel des Invalides, one of the finest classical buildings in the city, as a home for crippled soldiers. Colbert and Le Brun inspired much planning, including the creation of the quais along the Seine, the first layout of the Champs Elysées, some new town gates in classical style, and the design of more streets with vistas and *rond-points* at their intersections. The theatre was not neglected. In 1680 the King set up the Comédie Française to ensure worthy performances of classical French drama. But there were no new works to add to the repertoire except for Racine's last works, the great religious plays *Esther* and *Athalie* produced in the early 1690s at the request and for the glorification of Mme de Maintenon, for performance before her and the King by the girls of her academy of St Cyr.

The progressive urge which had given a new image to the Bourbon administration of France had spent itself. As France became a vastly more formidable military machine and Versailles imposed itself more and more on the imagination of France and Europe, the King lost his control of the best minds of his country, and became a brake on necessary reforms and new ideas.

The Court

The important changes in the King's own outlook which took place in this period may be summed up by reference to two events, the settlement of the Court at Versailles in 1682, and his marriage to Mme de Maintenon, probably in 1683.

Louis devoted himself to the creation and organization of Versailles as an artist devotes himself to a work of art. It was his greatest creative work. In the early years of his rule the small château of Louis XIII, with its grounds more and more elaborately embellished by Le Nôtre, was his favourite place of amusement and relaxation. Between 1670 and 1674 a new façade was built to the designs of Le Vau facing the splendours of the park, and when it was finished Louis edited a guide for visitors and enjoyed showing the building to favoured guests. Meanwhile the town of Versailles had been planned and begun. From this time the Court stayed at Versailles for longer periods. Hardouin-Mansart became the chief architect in 1677, and work was renewed and pressed by the King with great energy. The almost new Italian façade was replaced by the Galerie des Glaces, and two enormous wings were built, making a façade on the garden front of 1,800 feet. The interior was entirely remodelled and decorated lavishly to the plans of Le Brun. The working force was prodigious – in 1685 it was estimated at 36,000. The total cost was 70 million livres.

There is a certain stately monotony about this massive work of classical grandeur. It is an altogether appropriate monument to the great king who was its creator. The park with its fountains and statues, though formal, is a much livelier baroque creation, as befits the site of the fêtes consecrated by the royal lover to his mistresses, above all to Mme de Montespan. She was so dominant during the building of Versailles that when Louis was away on campaign and she was in Paris he instructed Colbert to consult her about every detail of the work.

Throughout the 1670s Mme de Montespan lorded it arrogantly. She had all the pride of a member of one of the oldest families in France. But her hold on the King grew less as she aged and grew

fatter, and he became tired of her outbursts of temper. In the end
she dabbled in sorcery to keep the King's affections, but unfortunately some of the sorcerers were also poisoners, and there was
a great scandal at the Court. Louvois was her friend and saved
her from disgrace, but by the time the Court made its final move to
Versailles she was no longer the reigning mistress, though she
continued to live at the Court for many years.

Mme de Montespan had borne several children to Louis, and
he employed as the governess of the four survivors Françoise
d'Aubigné, Mme Scarron, whom he made Marquise de Maintenon.
Louis was fond of these children – later he declared them legitimate – and when he visited them he was much attracted by the
serenity and beauty of their governess. When he broke with
Mme de Montespan he had one or two brief affairs and then
turned once and for all to Mme de Maintenon. In 1683 the neglected Queen Maria Theresa died, and probably in the same year
Louis secretly married Mme de Maintenon as his morganatic wife.
His adventures in love were over. This represents a remarkable
crisis in Louis's private life, a very important aspect of the
process of settling down which was going on at this time. The
woman he chose was already 48, a bourgeoise three years older
than the King. She had been born in a prison, and for a time
during her girlhood she was a Protestant. She had become the
wife of the satirical poet Scarron, and mixed with a group of
clever intellectuals who frequented her salon. After living as a
widow for many years she took charge of the Montespan family,
won the affection of the children, and was far more a mother to
them than Mme de Montespan was. She had no children of her
own. A serious and virtuous woman, she was a strong Catholic
dévot, influenced and used by the clergy; Bossuet had the most
permanent influence. She gave a new stability to Louis's life.
Her room at Versailles was a haven from the crowds and the
strain, which perhaps even the King felt, of being almost per-
petually on view. Many of the King's most important interviews
with ministers and officials took place there, and throughout the
later years of the reign it was the meeting place of the Conseil
d'en Haut.

There has been much argument about the extent of Mme de Maintenon's political influence. She undoubtedly wanted to influence the King's religious outlook and policy, and she succeeded in effecting his conversion to an outwardly more decent and sober life and an appearance of devotion. Her first concern was the King's salvation, and she may have helped to bring about his reconciliation with the Pope. She longed for the conversion of the Huguenots, but there is no evidence that she approved of the Revocation of the Edict of Nantes. She hated Louvois and may have undermined his position to some extent, and she promoted the interests of the Colbert family who shared her religious zeal. She sat silently and worked at her tapestry during meetings of the Council of State, unless the King asked for her opinion. Clearly her influence on his policies was not negligible, but it was indirect, and she was very often thwarted.

Mme de Maintenon played a very discreet and inconspicuous part in the pageantry now established at Versailles. Eventually some 15,000 persons lived there regularly, and innumerable visitors increased the crowds; any one properly dressed was welcomed as a guest, and it is said that on one day alone there were 60,000 visitors. Even the King was sometimes unable to take his accustomed walk because of the jostling crowds. Life was difficult for most of the inhabitants. Sanitary arrangements were very neglected. The palace was so cold that water for washing sometimes froze in the ewers. The fixed routine of daily activities became extremely boring to many courtiers, and the King was a stickler for punctuality and the strict observance of every nice point of etiquette. Intrigues and gossip abounded, but it was always felt that the King oversaw everything that went on. He was interested and had many spies to keep him informed. Coarseness and elegance were incongruously mingled, yet the courtiers remained hypnotized by the spectacle of royal splendour, sought Court offices and privileges, and knew that the only hope of royal favour lay here at Versailles. In the end they became incapable of any other kind of life.

At the centre of the pomp and ceremony surrounding the King were the proliferating Bourbons, legitimate and illegitimate; not, on the whole, an edifying spectacle. His lethargic son the Dauphin Louis married a Bavarian princess and had three sons to continue the succession, and the future of Louis's direct line seemed assured. His brother Philippe d'Orléans married as his first wife Henrietta Stuart, but she died in 1670, and he then married the Princess Palatine, and had a son – who became the Regent when Louis died – and a daughter who was unhappily married to the feeble King of Spain. Orléans was a homosexual who caused much scandal at Court. He was a good soldier, and won a battle against William of Orange, but Louis was jealous of this success and never allowed him to command an army again.

The members of the royal family held the highest Court offices, and there were hundreds of other offices, graded in rank, to satisfy the ambitions of the principal courtiers. The whole little world of Versailles resolved around the movements of the King, timed, orderly, calculable. Everyone at Court knew precisely his rights and duties and his means of access to the Roi Soleil, and the aim of all was to be seen and heard if possible. The King's love of all this detail and routine, and his amazing memory for faces and facts about people ensured the working of this system.

The settlement of the Court at Versailles isolated the King more than ever from the French people. He neutralized the nobles and ecclesiastics who lived at Court, but at the expense of seeing the world largely through their eyes. Louis's visible grandeur increased his arrogance. As he aged his sympathies narrowed and he became less affected by ordinary human emotions. Like the King the government responded sluggishly to the needs of the nation. It lived on the impetus of Colbertian reforms. The King's administration became more effective, but for a national policy he substituted a series of dubious foreign adventures. The main interest in home affairs shifted to religious questions, to the conflict with the Pope and the suppression of the Huguenots.

[22] THE FRENCH CHURCH AND THE PAPACY

The French Church in Louis XIV's reign was very much alive and full of contradictions. The dévots found new forms of religious expression. In 1664 the austere Trappist order of monks was founded, and in 1680 the very important teaching order of the De La Salle Brothers. Mystical beliefs revived in the form of Quietism, propagated by Mme Guyon and Fénelon. Jansenism, freed from persecution by the Peace of the Church of 1668, and now far more concerned with morality than theology, spread among the curés of Paris, and, in opposition to Jesuits and mystics, among the French regular clergy, especially the Oratorians. The Jesuits themselves flourished; they had a firm control of the King's religious views through La Chaise, his confessor, and they dominated in the field of education – there were 97 Jesuit colleges by the end of the reign. The upper bourgeoisie and the noblesse de robe maintained their enthusiasm for the Catholic faith. On the other hand the mass of the provincial clergy were still so ignorant as to be useless in the effort to convert the relatively enlightened Huguenots. They were very poor as well as ignorant, and their poverty was largely the consequence of creaming off the revenues of the Church for the upkeep of the younger sons of the upper classes, a form of patronage which played a great part in the King's control of the courtiers and officials. Versailles swarmed with absentee ecclesiastics. These abuses could not be reformed.

Such a church seethed with conflicts, but the servility of its upper clergy to the King was assured by the system. In the early years of his rule Louis had taken up a strongly anti-papal attitude, encouraged by Lionne and Colbert. The Parlement of Paris strongly supported Gallicanism, more so than the King. It constantly opposed papal interference in France, whereas the King made use of the Pope whenever it was convenient and possible to do so, and dropped Gallicanism altogether during his last struggle with the Jansenists. On the whole the Parlement was permanently pro-Jansenist and anti-Jesuit. The Sorbonne was divided, but was the only university in Catholic Europe which did not officially teach Catholic infallibility – although this did not become part of Catholic dogma until 1870.

Throughout most of France the King exercised important rights, known as the regale. When a bishop died and before his successor was installed, he could collect the revenues of the see, and nominate to certain benefices within the gift of the bishop. Colbert persuaded the King to issue a decree extending the régale to the whole of France, and even the French Jesuits supported him. The outstanding opponents of this decree were the bishops Pavillon of Alet and Caulet of Pamiers, both Jansenists of Languedoc, who appealed eventually to Rome, where Innocent XI, the pope elected in 1676, combined Jansenist sympathies with vigorous opposition to the King's rights. After Pavillon's death Caulet kept up his defiance, and in 1678 the King seized his temporalities. Innocent XI issued three briefs condemning the King's claims and actions. When Caulet died in 1680 the intendant installed a royal administrator at Pamiers with the help of an escort of cavalry, and the Pope excommunicated the administrator and threatened the King.

During the Dutch War Louis had been concerned about the Pope's diplomatic support, but he had been at peace since 1679 and felt free to act against the Pope. (At the same time, no longer worried about the reactions of Protestant states, he mounted an attack on the Huguenots.) Louis could count on the more or less embarrassed support of the French clergy in his quarrel. The regular Assembly of Clergy in 1680 had protested against the Pope's attitude: 'We are so bound to Your Majesty that nothing is capable of separating us'. In 1681 the King assembled all the bishops present in Paris – 52 were available – in an emergency meeting which proposed the calling of a special Assembly of Clergy to deal with the crisis. This body met in November 1681, after elections largely controlled by Colbert. Harley, Archbishop of Paris, an extreme Gallican, presided, but the direction of affairs fell more into the hands of Bossuet, a moderate supported by Le Tellier. In a brilliantly eloquent opening sermon Bossuet avoided any commitment. He secured from the King important concessions as to the régale spirituelle, but in the end he was driven to formulate the Four Articles of March 1682, which were adopted by the Assembly. The first article was a clear and un-ambiguous statement of the King's temporal authority: 'Kings and sovereigns are not subject to any ecclesiastical power, by God's command, in temporal concerns; they cannot be deposed directly or indirectly by the heads of the Church'. The other clauses, rather confusingly expressed, were inserted to satisfy the Gallican bishops, and were of minor interest to the King. The second asserted the superiority of Church Councils to the Pope. The third safeguarded the customs of the Gallican Church from papal interference, and the fourth rejected, with some circumlocution, the claim of the Pope to be infallible.

The Four Articles were really a challenge to the authority of the Pope to force him to make concessions. The claims of the King to the régale were not specifically referred to. La Chaise and the French Jesuits who supported the claim to the régale deplored the Four Articles. Le Tellier and Louvois also opposed them although they were strongly in favour of the régale. Bossuet worked for a compromise. Mme de Maintenon grieved over the dispute and stirred the King's conscience. On his side the Pope did not push the quarrel to extremes. He granted a dispensation to allow the eldest son of Louis and Mme de Montespan, aged 10, to receive certain abbeys in commendam, and in 1686, at Louis's request, made Fürstenberg, one of the chief supporters of France in Germany, a cardinal.

Yet neither side would give way. Louis, not without difficulty, secured the registration of the Four Articles by the Sorbonne and the universities of France. Twelve recalcitrant members of the Sorbonne were exiled by lettres de cachet. The Parlement of Paris enthusiastically supported the enactment of the Articles and all bishops and teachers of theology had to subscribe to them. As the Pope would not institute the King's subscribing nominees, more and more bishoprics became vacant, 35 by 1688. Louis hoped that the persecution of the Huguenots would win the Pope's approval, but Innocent XI denounced the forced conversions. In 1688 the quarrel became more acute as France moved towards another European war. The Pope had been hostile for years to Louis's aggressive foreign policy, and now refused to appoint the French candidate, Cardinal Fürstenberg, to the archbishopric of Cologne. He also took away certain privileges of sanctuary from the French embassy in Rome, and when the French ambassador defied the Pope he was excommunicated. Louis responded by forcibly installing Fürstenberg at Cologne, and occupying the Pope's territory of Avignon. Heated words were used; Colbert de Croissy denounced the Pope as a Jansenist, a Quietist, and an ally of the heretic William of Orange.

Much of this was bluff and bluster. Louis at war with half Europe needed at least a neutral pope. Innocent XI's death in 1689 eased the situation, and negotiations followed with his successors Alexander VIII and Innocent XII. France restored Avignon and gave up her claims to sanctuary rights in the Rome embassy. At last in 1693 the King wrote a letter to the Pope disowning the Four Articles – although they were not repealed by the Parlements – and the Pope agreed to institute the King's nominees to bishoprics provided that they too disavowed the Articles. Louis retained the régale temporelle throughout France. It was a compromise, but on the whole a defeat for Gallicanism. In the disputes over doctrine which were once more beginning in the French Church Louis needed the support of the Pope against Quietists and Jansenists, and he abandoned Gallicanism. The ambiguous outcome of an ambiguous dispute left the French Church more confused than ever, with the serious risk to the King of Gallican opposition.

[23] THE PERSECUTION OF THE PROTESTANTS

The Bourbons appeared to have succeeded in a policy of toleration which was unique in Europe. Since Richelieu had destroyed the military and political power of the Huguenots they had given no trouble to the government. Mazarin acknowledged this in a letter to the last national synod of the Protestant Church in 1659: 'I beg you to believe that I have a great esteem for you, as you are good and faithful servants of the King'. Turenne headed a distinguished group of Protestant army officers, and Admiral Duquesne, the conqueror of De Ruyter, was a Protestant. La Rochelle continued to flourish as a great port. Nîmes, with a majority of Protestant families, was one of the main growing points of the silk industry. Everywhere the Protestant bourgeoisie devoted itself to the accumulation of wealth. In Paris, now the home of a large Protestant community, they were important among the leaders of finance. Samuel Bernard, a Huguenot banker, was the key figure in the financial transactions of the government.

Richelieu had assured the Protestant leaders that they could rely on the King's promise to maintain the Edict of Nantes. Louis XIV felt bound by the letter of the Edict, but he had no feeling whatever for its spirit, and as soon as he began to rule the Huguenots felt a cold blast of royal disapproval. The King would not sanction any more meetings of a national Protestant synod, and provincial synods were forbidden to correspond with one another. Toleration was an unpopular policy, and the King was unlikely to forgo popularity for a policy he disliked. He agreed with a demand of the Assembly of Clergy of 1661 for an inquiry into the Edict, and in each province a Catholic, usually the intendant himself, and a Protestant, normally chosen by the intendant and a dubious supporter of the cause, made an investigation and closed a great many Protestant churches which – it was claimed – had been irregularly established. In 1666 there appeared an interpretation of the Edict by a lawyer showing how the privileges it accorded could be whittled away without a breach of the letter of the law, and local authorities began to adopt these methods with the approval of the royal administration. Protestant marriages and funerals were placed under irritating restrictions, and their schools were hampered. An unenforceable decree of the Council restricted entry to guilds to Catholics.

Against these pressures the Protestants showed little fight. There was a steady stream of upper class conversions, and it was a heavy blow to the Huguenots when Turenne became a Catholic in 1668. More surprisingly a serious defection of Protestant pastors took place, caused in part by internal disputes between strict Calvinists and Arminians (believers in free will), in part by the attractions of the dévot movement in the French Church, especially in its Jansenist form, and the strength of feeling in favour of church unity. A third of the pastors abjured. Down to 1679 the official Catholic policy, keenly supported by Bossuet and the Jansenists, was a strong propaganda drive for unity by conversion. A very crude application of this policy was made in 1676, when Pellisson, a convert, was given control of a sum of money to buy conversions. It is surprising to find that Bossuet, Arnauld, and Vauban approved of this method, and that by the payment of small sums – from 6 to 12 livres – Pellisson was able to secure 58,000 conversions. However, many were fraudulent.

The signs of weakness among the Protestants were an encouragement to the extremists among the Catholics. When the Peace of Nymegen freed the King from the need to consider Protestant opinion abroad he decided that a severe persecution would produce an easy victory over Protestantism. In this he had the backing of nearly the whole Catholic community, and it was one of the most popular decisions of his reign. Colbert dreaded its effects, but was not strong enough to resist. Le Tellier and Louvois have been regarded as the chief exponents of this policy, and there is no doubt that they supported it vigorously, but Louis hardly needed to be prodded into action by ministers. He believed that the Protestant Church would collapse like a house of cards. Toleration had not struck roots in France, and Louis merely shared the general European opinion of the time when he insisted that unity in the state was impossible without unity in the Church. In England at this time two priests were executed for the crime of saying mass. But no other state in Europe had so large a minority to persecute – the number of Protestants in France was probably over a million and a half – and at a time when in most countries religious passions were becoming less fierce, the hunting down of the Huguenots, and the flight of so many, shocked Protestants abroad and even many Catholics.

Before Louis revoked the Edict in 1685 he reduced it to a farce. The legal safeguards of the Protestants were removed when the Chambres de l'Édit were abolished in 1679. Their equal privileges vanished when they were formally excluded from public offices and eventually from the legal profession, medicine, printing and publishing. Their children might be converted to Catholicism at the age of seven, and if so might be taken from them and educated at their expense in the Catholic faith. On the slightest pretext, as for example the solemnization of a mixed marriage, their churches were pulled down. In some provinces the intendants took the law into their own hands and destroyed churches without looking for an excuse; in Béarn, for example, Henry of Navarre's home territory, which had been entirely Protestant when it had become part of France, all the Protestant churches were destroyed.

The most successful methods of inducing conversions were applied first in Poitou by the intendant Marillac. He exempted the newly converted from taille and surcharged Protestants, sometimes making them pay three or four times as much as before. He also began the practice of dragonnades, the billeting of soldiers on Protestant families, with every encouragement to behave as brutally as they liked – this had already been tried out successfully on seditious subjects. The sensational result was that 30,000 Protestants were converted in a year in Poitou alone. But complaints reached the King, and Louis first ordered Marillac to keep the soldiers in better order, and then had him transferred to Rouen. His successor Basville and other intendants in the Midi continued the dragonnades. The King and Louvois turned a blind eye to the violence in their delight in the results, although official instructions were that troops were to behave in an orderly way; Louvois wrote to one intendant: 'Violence is not to the taste of His Majesty'. But they did not punish anyone for disobedience, and there was a reign of terror in Protestant France and a spate of conversions, so many that Louis believed that the Protestants would disappear without any further legal action, which indeed hardly seemed necessary when the intendants could flout the law with impunity. In Nîmes all who did not abjure within twenty days were threatened with confiscation of goods and a life sentence to the galleys.

Why then did Louis decide to revoke the Edict? The enormous numbers of new converts created a problem. They were exempted from taille and from billeting, and this was causing discontent among Catholics who had to bear the additional burden. Frequently the converts were insincere, and were sustained as secret Protestants by the ministers of the Protestant Church. The legal prohibition of the religion would obviate further bribery and do away with the church organization which disturbed the Catholicism of the new converts.

The Revocation of the Edict of Nantes, drawn up by the Chancellor Le Tellier, was registered in October 1685. It was aimed largely at the ministers, who were banished from France – 600 of them were executed in the Midi. Lay Huguenots were forbidden to emigrate and compelled to have their children baptized as Catholics. Protestant worship was banned, even in private houses, and although rights of conscience were nominally safeguarded, many intendants, and for a time the government itself, treated all Protestants as Nouveaux Convertis, and in some regions they were compelled to attend mass.

There was a chorus of praise in France, most eloquently expressed by Bossuet in his funeral oration for Le Tellier a few weeks after the Revocation: 'Let us proclaim the miracle of our time. Let our hearts swell at the piety of Louis: let us lift our praises to the sky, and say to this new Constantine, this new Theodosius, this new Marcian, this new Charlemagne: "It is the worthy achievement of your reign, true to its character; thanks to you heresy is no more; God alone could perform this wonderful deed." ' Abroad the effects were less happy. The King had undoubtedly intended to show the Pope and the Catholic world that he could achieve what the Emperor could not, the elimination of Protestantism in his own lands. But the Revocation was disapproved of by most foreign Catholics and roused the fears and indignation of Protestant Europe. The stream of refugees, about

200,000 just before and after the suppression, reinforced the hatred that was already growing for the tyranny of the French King.

It is generally agreed that Louis made a colossal blunder in his attack on this large peaceful community. The hard core of resistance was much larger and stronger than the government had anticipated. The emigrants were a heavy loss to France. Seignelay was greatly worried by the defection of sailors; the army lost at least 600 officers, including Marshal Schomberg and Ruvigny – the later Earl of Galway – to William of Orange, and some 10,000 Huguenot soldiers fought in the enemy ranks in the next war. The industry and trade of Protestant countries, above all England and Brandenburg, benefited much from the skill of the immigrants. In England, for example, they established a silk manufacture which cut down the country's dependence on imports from France.

Many historians have believed that the Revocation, by destroying a community so vital to the French economy, was the major cause of the decay of French industry and trade in the later years of Louis's reign. However, a detailed investigation by W. C. Scoville, an American historian, *The Persecution of the Huguenots and French Economic Development*, has made it clear that other factors were much more important in this decline, above all the wars themselves.

The Revocation failed. By 1698 moderate counsellors induced the King to oppose the excesses of the more violent intendants, to give up the pretence that all the Huguenots were now new converts, and to refer to them as of old as the Religion Prétendue Reformée (R.P.R.). They need not abjure, although of course religious services were forbidden, and there seemed little hope for the future of a community whose children were to be brought up as Catholics.

Illegal Protestantism survived. It was impossible to prevent conventicles in the wilder parts of the Midi. Severe action against them provoked the revolt in the Cévennes in 1703, which was such a grave embarrassment to the government during the Spanish Succession War that the best French general, Villars, was given the task of suppressing it. Most of the Huguenots confined themselves to passive resistance, but steadfastly kept their faith alive. There were probably over a million at the end of the reign.

[24] AGGRANDIZEMENT IN EUROPE

The Dutch War

It is difficult to overestimate the significance of the Dutch War of 1672–8 in the history of Louis's reign. It set the pattern for the rest of the reign. From its beginnings the Dutch Republic had looked to France for support against Spain, though never without fears of French expansion in the Netherlands. That alliance was still in force, however threadbare after the French tariff of 1667 and the Triple Alliance. Now it was broken for a hundred years, and in the crisis the House of Orange, in the person of William of Orange, once more came forward to save the Dutch, this time from France. Holland in diplomacy and war opposed all Louis's aims for the rest of his life. Europe became hostile through fear of a military power such as Europe had never before seen since Roman times. The crushing burden imposed on the French brought to an end the years of Colbertian reform; the war weakened Colbert's position in the Council and posed a new threat to the finances. It began the closer association of Louvois with the King which continued as long as Louvois lived, and although there is a lack of evidence for the view that Louvois was Louis's evil genius, there is no doubt that his promptings would favour the arrogant behaviour which characterizes the rule of the King in this period.

Louis needed a quick success such as he had achieved against Spain in 1667–8, and his failure to achieve it was largely his own fault. The preparations were thorough, and the French armies, avoiding the Spanish Netherlands, mounted a strong attack from the east, crossed the Rhine, and got within ten miles of Amsterdam. But Turenne was slow, the King was always a brake on

military movement, and the more impetuous Condé was held
back. The Dutch had time to put the young Prince of Orange in
charge of their defences and to flood the land around Amsterdam.
At sea De Ruyter managed to keep the sea lanes open by defeating a stronger but badly coordinated Anglo-French fleet in
Southwold Bay. Even so the Dutch offered terms of peace which
would have given France an indemnity and all Dutch territory
south of the Maas. With that gain the French must have been
able to conquer the whole Spanish Netherlands. But Louvois
pressed for harsher terms, England wanted a partition of the
Dutch Republic, and Colbert dreamed of acquiring the mercantile
marine of Holland. The rejection of these Dutch offers was the
biggest of many blunders in Louis's foreign policy. De Witt was
destroyed and William of Orange installed as Stadtholder. The
inundation of Holland continued. The French troops lost their
hold on most of the country and by order terrorized the occupied
territory. The Dutch were spurred on to a desperate resistance –
it is said that the French atrocities were not forgotten a hundred
years later – and they found allies in Brandenburg, the Empire,
and Spain. The instability of the English alliance was revealed
when parliamentary pressure forced Charles II to make a
separate peace with the Dutch in 1674, and henceforth he
remained neutral with some difficulty in face of demands for
intervention in support of the Dutch.

The war had completely changed its character. The Dutch had
won their independence, though at a heavy cost. France had to
fight defensively in the main. Colbert's finance enabled her to
raise the largest army in Europe, 280,000 strong by the end of
the war, and a navy to match the Dutch. To the annoyance of
the generals the military effort was centrally directed by the King
and Louvois. The old generals disappeared from the scene.
Turenne, after laying waste part of the Palatinate to impede
Imperial attacks, and fighting his most brilliant campaign of
manœuvre in Alsace in the winter of 1674–5, was killed in action.
Condé, deprived of opportunities for brilliance, retired at the age
of fifty-four later in 1675. Vauban, besieging and fortifying, was
the outstanding military figure, and with his help the King as

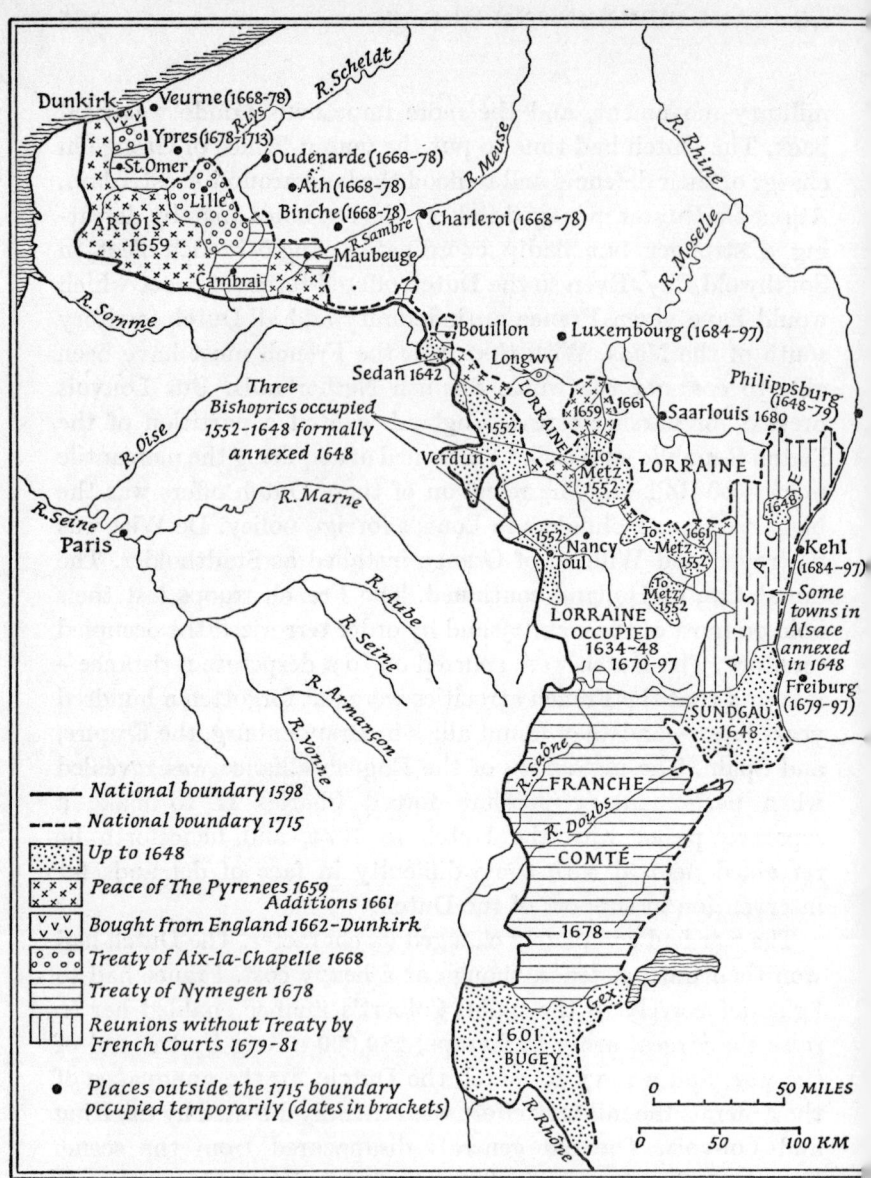

3 THE UNTIDY FRONTIER – FRENCH ADVANCES IN THE NORTH-EAST

Map labels:

Dunkirk
Veurne (1668–78)
Ypres (1678–1713)
St. Omer
Oudenarde (1668–78)
Ath (1668–78)
ARTOIS 1659
Binche (1668–78)
Charleroi (1668–78)
Lille
Cambrai
Maubeuge
R. Scheldt
R. Lys
R. Meuse
R. Rhine
R. Moselle
R. Sambre
R. Somme
R. Oise
Bouillon
Luxembourg (1684–97)
Sedan 1642
Longwy
Philippsburg (1648–79)
Three Bishoprics occupied 1552–1648 formally annexed 1648
Verdun
1552
LORRAINE
1659
1661
Saarlouis 1680
To Metz 1552
LORRAINE
R. Seine
Paris
R. Marne
R. Aube
R. Seine
R. Armançon
R. Yonne
1552
Nancy
Toul
To Metz 1552
1661
To Metz 1552
1648
Kehl (1684–97)
Some towns in Alsace annexed in 1648
A L S A C E
LORRAINE OCCUPIED 1634–48 1670–97
Freiburg (1679–97)
SUNDGAU 1648
R. Saône
FRANCHE
R. Doubs
COMTÉ
1678
Gex
1601 BUGEY
R. Rhône

Legend:

—— National boundary 1598
----- National boundary 1715
⠿ Up to 1648
✕ Peace of The Pyrenees 1659 — Additions 1661
v Bought from England 1662 – Dunkirk
○ Treaty of Aix-la-Chapelle 1668
═ Treaty of Nymegen 1678
‖ Reunions without Treaty by French Courts 1679–81
● Places outside the 1715 boundary occupied temporarily (dates in brackets)

0   50 MILES
0   50   100 KM

commander conquered Franche-Comté in 1674. French army organization was so superior that every year the French armies were able to take the field a month before their opponents. Nevertheless the land warfare was static and indecisive. At sea Tromp controlled the Atlantic trade routes, much troubled by French privateers. But in the Mediterranean there were sensational events. The French Admiral Duquesne was helping some rebels in Sicily in 1676 when De Ruyter arrived with a superior Dutch fleet. In three naval battles off the Sicilian coast Duquesne defeated the Dutch and De Ruyter was killed. France ended the war strongly, benefiting from a unified command against an alliance as usual falling apart.

The peace, under negotiation at Nymegen from 1676 onwards, came about when the French army took Ghent in 1678, and William at last gave way to the pressure of the Dutch merchants. By making a separate peace and abandoning his German allies including Brandenburg he created confusion in Germany and opportunities for the French. Louis saved his ally Sweden from the consequences of a severe defeat, and made the shrewd Elector of Brandenburg, Frederick William, realize that there was little to be gained from anti-French coalitions.

The gains of France at the Peace of Nymegen were the French-speaking Spanish province of Franche-Comté and a frontier rectification in the north – the French gave up some isolated and advanced positions but gained a much straighter frontier by annexing Flemish border areas. Vauban could set to work on his system of frontier fortresses. In the east Franche-Comté linked Burgundy with Alsace, but Alsace was a territory of confused sovereignties; Lorraine was still the property of its Duke, but his refusal to come to terms with France allowed the French to continue in occupation.

Aggression between wars

By the disintegration of the opposition Louis found himself once more dominant in Europe, with a new group of allies in Germany. He kept his army on a war footing and used his power to extend his rule eastward by piecemeal aggression. He calculated on the isolation of William and the Dutch, the feebleness of England under Charles II, and the preoccupation of the Emperor with a Turkish invasion. By overplaying his hand, underestimating the Emperor and William of Orange, and antagonizing the Protestants of Europe by the Revocation, Louis isolated himself and came face to face with a much more formidable alliance ten years later. The only excuse for this was the need to obtain a sound strategic frontier in the east such as had already been achieved in the north, but Louis's measures went far beyond any such modest aim, and expressed an arrogant pride which alarmed Europe.

Colbert de Croissy brought to the direction of foreign affairs his special knowledge of the eastern frontier, gained as an official first in Alsace and then at Metz. He proposed a policy of reunions, and was strongly supported by Louvois, who henceforth encroached more and more in the field of foreign policy. Louis claimed sovereignty over all the dependencies of territories he already held in Alsace, Franche-Comté, and the bishoprics of Metz, Toul and Verdun. His own courts pronounced the verdicts on these claims and his own troops enforced them. This was so easy that Louis was tempted to go further. Some places in Luxembourg were claimed and seized as dependencies of Verdun, and then the city of Luxembourg was demanded in exchange for the abandonment of these claims. In 1681 the King and Louvois with 30,000 troops seized Strasbourg, a free city of the Empire to which the French could lay no claim, and on the same day French forces seized Casale in North Italy. He now offered to negotiate a settlement with the Emperor, who was facing the greatest Turkish threat since the battle of Mohacs. During the crisis Louis weakened the Emperor by giving encouragement to the Hungarian rebels and eventually trying unsuccessfully to dissuade John Sobieski, King of Poland and a former client of France, from going to the rescue of Vienna. When in October 1683, in the greatest battle of the century fought on the Kahlemberg outside Vienna, the Turks were defeated, Louis's own policies suffered a severe blow.

Already in the summer of 1683 the French army had invaded the Spanish Netherlands with orders to spread terror. A short war with Spain followed, and the French besieged and took Luxembourg. To enforce the submission to France of Genoa, the ally of Spain in the Mediterranean, Duquesne bombarded Genoa and destroyed most of the city. This minor war was wholly successful. The Doge of Genoa had to visit Versailles and accept the French terms. Spain gave way and the Emperor, not yet ready to fight, accepted the Truce of Ratisbon in August 1684, by which France was to retain all her reunion gains and Strasbourg, Kehl, and Luxembourg.

Louis had reached the height of his greatness in Europe, but his position was insecure. He had offended against the canons of normal behaviour of European monarchs. At home and abroad his troops had used terrorization as an instrument of policy, and his military might spread fears of tyranny. The ruthlessness with which the Revocation was carried out destroyed his Protestant alliances. Two important Protestant chiefs had personal grievances. The French had seized Orange, William's principality on the Rhône, a Protestant refuge full of refugees, and had imposed intolerant Catholicism; Louis had demanded, unsuccessfully, an oath of homage from Charles XI of Sweden for his German principality of Zweibrücken. England, which had so far been controlled by the payment of subsidies to Charles II, was shaken by a new crisis when James II his Catholic brother succeeded to the throne in 1685. Louis found James much more stubbornly independent than Charles had been; hence he was inclined to do nothing as English Protestants, outraged by James's policy, turned to thoughts of revolt and looked to William of Orange to lead it. Louis regarded all this as a distraction to William, removing his attention from Germany, the main centre of Louis's interests. He disregarded the risk that William, who was himself a Stuart through his mother, and whose wife Mary was the elder daughter and heiress of James II, might get control of England. Throughout his career Louis underrated William, his most dangerous and persistent antagonist, and this was the time when this attitude had the most serious effects.

Meanwhile the core of resistance to Louis was the League of Augsburg, formed in 1686 for the defence of Germany, and joined by the Emperor, most German princes, Spain, and Sweden. The King took little notice of it, and he appeared to think that his high-handed methods could pay dividends indefinitely. At the height of the quarrel with the Pope the French seized Avignon in 1688. In the same year Louis intervened with troops to impose his candidate for the archbishopric of Cologne, Cardinal Fürstenberg, against Clement of Bavaria, the Pope's nominee. He also ordered the occupation of the Palatinate, the succession to which he claimed for his sister-in-law the Princess Palatine, Duchesse d'Orléans – against her wishes. His council ordered the devastation of the Palatinate and it was systematically carried out. Heidelberg and Mannheim were destroyed; the French troops shot the people of Mannheim who returned to live in the rubble. Germany was roused to a fierce resistance.

These actions had involved neglect of the English Revolution which overthrew James II and installed William III as ruler of a kingdom with the resources to become the centre and paymaster of the great alliance now formed to fight France. In 1689 Louis, standing alone, was to put his motto, *Nec pluribus impar*, to its supreme test.

Principal Events, 1672—89

FRANCE AND COLONIES		EUROPE AND OVERSEAS
Pomponne Foreign Secretary.	1672	Outbreak of Dutch War.
Pondicherry founded.		William of Orange Stadt-
Frontenac Governor of New		holder of Netherlands
France		
Molière dies.	1673	Assassination of De Witt.
Beginning of *régale* dispute		Coalition against France
Revolt in Bordeaux	1674	Anglo-Dutch peace. French
		conquest of Franche-Comté.
		John Sobieski King of Poland
Turenne killed. Condé	1675	Battle of Fehrbellin
retires. Revolt in Brittany		
Conversion fund for	1676	Innocent XI Pope.
Protestants.		Duquesne's naval victories in
French at Chandernagore		Mediterranean
Le Tellier Chancellor.	1677	William of Orange marries
Racine: *Phèdre*		Mary
King seizes bishopric of	1678	Peace of Nymegen.
Pamiers.		Popish 'Plot' in England
Croissy Foreign Secretary.	1679	Treaty of St Germain.
Intensified persecution of		Chambres de Réunion set up.
Protestants		Exclusion crisis in England
First *dragonnade*. Farmers-	1680	Charles XI's coup d'état in
General–*Cinq Grosses Fermes*		Sweden
Church Assembly meets. Canal	1681	French take Strasbourg and
des Deux Mers completed		Casale
Four Articles of Religion.	1682	Pennsylvania founded
Court moves to Versailles.		
Cavelier de La Salle sails		
down Mississippi to mouth		
Colbert dies. Maria Theresa dies	1683	John Sobieski defeats
Louis marries Mme de		Turks at Kahlenberg
Maintenon		(Vienna)
Widespread dragonnades	1684	Truce of Ratisbon.
		Genoa subdued by French
Revocation of Edict of	1685	James II King of England –
Nantes. Le Tellier dies		Monmouth Rebellion

FRANCE AND COLONIES		EUROPE AND OVERSEAS
Mme de Maintenon founds St Cyr	1686	League of Augsburg formed. Turks driven out of Hungary
Cavelier de La Salle killed. Lulli dies.	1687	Newton: *Principia*
	1688	French occupy Cologne and devastate Palatinate Great Elector dies. English Revolution
	1689	Innocent XI dies. William III King of England. War of League of Augsburg

PART VI
The Decline of Absolute Monarchy

[25] THE GOVERNMENT IN THE LATER YEARS

When the War of the League of Augsburg broke out in 1689, Louis XIV had for seventeen years been following an aggressive foreign policy. The brilliance of the early years had faded, and the enthusiasm of the people was giving way to weariness and disillusionment. The interests of the King, centred on military glory, religious uniformity, and the splendour and isolation of Versailles, had of course prevailed over those of Colbert. At fifty Louis was a very shrewd ruler, but the good work of his reign was largely nullified by his outbursts of pride, brutality, and sudden aggression. Now he had to face a hostile Europe.

Louis was in many ways a changed man. He cared far less for Court and society, worked at the business of state for a full day, and rested quietly with Mme de Maintenon. Her room was the centre of government. Her Academy of St Cyr was a refuge from society, and she and the King were really at home there. It was there that they enjoyed the performance of Racine's *Esther* in 1690, with its allegorical politics – the heroine a thinly-disguised Mme de Maintenon, the villain pointing at Louvois. The King's other refuge was Marly, a palace built in the form of a royal pavilion surrounded by twelve satellite pavilions – like a glorified motel – to which the King and Mme de Maintenon paid short visits, and to which he invited specially favoured courtiers to

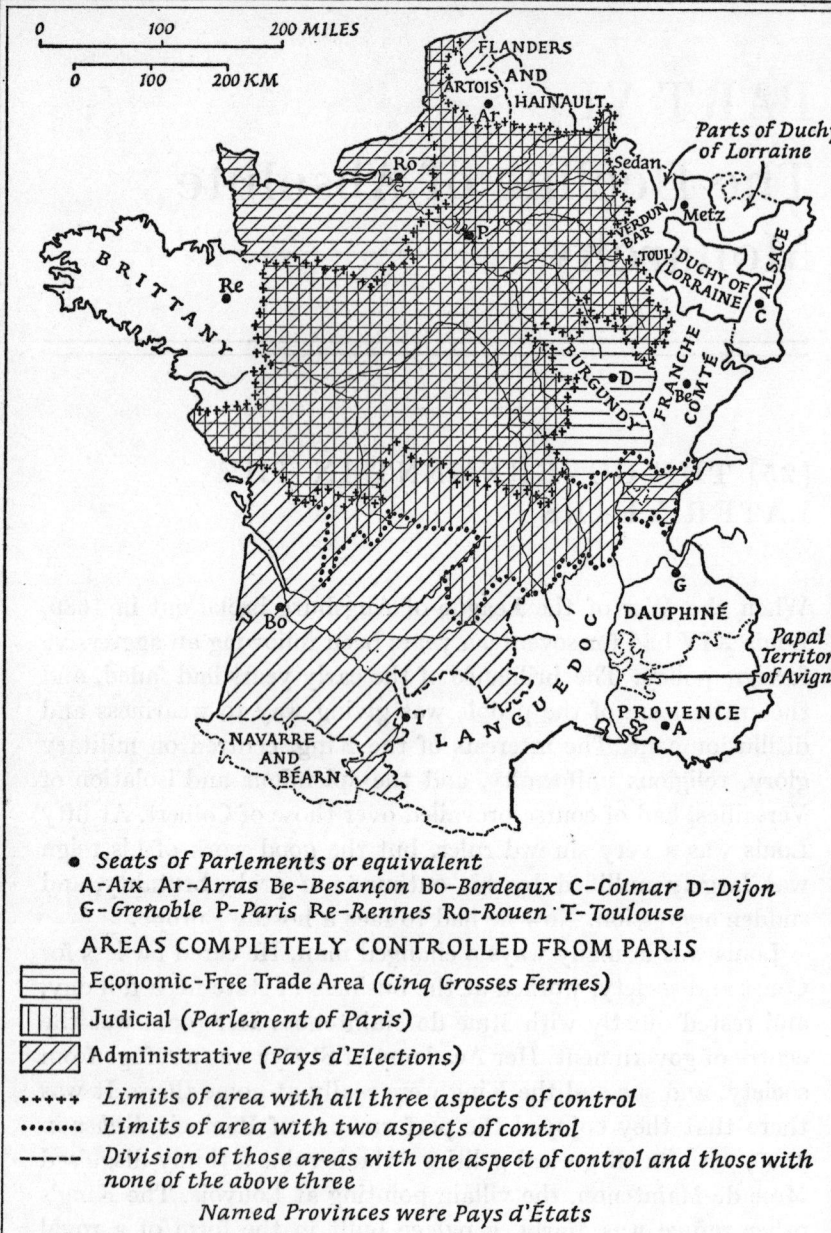

4 PARTIALLY CENTRALIZED FRANCE 1715

relax in a less formal atmosphere. But the routines of Versailles still persisted. The King hunted every afternoon, though often in a carriage. Ceremonies were organized with less care and etiquette became less strict; gambling was more and more the main activity. The King and Mme de Maintenon tried in vain to impose decency on a growingly dissolute society.

The King had a wonderful constitution, which enabled him to survive in spite of his very greedy eating habits and the attentions of the doctors, who imposed on him excruciating and often senseless treatments for his complaints and illnesses. He bore suffering stoically, but became more brutal when he suffered most pain.

The saddened Court of the ageing King was enlivened by Marie Adelaide, the princess of Savoy whom the Duc de Bourgogne married in 1697. She was a charming spoilt child who fascinated the King, and as she grew up she became the centre of the social life of the court, secure of her position through her hold on Louis. The heavy Dauphin was almost a cipher in public affairs and society, and the solemn, priggish, and devout Duc de Bourgogne and his brilliant wife took the place of the heir to the throne.

By a series of marriages between his illegitimate children and members of the royal families of Orléans and Condé Louis tried to consolidate the interests of the Bourbons. One sign of his extraordinary authority was the respect paid to his illegitimate children, whom he legitimated by decree. The ablest and least manageable of his royal relatives was Philippe Duc de Chartres, who became Duc d'Orléans when his father died in 1710. He was a freethinking libertine, intelligent and unscrupulous, whom the misfortunes of the royal family made Regent of France after Louis XIV's death.

None of these royal persons was allowed to have the slightest influence on government, which was still conducted by the King and his ministers. Louvois lost his influence with the King when the war did not go according to plan in 1689; one sign of this was the appointment of Seignelay, his opponent and a protégé of Mme de Maintenon, as a minister. But Seignelay died in 1690 and Louvois the next year, virtually in disgrace. The King is reputed to have been particularly gay just after Louvois's death; perhaps he felt free at last to disregard all ministerial opinion. The ministers he chose were generally worthy but of second-rate ability and completely manageable. In 1692 the Conseil d'en Haut consisted of the Dauphin, Colbert de Croissy, Pontchartrain who was now the Controller-General of Finance and successor to Seignelay in charge of the navy, Pomponne who had been dismissed in 1679 and was now recalled, and the Duc de Beau-villier – the only member of the noblesse d'épée ever in Louis's council, governor of the Duc de Bourgogne, a son-in-law of Colbert, and one of the dévot group surrounding Mme de Main-tenon. When Croissy died in 1696 his much more able son Torcy succeeded him, and replaced Pomponne in the ministry in 1699; he conducted foreign affairs with marked finesse and acted as a kind of secretary to the council. The worst that can be said against these ministers is that they were uninspired and had no independent spirit to oppose the King. The only pressure on him, and it was largely ineffective, came from the dévots operating through the backstairs influence of Mme de Maintenon and another of Colbert's sons-in-law the Duc de Chevreuse, who became a secret adviser of the King; St Simon says that the King ordered in 1703 that all state papers should be shown to him. But as this group opposed the war policy it is clear that they had little influence on the King's actions.

The least satisfactory and the strangest of Louis's appoint-ments in this period was that of Chamillart in succession to Pontchartrain when the latter became Chancellor in 1700. Chamillart became a friend of the King by playing billiards with him, and was given not only the controller-generalship but the war ministry as well. Chamillart protested and proved his own inadequacy, but Louis persisted in keeping him in the two most important posts in the country, either one of which was too heavy for him, during some of the most disastrous years in the history of France. When he was at last allowed to go in 1708 Louis appointed as Controller-General Desmaretz, a brilliant, un-scrupulous, and cynical official, a nephew of Colbert, who had been the real power behind the scenes in the Treasury during the previous twenty years.

Whatever ministers he had Louis decided his own course of action. He gave the other councils no part in government. Two very important new taxes, the *capitation* and the *dixième*, were imposed without consultation with the Conseil des Finances. As the King ruled in a more personal way the chief clerks and secretaries became more powerful, and often saw the King on state business. The administration was more bureaucratic because it was impossible for the ageing ruler to oversee it effectively, especially as he had to give his first attention to the detailed oversight of the wars.

The death of Colbert had removed all restraints on the growth of a local bureaucracy. Brittany, the last province without an intendant, obtained one in 1687. These intendants were now always chosen from the maîtres des requêtes, themselves appointed from counsellors of one of the Parlements, and therefore venal officials. Yet by a last saving display of common sense the office of intendant was not purchasable or inheritable, and was usually filled by a man of first-class ability. It was now the regular practice for intendants to remain many years in the same place; Basville de Lamoignon, the notorious intendant of Languedoc, remained there for over thirty years. They managed their généralités through an increasing number of minor functionaries chosen from the venal officials, paid largely out of fees from the public. Their work became rapidly heavier. As magistrates they concerned themselves with more and more cases, including those formerly dealt with by the assizes of the Parlements known as the *grand jours*. They administered all direct taxation except in the pays d'états. They had great powers of intervention in industry and trade, were responsible for welfare, and made periodic surveys to provide statistical information. The Revocation threw an enormous burden on those intendants who had to deal with large Protestant communities. The great famines of 1693–4 and 1709 created problems which required drastic emergency treatment.

Through the intendants the King's administration was felt

throughout France. They were unpopular instruments of royal power; even when they were completely efficient they were arbitrary, and hence were harshly judged. Yet they were by no means merely instruments. Communications with Paris were slow and if anything became worse as the state of the royal finances prevented expenditure on roads and bridges. The overburdened central administration could not effectively supervise from a distance the action of these petty kings. They used their discretion, sometimes to temper the wind to the shorn lamb. The intendant of Tours wrote in 1700: 'One is very much embarrassed with on the one hand the obligation to lighten the burden of the people and on the other to obey the King'. Frequently they objected to new taxation and sometimes secured local modifications of the policy. Often, however, they were excessively harsh, especially in dealing with obstinate dissidents such as the Huguenots – whose treatment varied greatly from one généralité to another. They appeared at their best in the newly annexed provinces, Alsace, Flanders, and Franche-Comté, where their reasonable handling of the problems of assimilation did much to attach the people to France.

In spite of the great work of unification being carried out by the intendants France remained essentially a federation of provinces with extraordinary differences of law, government, taxation, and customs. The governors were no longer of any importance, but where there were local Parlements these still challenged the powers of the intendants, more so towards the end of the reign. The new police, established throughout France by 1699, fell in the provinces mainly into the hands of venal officials, and these encroached considerably on the powers of the intendants. No law, not even the Revocation, applied to the whole of France – in this case Alsace was the exception.

The government gradually became an ossified bureaucracy. Pagès goes so far as to describe it as 'an anonymous irresponsible despotism'. It could administer with some effectiveness, but made few reforms. Royal absolutism was largely a façade. The richest and most populous state in Europe was so imperfectly unified that even in desperate crises it could not realize its full potential.

[26] FINANCE AND THE ECONOMY AFTER COLBERT

Finance

Colbert had firmly established a workable if not equitable administration of the finances, and this was on the whole maintained by conscientious successors. Their circumstances were much worse than his. The scarcity of money depressed the economy – the copper coins most used by the common people were in a deplorable state. Two of the worst famines which afflicted the French of the ancien régime occurred in this period, in 1693–4 and 1709. The country was on a war footing for the rest of the reign, and actually fought two wars lasting for twenty years altogether. No one, not even Colbert, could curb the King's extravagance. The Controllers-General for the last part of the reign, Le Pelletier, Ponchartrain, Chamillart, and Desmaretz, were forced by circumstances to use all the old expedients of the times of Richelieu and Mazarin. By the end of the reign the state was far more deeply in debt to the private bankers and financiers than ever before.

The War of the League of Augsburg resulted in a debt of 600 million livres. The revenue from the old sources was falling slightly. Many new offices were created, often by the duplication of existing offices. Merchants and manufacturers had to pay fees to a host of unnecessary and vexatious new inspectors. The honour of becoming a member of the official order was still the chief bait, and in the short run the King did very well out of this. Pontchartrain said: 'Every time Your Majesty creates an office, God creates a fool to buy it'. Some offices were held in rotation. In six years Pontchartrain sold offices for 170 million livres. In 1701 two new posts of Directors of Finance sold for 800,000 livres each.

Even in Colbert's lifetime some criticism of French methods of taxation had appeared. Vauban, the most successful and most

penetratingly intelligent of the King's officers, developed these
criticisms in the 1690s, and brought out a plan, the most radical
of the century, for an income tax of 7 per cent without exemptions, to yield 60 million livres. This appeared at the time of
greatest difficulty in this decade, in 1694, and Pontchartrain,
probably inspired by Desmaretz, was driven by desperation to
adopt a variant, the capitation or poll-tax in 1695. The whole
taxable population, including those exempt from taille, was
divided into 22 classes according to rank rather than wealth,
to pay on a graduated scale. The members of the first class
were to pay 2,000 livres a head, and the twenty-second 1 livre.
Financiers, the richest men in France, paid less than many high
officials. The clergy gained exemption by payment of a higher
don gratuit. Languedoc opted out for a lump sum. Nobles deeply
resented the loss of their privilege, and soon began to gain new
exemptions. But at least this was the first attempt to make the
rich pay something towards the costs of war. The yield, $22\frac{1}{2}$
million livres in the first year and a little more later, was disappointing. The privileged paid about a third of this sum. The
tax, repealed at the peace, was reimposed when war broke out
again, but it was unpopular with the overworked intendants, and
they usually converted it into a mere supplement to the taille.

During the respite between the wars Pontchartrain reduced the
taille, and reduced the interest on rentes by enforced conversions
from $8\frac{1}{2}$ per cent to 5 per cent. In 1699 he was still anticipating
revenue, but only to the extent of 25 million livres. The armed
truce lasted all too short a time, however, and the renewal of
war destroyed the faint hope of financial stability. During this
war a far larger proportion of the mounting costs had to be met
by borrowing. By the end, in spite of new taxation, net receipts
from taxes had fallen to about 70 million livres. The debt had
soared to 2,300 million livres.

In 1706 Vauban published his *Dixme Royale*, a trenchant
criticism of the royal administration, and a proposal that the
whole revenue should be raised by a single direct income tax. The
book was banned and he was dismissed from his offices and disgraced by the angry King. But the financial situation was so

critical in 1710, following the great famine and Marlborough's invasion of France, that Desmaretz persuaded Louis to impose an income tax known as the *dixième*. It was impossible to get a correct return, except from salaried officials and holders of rentes, from whom, in highly modern fashion, tax was deducted at source. The yield of 22 million was accordingly far below expectations. So income tax started on its chequered career in Europe. There were risings against it in Béarn, Limousin, and Normandy. Some of the more distant provinces escaped its imposition – Languedoc, Provence, Burgundy, Brittany, Lyon, Alsace, Strasbourg, and Flanders were exempted. The clergy escaped again, but only on the payment of another 8 million. The dixième became a permanent tax, but soon fell entirely on the less rich. Unwilling financiers were encouraged to lend to the government by offers of exemption. Inadequate single payments redeemed the tax for all time. The results of these attempts at fair taxation were disappointing, but Desmaretz deserves credit for trying – had Colbert made the effort he might have been able to solve the administrative problems. As it was the capitation and dixième together more than doubled the yield of direct taxation.

Desmaretz was facing a very serious crisis, and he was unscrupulous as well as bold. Frenchmen lost confidence in their financial bureaucracy as arbitrary acts became more and more common – forced conversions to lower the interest on rentes, arrears of interest followed by repudiations. Forced loans were imposed on certain classes, for example foreigners. The government instituted interest-bearing money bills in 1710, and partly owing to the great shortage of specie they circulated as paper money. This steadily depreciated; it was worth little more than a third of its value in 1706, and less than a fifth by 1713, yet in 1707 these notes were made legal tender at face value for up to a quarter of the total payment in any transaction, and government debts were often paid entirely in paper money. Several times the livre was devalued. There were no livre coins – it was only money of account – and the chief coins minted were the gold louis d'or and the silver écu. Their value in livres was fairly frequently altered, and the government made a profit each time.

The louis d'or, worth 11½ livres in 1692, was raised in stages to a value of 20 livres in 1705. Paper money and devaluation did in fact counteract deflation and in that way helped the economy. But credit, and faith in the competence of the government, were shaken. It proved itself incompetent to collect the customs and excise duties when the tax-farmers refused to continue in 1709. The Bureau of Finance set up its own department, but the revenue dropped by over 20 millions, and eventually the tax-farmers were persuaded to resume.

The financiers, although subject to the whims of the government, flourished amid the wreck of the finances. Samuel Bernard, the former Huguenot, was the greatest of these, a confidential adviser to the Controller-General. In 1708, when he had just lent 11 million livres to the government he was invited by the King to Marly – the most exclusive of privileges – and persuaded to part with another 19 million. (This was at the time when only the arrival of a Spanish ship containing silver at St Malo saved France from immediate bankruptcy.) Most financiers preferred the recklessness and uncertainty of the French situation, with the possibility of immense profits, to any stability such as had been achieved by England. When Bernard proposed a state bank his fellow financiers opposed it strongly and the plan was abandoned. At the time of the King's death the debt, apart from the rentes, was a floating one. Revenue for three years ahead had already been anticipated, and Desmaretz was proposing bankruptcy. No wonder the Regent Orléans turned to the brilliant Scots financier John Law to perform a financial miracle.

The economy

Colbert had both stimulated and regulated industry and trade. His successors confined themselves to more and more meticulous regulation and closer inspection, not to bring about change, but to keep things as they were. The reductio ad absurdum of this regulative mania is seen in the regulation for the sowing of woad (a home-produced source of blue dye): 'The seed . . . is to be sown during the last quarter of the moon in February or the first quarter of the moon in March and at all the full moons until the month of May'. Tariffs were steadily increased to protect home manufactures. The importation of cotton goods from India was restricted and then banned altogether, to the detriment of the East India Company. The guilds were made more powerful and at the same time more expensive and exclusive. Luxury trades were affected by the general depression and the financial difficulties of the government at war; the Gobelins, after the crisis of 1693, was closed for three years, and the Savonnerie declined until in 1712 it was taken over by the Gobelins. Iron production expanded to meet the demand for munitions. Cloth manufacture flourished in Languedoc because of the growth of the Levant trade from Marseille, successfully resisting the efforts of the government to put it in a strait waistcoat. The silk industry in Lyon was well maintained by government favour at the expense of the newer centres of Tours and Nîmes, where it had been largely in Huguenot hands and where there was a sad decline. Glass manufacture, technically very advanced, continued to flourish.

But the overall picture is one of stagnation or decline, aggravated by war. The great agricultural crises of 1693 and 1708 prevented the creation of a stable internal market. Entrepreneurs were lacking, and hence there was no technical progress, and they were not likely to appear in a country without a sound credit mechanism and constricted by bureaucracy, whose capital was drawn off into unproductive fields by social snobbery. According to Montesquieu the first man to say 'laissons-nous faire' was a manufacturer called Legendre speaking to Colbert, and now many French manufacturers and merchants were taking up the cry, and they had an exponent in Boisguilbert, the opponent of rigid Colbertian principles.

It was in foreign trade that greater freedom appeared at this time. The War of the League of Augsburg was very harmful to overseas ventures because of the naval superiority of England and Holland after 1692, but it gave scope to the adventurous merchants of St Malo, Nantes, Bordeaux, and La Rochelle who were prepared to take big risks for big prizes. During the five years of peace between 1697 and 1702 ships were built in large numbers, and the uncontrolled trade with Spain developed rapidly, and above all the contraband trade with Spanish possessions throughout the world. The alliance with Spain enabled some of this trade to continue during the War of the Spanish Succession, in spite of England's control of the sea. Even Louis XIV became aware of the importance of the struggle for trade and stated that *'le principal objet de la guerre presente est celui du commerce des Indes et des richesses qu'elles produisent'*.

More than any other port, St Malo heralded the growth of French overseas interests. A remarkable Malouin merchant, Danycan, organized a company which for a number of years had a monopoly of the Pacific trade. At least ten French ships a year entered the Pacific from 1705 onwards, and there were seven French ships at once in a Chilean port in 1708. The *Grand Dauphin* of St Malo sailed round the world between 1711 and 1713, and again between 1714 and 1717. Danycan was probably the richest merchant in France; when his youngest three daughters married they had dowries of 800,000 livres each, nearly as much as Colbert could manage with help from the King. It is amazing how well this trade was maintained during all the immense troubles and disorders of the Spanish Succession War and in spite of losses caused by the enemy. In the middle years of the war an average of about 1,000 ships a year were entering St Malo; the figure dropped to 543 in 1713, but rose to 1,921 in 1714. The heavily indebted East India Company handed over its trade monopoly to the St Malo merchants in 1708 in return for an annual payment to redeem its debt.

The government had made a great concession to private trading interests by setting up a Council of Commerce in 1700, in which there was representation for the merchants of twelve towns. The deputies generally supported freer trade. In 1701 two of them demanded lower tariffs, and a memoir on the Guinea slave trade put forward the view that 'nothing but competition and freedom render commerce useful to the state and . . . all exclusive trades are infinitely burdensome . . . especially when in the hands of Parisians'. There was abundant vitality in the French ports.

To all this reviving life Louis was blind and deaf. Fortunately ministers, notably Pontchartrain and Desmaretz, had more interest in the lively growth of French overseas interests.

Colonies

The wars naturally created difficulties in the colonies. In the East the French failed in their effort to establish an interest in Siam. They evacuated Madagascar. The Dutch took Pondicherry in 1693, but it was restored at the peace. A factory had been opened at Chandernagore in Bengal, but development in India was very slow and the trade was hampered by the prohibition on imports of cotton goods into France.

The French West Indian colonies continued to grow, but much of their trade was contraband, often with the enemies of France. Canada, strongly ruled by Frontenac, more than held its own in conflict with the English during the War of the League of Augsburg. An adventurous overland expedition seized all the Hudson's Bay Company's forts except one, but they were restored at the peace of Ryswick. Cavelier de La Salle's attempt to found a colony at the mouth of the Mississippi led to disaster in 1687 – he was assassinated while searching overland for the great river whose mouth he had been unable to rediscover. But D'Iberville disembarked with a shipload of colonists in the Mississippi delta in 1699, and Louisiana was successfully founded.

The Spanish Succession War meant a hard struggle in America. Louisiana was saved from English attacks, and an English expedition to Quebec in 1711 was a failure; once more England's Hudson's Bay forts were seized. But at Utrecht the French had to pay for their defeat in the war by the loss of Acadia (Nova Scotia) which the English had seized during the war, and Newfoundland – though here certain fishing rights were preserved – and the restoration of the Hudson's Bay territory.

The Peace of Utrecht established English preponderance in the world overseas. But the French, with little aid from a preoccupied and largely indifferent government, had kept open possibilities for the future. Louis XIV had shown himself a true pupil of

Mazarin in his concentration on Europe and neglect of the overseas interest of France and of the navy. If he could have been inspired by Richelieu's vision, or if Colbert had been the kind of man to inspire anyone, the foreign policy of France might have given its rightful place to the aim of world power.

[27] FRANCE AGAINST EUROPE

The War of the League of Augsburg

In 1688 Louis XIV occupied Cologne and made a wanton attack on German territory, devastating the Palatinate. He and Louvois no doubt calculated on a short struggle and quick surrender similar to Spain's in 1684, and they certainly imagined that the stiff-necked Catholic King of England and William of Orange would be engaged in a new civil war for some time. On the contrary England settled its crisis with astonishing speed by the proclamation of William III and Mary II, James II was Louis's guest at St Germain, and England and Holland were ready to join the Emperor in war against France. In Germany there was virtually unanimous resistance to the French. Louis alienated his former friends in Protestant Germany by the Revocation, and Bavaria by his behaviour over the Archbishopric of Cologne. Spain joined the great coalition, and France, without an ally, had to face most of Europe.

Although he had not the resources for a long conflict against such a big alliance, Louis had certain immediate advantages. William, secure in England, had to meet a Jacobite revolt in Scotland and the refusal of the Catholic Irish to accept his rule. The Emperor had to continue the war against the Turks, who refused to make peace even when Belgrade fell in September 1688. The French army was large, well drilled, and well equipped, and a form of conscription had just been adopted to maintain its strength; a militia of 24,000 was recruited by lot, to serve for two years – later increased to three. The navy was at the peak of its comparative power, thanks to the untiring zeal of Seignelay. There was a central command – the King and Louvois, and after Louvois's death in 1691 the King alone, advised by the expert Chamlay – who gave the generals more independence of action than Louvois had done. One great tactician remained; the veteran Luxembourg, Louvois's enemy, was brought out of the Bastille in 1690 to command in the Netherlands. And France had the finest of military engineers in Vauban.

There was to be no speedy success. The French decided that their main effort should be directed against William III, insecure in the British Isles and vulnerable in Holland. The navy was able to ensure the passage of troops to Ireland, and for a time won command of the Channel by Tourville's victory off Beachy Head. James II with a small French force landed in Ireland, but the jealousy of Louvois concerning an enterprise within Seignelay's province prevented the sending of sufficient troops to ensure success, and the battle of the Boyne in 1690 ruined the hopes of James II in Ireland. Then in 1692 at La Hogue the English fleet and the weather largely destroyed the French fleet which was preparing to escort James on a second attempt to regain his English throne. Seignelay had died, and the King had given control of the navy to Pontchartrain, who knew nothing about it and wanted to economize by confining naval activity to privateering and by fortifying the coast against invasion – Vauban's policy. A great French naval success in 1693, when Tourville attacked an escorted Anglo-Dutch merchant convoy off Cape St Vincent and destroyed 83 ships, was the last victory at sea for many years, although the French privateers such as Jean Bart did enormous damage to enemy shipping. The French, on the defensive, lost ground in Germany. The main military effort in the Spanish Netherlands never looked like producing decisive results. It was a war mainly of sieges; Louis himself nominally commanded for the last time at the successful siege of Mons in 1691. Luxembourg won victories over William at Steenkirk in 1692 and (more decisively) at Neerwinden in 1693, but was not very skilful at exploiting them, and William held his ground stubbornly.

The severe famine and crisis in France in 1693 and 1694 destroyed the last hope of a victory for France. The resources of the country were exhausted. The Conseil d'en Haut consisted of cautious men who wanted peace, and negotiations had begun in 1693, but Louis could not for a long time reconcile himself to the deposition of James II. When Luxembourg died in January 1695 Louis appointed an incompetent commander in the Netherlands, his friend Villeroy, and William was able to retake Namur, thought to be impregnable since Vauban had remodelled its fortifications. In 1696 France seized the opportunity of coming to terms with Savoy, by abandoning Casale and Pinerolo and arranging the marriage of a Savoyard princess with the Duc de Bourgogne. This defection and general exhaustion brought the allies to terms in the Treaty of Ryswick in 1697.

Louis had fought an unnecessary war to no purpose whatever. He had already made his peace with the Pope by giving up royal Gallicanism. Now he had to recognize William III as King of England, admit failure in the Palatinate and the Archbishopric of Cologne, give up all his gains made since 1679, except those made in Alsace including Strasbourg, and effectively restore the Duke to Lorraine, which France had occupied for over sixty years. Overseas French gains and losses had been fairly balanced, and all colonial conquests were to be restored by the peace. Spain lost nothing in the war. The Emperor was most successful in restoring the position in Germany, and in 1699 consolidated his successes by a victorious peace with the Turks. England was now a strong European power, dominant at sea and sure of the Dutch alliance. Holland gained the right to garrison a number of fortresses in the Spanish Netherlands against the danger from France.

Excessive pride, arrogant behaviour stimulated by Louvois, gross misunderstanding of the European situation, and failure to mobilize the full financial resources of France, had brought Louis to this humiliating position. He and his cautious ministers wished to avoid further adventures, and the influence of Mme de Maintenon and the dévots who were powerful behind the scenes was strongly against further wars. Yet an even greater struggle followed after five years.

The War of the Spanish Succession

A new European war became almost certainly inevitable when
Charles II of Spain died in 1700. This time Louis strove hard to
find a peaceful solution, brilliantly assisted by Colbert de Torcy.
There was no clearcut legal heir. If Maria Theresa's renunciation
was invalid because of the nonpayment of the dowry, the Dauphin
was heir to the Spanish throne, and it was understood that he
handed on his claims to his second son Philippe d'Anjou. If the
French claim was legally inadmissible, the heiress was Maria
Antonia – daughter of the Emperor Leopold I and the Spanish
princess Margarita Theresa – who was the Electress of Bavaria.
But her father had compelled her to renounce her claim so that
he could put forward his own as the next in line of succession, and
he proposed to pass on his claim to his second son by an earlier
marriage, Archduke Charles. This tangle could hardly be peace-
fully solved, but in preparation for the death of the Spanish King,
Louis and William, but not the Emperor, agreed on two partition
Treaties, the first making Maria Antonia's small son Joseph
Ferdinand the heir to Spain, with compensations to France and
Austria from the European possessions of Spain, and the second,
after Joseph Ferdinand's death from smallpox, making the
Archduke Charles the heir with compensation to France. It was
clear that Spain would not accept partition, and after an intense
struggle around his deathbed, Charles II made a will leaving the
whole inheritance to Philippe, or if Louis XIV refused this, to
Archduke Charles.

When the offer was brought to France there was a long and
serious consultation in a divided council. The Dauphin and Mme
de Maintenon urged the King to accept the will and make a
Bourbon king of Spain. Louis decided in favour of the will because
he assumed that the Emperor would fight for the whole inheritance in any case, and it was clear that William's partition policy
was very unpopular in England. Louis had broken his word to
William, but the circumstances very nearly excused him. England
and Holland accepted the will and recognized Philip V of Spain,
while the Emperor prepared for war. French diplomacy found

allies in Portugual, Savoy, Bavaria, and Cologne. The war would begin at a distance from the borders of France. But Louis reverted to arrogance as the war with Austria began, and his indiscretions in 1701 ensured that he would have to fight England and Holland as well as Austria. He refused to cancel the right of Philip V to succeed to the French throne, and had Philip's place in the succession registered in the Parlement. His troops seized the Dutch barrier fortresses in the Netherlands and made their garrisons prisoners. The French secured a monopoly of the trade with Spanish America, including the slave traffic. War fever swept through England and Holland, and William III once again enjoyed popular support. He formed the Grand Alliance before his death and left Marlborough and Heinsius to direct it. The drawing power of this alliance brought about the defection from France of Savoy and Portugal in 1703, and in Spain itself Catalonia proclaimed Charles III as King of Spain.

The French army was better armed than ever before, with the flintlock musket and the ring bayonet and a powerful artillery. It was also bigger, with 300,000 men in 1703 and 400,000 at its height, an immense achievement. But in the earlier years of the war Louis preferred courtiers to able officers as commanders, while the allies with at least equal forces had generals of genius, Marlborough and Prince Eugène, to command in the main theatres of war. Villars won early victories in Germany which endangered Vienna, but was sent to subdue Huguenot rebels in the Cévennes because he could not get on with the Elector of Bavaria. Tallard and Marsin, his successors in Germany, were crushed by Marlborough at Blenheim. Villeroy once more demonstrated his incompetence when he lost the Netherlands at Ramilles. Divided and confused leadership in Italy allowed Eugène to drive out the French by his victory at Turin. Louis took full responsibility for these defeats and nobly refused to cast the blame on his generals. Until 1708 he clung to Chamillart, the leading minister in charge of war and finance. St Simon, who was a friend of Chamillart, wrote of him: 'The rare thing is that the great source of the King's tender affection for him was actually his incapacity. He avowed it to the King at every turn, and the King took pleasure in directing and instructing him; so that he was as zealous for his success as for his own and excused everything.'

Louis was convinced after Ramillies that he would be compelled to make a disadvantageous peace, and Torcy began negotiations in 1706. Then in 1708 the Flemings rebelled against their new Dutch overlords, and the French army advanced to Ghent. But this time Louis had given the command to his grandson the Duc de Bourgogne, a young, inexperienced, and timid commander who detested the war, with Vendôme, brilliant but lazy and dissipated, to advise him; and Marlborough won another crushing victory over this incongruous dual command at Oudenarde. France was invaded and Lille fell.

The worst crisis of the reign had begun. Voysin, an able minister, took charge of the war when Chamillart was at last allowed to resign. Villars, by far the best French general, was given the Netherlands command. Vendôme went to Spain, where his leadership played a large part in the final success of the French forces. But the winter of 1708–9 saw the worst famine of the century, great outbreaks of rioting, and open criticism of the King. The peace-at-any-price party at Court, inspired by Fénelon behind the scenes, represented by Beauvillier and the Duc de Bourgogne in the inner counsels, and countenanced by Mme de Maintenon, gained in strength. The King went to nearly all lengths to get peace, offering sacrifices of territory – Strasbourg and land on the Flemish border – and accepting the deposition of Philip V in favour of Charles III in Spain. When the allies would accept nothing less than the turning out of Philip V by his grandfather's army Louis's pride and sense of decency forced him to refuse, although he could see only ruin ahead. The last act of this tremendous reign opened with this decision to make a desperate stand.

[28] CULTURAL AND RELIGIOUS OPPOSITION

In spite of Louis XIV, France with all Europe was moving towards the Age of Reason. Against change the Catholic orthodoxy of the King and the Church fought a rearguard action, but new ideas permeated Versailles itself. Even Bossuet made many concessions to Cartesianism. Because French orthodoxy was unfriendly to the new science France contributed little to the Newtonian revolution; but Fontenelle, a scientific popularizer, spread the new knowledge and outlook in France, and stimulated a belief in progress which became characteristic of the new age.

Knowledge of lands with non-Christian cultures, powerfully assisted in France by the colonial policy of Colbert, created new perspectives in which morals and culture could be considered apart from religion. Reports of the life of the American Indians were already giving rise to the cult of the noble savage. Chinese civilization, built on utterly different foundations from that of Christian Europe, enjoyed great prestige. Montesquieu, a rationalist and deist, a man of twenty-six at the end of the reign, was able to use this new knowledge to create a comparative world view of human societies.

Criticism was necessarily muted under the harsh censorship of Louis XIV, but nevertheless by the end of the reign the bases of the French Enlightenment had been firmly laid. Voltaire cultivated his sceptical spirit – he was twenty-one when Louis XIV died. (There is no better proof of the spell cast by the great King than the fact that Voltaire, living in the shadow of past greatness, wrote the most complete panegyric of the reign in *Le Siècle de Louis XIV*, and kept a lifelong belief in the superiority of absolute monarchy over any other form of government.) The rationalism of Descartes was now reinforced by the atheistic philosophy of Spinoza. In France the Oratorians in particular were seeking for a compromise, a reconciliation of faith and reason, of science and God. The most influential was

Malebranche. He discredited the supernatural and claimed as a right unlimited freedom of thought. All his books were condemned by Rome, yet the King's confidant the Duc de Chevreuse, Quesnel the Jansenist leader, and Fénelon were all more or less his disciples. The critical spirit of the Oratory, and its courageous resistance to authority, was also displayed by Richard Simon, who in spite of the suppression of his first work on the Old Testament, published a textual criticism of the New Testament in 1689. He found some support from Catholics because he undermined the reliance of Protestants on the verbal inspiration of the Bible, but the censorship prevented any widespread knowledge of his work.

Protestants in exile were much freer to publish their works. Of these the most outstanding was Bayle, a rationalistic thinker who became a Unitarian. His *Dictionnaire Critique* (1692) was a basic work of the Enlightenment; he questioned the veracity of much of the Old Testament and put forward views which horrified many of his fellow refugees. Bayle himself was a monarchist who disagreed strongly with the political views of another Huguenot, Jurieu, who took from Locke a whiggish theory of government – the sovereign people had given power to the king only provisionally, and had the right to rebel if he did not keep to the terms of the contract. Such extreme opinions had little influence in France as yet.

The classical outlook of the great age died hard; its most important product in this period was the dictionary produced by the Academy in 1694. Scholars had a long and bitter debate about the merits of classical as against modern literature, initiated by Charles Perrault, the champion of the moderns. He accepted the greatness of the classical writers of his own time, and insisted on their superiority over Greek and Latin authors – a doctrine repudiated by Racine, Boileau, La Fontaine, and La Bruyère. The moderns triumphed in this controversy; only Bossuet continued to uphold the classical case, and he, like the King, seemed to belong to a past age.

There was a new freedom and humanitarian realism in the literature and art of the end of the reign, no longer subject to royal patronage. La Bruyère's *Caractères* embodied social criticism, and presented the common people, especially the peasants, as the real force of the nation. Boisguilbert was a very hostile critic of mercantilism, and he stressed the importance of agriculture as the basic economic activity. Vauban showed a concern for the poor which reflects the new humanitarian outlook. Le Sage, the most popular writer of the last years of the reign, author of picaresque novels, presented documentary detail of everyday life. Watteau, the leading painter, born at Valenciennes within the range of Flemish influence, introduced a new note of realism into painting.

Humanitarianism also found expression in the writings of a thinker who in this period was by far the most dangerous opponent of Louis XIV, the Abbé Fénelon. The danger came from the action of Louis himself in making him, at Mme de Maintenon's request, tutor to the Duc de Bourgogne in 1689. Fénelon retained to the end an extraordinary hold on the mind of his royal pupil, and remained very close to the Colbert sons-in-law, Beauvillier and Chevreuse, even when he became an open opponent of the King. His fine style ensured that his writings would be read. His religion was mystical and his politics pacifist. He was deeply influenced by the Quietism of Mme de Guyon, a mystic whose religious outlook might have been acceptable in the time of Henry IV or Louis XIII, but now met the bitter hostility of Bossuet and the King. Mme de Maintenon, alarmed possibly about her own position – she allowed Mme Guyon to acquire a strong hold on her academy at St Cyr – abandoned Fénelon and Mme Guyon, and Bossuet began a violent onslaught. Mme Guyon was imprisoned. Fénelon defended Quietism in his *Maximes des Saints sur la Vie Intérieure*, and appealed to Innocent XII, but the Pope condemned his book and so cemented his new alliance with Louis XIV. Fénelon, who had been made Archbishop of Cambrai, was exiled to his province, but remained a very active force. He partly redeemed his religious position by leading the attack on Jansenism, but his political views were more and more openly expressed and were a menace to everything the King stood for, all the greater because he might well, if the Duc de

Bourgogne succeeded to the throne, become the prime minister. Fénelon's views were expressed in his philosophical novel *Télémaque* and in the notes of his discussion with the Duc de Chevreuse at Chaulnes in 1711.

Fénelon believed that the King should live simply and economically with a small court, concern himself with the welfare of the people, foster agriculture and discourage large-scale industry and commerce, and avoid war. He idealized the aristocracy and wanted to abolish in its favour the King's absolute power, the bureaucracy, and the venal office-holders. He advocated frequent and regular meetings of the Estates General under noble domination, and Estates for all the provinces on the lines of those in Languedoc. Many 'enlightened' French nobles of the eighteenth century took up these ideas, and they were very important in the events leading to the Revolution. They were impracticable, however, as was shown by the Regent Orléans's experiment in aristocratic rule after 1715. Fénelon was a pacifist who believed that 'all wars are civil wars'. He was a determined opponent of the War of the Spanish Succession, and took the extreme view that Louis must bear the exclusive blame for it. For the avoidance of future wars he proposed a league of states, kept going by a triennial meeting of the kings and rulers of Europe. Fénelon was a utopian thinker rather than a practical politician, but his sincere idealism and his powers of expression made him an incalculable force in opposition. By a stroke of fate he and all his patrons died before the old King.

Fénelon's following was influential but small, but his enemies the Jansenists had won wide popular support. This was largely the work of a remarkable Oratorian priest, Quesnel, who succeeded Arnauld as the leader of the movement. Quesnel was not primarily interested in the theological controversies which had so far occupied the Jansenists. He shared with the earlier leadership the austerity, the conception of a profoundly demanding Christianity, and the determination to uphold individual judgment against the crushing orthodoxies of Church and State. His book *Réflexions sur le Nouveau Testament*, was concerned more with morals than with theology, and attracted much wider support for Jansenism from serious dévots. The movement spread rapidly among the curés of the parishes, partly because it took up their cause – known as Richerism in France – against the power of the bishops. Nevertheless Quesnel had the qualified support of Bossuet and the wholehearted backing of Noailles, the Archbishop of Paris appointed as a protégé of Mme de Maintenon and as an enemy of Quietism in 1695. Quesnel and Noailles were strong Gallicans, and from this time on the Jansenists could count on the support of the Gallican Parlement of Paris. Louis's Jesuit confessor La Chaise easily persuaded Louis that this popular religious deviation was a menace to his authority, and, while Fénelon led a new attack on Jansenism, the King induced the half-hearted Pope to issue a new bull – *Vineam Domini* – in 1705, condemning the 'respectful silence' which had been permitted to Jansenists since 1668. To overcome the Jansenists Louis once more, as in the case of Quietism, endangered the independence of the Gallican Church, though each time he safeguarded the forms of independence; the Sorbonne and the Parlement must pass judgment on the Bull however much this irritated the Pope. Noailles and the Parlement, though forced to submit, still protected the Jansenists from the consequences of the Bull, and Quesnel's own distinctive teachings – the advocacy of a simpler liturgy, the mass in French, the use of the French Bible, and more power to the curés, were still untouched.

The inconsistency of the leading Court figures in these religious controversies is important to note. Bossuet was a compromiser and at times ambiguous. Mme de Maintenon had made a protégé of Fénelon, then rejected him possibly for what may be regarded as political reasons, and had supported Bossuet and Noailles; then finally, under the guidance of a new confessor, turned very hostile to Noailles, the Gallicans, and the Jansenists. The King was less devout and much more a political opportunist. In religious matters he was dealing with the one power he could never hope to subdue, and he was capable of kaleidoscopic changes. H. G. Judge points out that during his personal rule there had been many different groupings: 'King, Pope, and Jesuits against Jansenists; King, Jesuits, and Gallicans against

Pope and Jansenists; King, Gallicans, and Jansenists against Quietists; King, Quietists, Jesuits, and Pope against Jansenists; and finally King and Pope against Jansenists and Gallicans' ('Church and State under Louis XIV', in *History*, Vol. 155). Although deeply divided among themselves, the dévots still had too much spiritual force, and too much solid power in Church and State, to obey unquestioningly the dictates of a despotic king.

[29] THE END OF THE REIGN

The famine of 1709 and his military defeat plunged Louis XIV into the worst crisis of government since the Fronde. For the first time he was openly derided. Lavisse quotes the verses composed at this time:

> *Le grandpère est un fanfaron,*
>   *Le fils un imbecile,*
> *Le petit fils un grand poltron,*
>   *Ohé! la belle famille.*

> *Que je vous plains, pauvres Français,*
>   *Soumis a cest empire.*
> *Faîtes comme ont fait les Anglais,*
>   *C'est assez vous en dire.*

A blasphemous parody on the Lord's Prayer has also survived: '*Notre père qui est à Versailles, votre nom n'est plus glorifié, votre royaume n'est pas si grand, votre volonté n'est plus fait sur la terre ni sur l'onde. Donnez-nous notre pain qui nous manque de tous cotés. Pardonnez à nos ennemis qui nous ont battus, et non à nos généraux, qui les ont laissés faire*'. The Dauphin visiting the opera was frightened by a hungry Parisian mob, and some market women attempted to march on Versailles to demand bread, but were turned back by the troops. There were innumerable risings in the provinces – in Languedoc 30,000 peasants rose in arms and Cahors was besieged for over a week.

Louis faced his defeat with phlegmatic courage, and his unpopularity with complete impassivity. He was so much insulated from the public that he may never have fully realized it, though he must surely have been affected by the fact that Mme de Maintenon dared not go out in the streets of Versailles, and it was impossible to go out hunting without coming across starving peasants.

France recovered from the famine, though it has been estimated that the population at the end of the reign was lower than at any time since the Bourbons came to power. With the help of a brilliant general – Villars – the ablest ministry since the Triad – Desmaretz, Torcy, and Voysin – and the English Tory government, Louis extricated himself from the war and avoided complete bankruptcy.

The end of the war and the Peace of Utrecht

The prospects of France in the war were at their lowest in the year of famine and insurrection, 1709. Louis came near to accepting complete defeat, and the group surrounding the Duc de Bourgogne would have been willing to sacrifice all Louis's gains and even Alsace to secure peace. But Villars by a firm and skilful stand at Malplaquet showed that Marlborough could be resisted; the French had to retreat, but inflicted crushing losses on the allied army. The French army recovered its fighting spirit, and although Louis continued to negotiate he resolved to fight it out. In 1710 Vendôme regained control of Spain, and the Tories, who believed that Great Britain was now fighting uselessly for the Spanish aims of Austria, gained power under Queen Anne. Soon the possibility of a separate peace with Britain opened up, and Torcy began negotiations with St John (later Viscount Bolingbroke) the British Foreign Secretary, who wanted not only peace but friendship and a commercial treaty with France. In 1711 the Archduke Charles became Emperor Charles VI when his brother Joseph died, and no one outside Austria any longer wanted him to be King of Spain as well. The allies were now hopelessly split. At the end of the year Marlborough was dismissed and threatened with disgrace. In 1712 the British army stood aside from the fighting and Villars defeated Eugène at Denain. Britain and France agreed on peace terms, and these were imposed on the Dutch at Utrecht in 1713 and on the Emperor at Rastatt in 1714.

France had made a remarkable recovery, and Louis's stubbornness was rewarded by terms of peace which preserved for France nearly all the gains made during his reign, and for the Bourbons the throne of Spain. Britain made big gains in America and in the Mediterranean (Gibraltar and Minorca), won trading privileges in the Spanish Empire, and became the leading world power. In Europe Austria established a very strong position with the annexation of most of Spain's former possessions in Italy and the Netherlands. The Dutch for many years to come still had the biggest merchant marine in the world, but had become dependent on Britain; in the Austrian Netherlands they gained a strong line of barrier fortresses to give them an illusion of security against France. France, with a sound frontier apart from Lorraine, Vauban's fortifications, the biggest army, and the greatest resources of any European power, was still immensely strong. At the end Louis was contemplating an alliance with Austria to revolutionize the European situation.

The coming commercial struggle, with trade with Imperial Spain as the main prize overseas, was now recognized as supremely important. For the first time French merchants were employed as negotiators, and Torcy planned a series of commercial treaties. But the control of Spanish policy by France, vital for French trade, suffered a heavy blow when Philip V in 1714 married for a second time. His bride, Elizabeth Farnese, was determined to control Spanish policy for her own Italian ends. Mme des Ursins, the representative of Louis at the Spanish Court, was promptly dismissed, and his hopes of reconciling Spain and Austria were in ruins.

Final religious conflicts

In his last years Louis XIV became once more excessively severe to heretics. Mme de Maintenon had acquired a much harsher confessor and demanded strong action. The approach of death increased Louis's fears for his soul; when his judicious confessor Father La Chaise died he was replaced by a much more extreme Jesuit, Father Tellier, who insisted that his salvation depended on the extirpation of heresy in France. This policy he maintained in spite of the opposition of two Gallican ministers, Torcy and Voysin, and his Gallican Chancellor, Pontchartrain. The first victims were the remaining twenty nuns of Port Royal, who had refused to accede to the Pope's Bull of 1705, and who were dispersed to other nunneries in 1709. With an excess of fanaticism Louis ordered in 1711 the destruction of the buildings of Port Royal and the desecration of the tombs. But the main problem was to deal with the widespread popular Jansenism which centred on Quesnel's moral teaching and had broad support from Gallican priests and laymen, led by Cardinal Noailles, the Archbishop of Paris. The King appointed a committee headed by the Duc de Bourgogne to investigate the conduct of Noailles, and it insisted on action against the Jansenists; Noailles refused to act and suspended all Jesuit confessors in his diocese. The King recklessly adopted an Ultramontane line. He pressed the Pope to condemn explicitly Quesnel's teachings, and at length and reluctantly – for fear of condemning orthodox Augustinianism – Pope Clement XI issued the Bull *Unigenitus* in September 1713. condemning 101 propositions from Quesnel's *Réflexions*, and the book as a whole.

The Gallicans roused themselves to resist, and summoned up the strongest opposition shown to any measure of Louis XIV. The Parlement of Paris first refused to register the Bull without the acceptance of the bishops. The King then called an ad hoc Assembly of thirty bishops, but they could not agree, and Noailles and eight other bishops appealed to the Pope for clarification, and meantime rejected the Bull. Noailles was excluded from Versailles and his supporters were banished to their bishoprics. Then in the Parlement the King's own chief officials, the Procureur-général Daguesseau and the Avocat-général, opposed the registration of the Bull, and only strong pressure from the First President prevented the adoption of remonstrances, proposed for the first time in forty years. Daguesseau, who had called Noailles 'the man of the nation' and refused to prosecute him, held firm in the King's presence although threatened with the Bastille. Some provincial Parlements also opposed the Bull, and in Brittany the Estates and the Parlement joined together to denounce it. In the end the Parlement of Paris registered the Bull – with qualifications safeguarding the Gallican liberties of the Church, and so, under threats, did the Sorbonne. But fifteen bishops refused to enforce it, and although Jansenists in many parts of France were thrown into prison, there was a still unsubdued opposition, whose strength was all the greater because it maintained that the King was betraying the interests of the French Crown.

The immunity of Cardinal Noailles is remarkable. He was greatly respected as an austere and saintly cleric, and almost the entire official order, as well as many of the clergy, were on his side. But Louis was passionately involved. He rejected the Pope's offer to discipline Noailles, but proposed to call a National Council of the French Church, perhaps even to preside over it himself, to crush the clerical opposition. This annoyed the Pope and still further confused the issue by antagonizing the Ultramontanes without reconciling the Gallicans. The Parlement was so much opposed to the proposal that Louis threatened to hold a lit de justice to enforce its acceptance. But he died before any further action could be taken.

In the meantime the Protestants had felt the lash of a new persecution. Doctors were forbidden to visit Protestant patients for more than two days unless they could present a certificate of confession. Finally in March 1715 it was declared that all who had remained in France were now Catholics and were to be treated as relapsed heretics. The answer of the Protestants of Languedoc, estimated at 800,000, was to call the first synod since the Revocation, led by Antoine Court, in the wilderness of the garrigues near Nîmes, and to elect a moderator and a secretary. As Louis died, the Protestant Church was reborn.

The succession

Towards the end of Louis's life the problem of the succession, which had apparently been solved beyond all risk, became very threatening as a result of an extraordinary series of sudden deaths in the royal family.

The King had only one son, but three grandsons and six great-grandsons, and the Bourbon succession seemed far safer than it had ever been. Of these one grandson had become Philip V of Spain, and he and his two sons could hardly come seriously into the reckoning for the French throne, although Philip made ceaseless efforts to keep his claim alive. The Dauphin died of smallpox in April 1711, and for a few months the prospect seemed very close of a reign in which Fénelon might be a prime minister committed to drastic changes. An epidemic of a virulent form of measles in February 1712 altered all that. First the Duchesse de Bourgogne, the shining light of the Court, caught the disease and died within a few days, possibly the victim of the drastic treatment prescribed by the doctors, and the Duc de Bourgogne soon followed her, and after him the new Dauphin, their eldest surviving son. The only other son, the later Louis XV, the fourth Dauphin of the reign, caught the disease, but survived, and this was generally considered to be due to the fact that his nurse protected him from medical attention. He was a weakly child of two, and was not expected to survive long. The next heir (apart from the Spanish King and his sons), the King's third grandson the Duc de Berri, died in 1714 – his only son had died in the previous year. Louis bore the crushing blows to his family with stoicism; the death of the charming duchess on whom he had lavished so much affection is said to have caused him the greatest sorrow of his life.

Philippe, Duc d'Orléans, was now a very important figure in France. He was a clever, cynical, dissipated man who had a far worse reputation than he deserved – many courtiers believed he had poisoned all the members of the royal family who had died in the past few years. He was now the second in line for the throne, and Louis felt that he would have to nominate him for the

necessary regency, but wished to limit his power. (Plans to re-
introduce Philip V broke down because he would not leave Spain
– he was offered an Italian kingdom in an exchange scheme with
the Duke of Savoy.) Then Louis declared his legitimated bastard
sons capable of inheriting the throne, and proposed giving the
eldest, the Duc de Maine, control of the boy Louis XV, and making him a key member of the Regency Council which was to
lessen Orléans's power.

The King's plan for curbing the power of Orléans as Regent was
set out in his will. Once more he had to recognize the place of the
Parlement of Paris in the constitution, for he deposited his will
there. Orléans, in a better position to act, and knowing well
what had happened at the death of Louis XIII, began to bargain
with the chief members of the Parlement for full powers as
Regent in return for the grant to the Parlement of the right of
remonstrance.

Louis XIV died peacefully on 1 September 1715. His illness had
been short – he went hunting as late as 9 August. He had prepared his last instructions for his grandson, containing the
famous admission that he had been too fond of war, and reconciled
himself tranquilly to the third successive minority in the
Bourbon succession. He took a ceremonious leave of all the great
court officials and his personal servants, and then spent the last
two days of his conscious life with Mme de Maintenon. The great
actor had played his part with dignity to the end.

To the French he seemed to have lived too long, and the general
feeling at the news of his death was one of relief, mixed with some
apprehension about the future of the monarchy; there were even
hostile demonstrations at his funeral. It was more like the end
of an era than a mere change of monarch – indeed the whole
reign of Louis XIV had endured longer than any system of
government has done in France since the Revolution.

The reign ended with a full foreshadowing of the evolution of
the ancien régime to the Revolution. The death of Louis removed
most of the restraints on the expression of the ideas of the Age
of Reason. The heretics inside and outside the Church were
unsubdued. The Parlement of Paris resumed its old position in

the state. Even the noblesse d'épee raised its head and attempted an aristocratic reaction under the Regent. The bureaucratic regime survived, but it had become too rigid to adapt itself to the changes in French society. Louis's excessively prolonged reign had greatly contributed to that rigidity.

Further Reading, 1672–1715

The books and articles covering this period have nearly all been mentioned already in the previous list at the end of Part IV. C. W. Cole has written a further volume on the economy, *French Mercantilism 1683–1700* (New York, 1943). There is an illuminating article by R. Mousnier, '*L'Évolution des Finances Publiques en France et Angleterre pendant les Guerres de la Ligue d'Augsburg et la Succession d'Espagne*', in the *Revue Historique*, Vol. 205.

On foreign policy M. A. Thomson has written three articles, 'Louis XIV and William III 1689–1697' in the *English Historical Review* (1961), 'Louis XIV and the Origins of the War of the Spanish Succession' in *Transactions of the Royal Historical Society* (1954), and 'Louis XIV and the Grand Alliance 1705–1710' in the *Bulletin of the Institute of Historical Research* (1961).

Principal Events, 1689–1715

FRANCE AND COLONIES		EUROPE AND OVERSEAS
Beauvillier governor, and Fénelon tutor, to Duc de Bourgogne	1689	War of League of Augsburg. Peter the Great sole Tsar. Toleration Act in England
Militia organized.	1690	Battle of the Boyne.
Racine: *Esther*. Seignelay, Le Brun and Louvois die.	1691	Battle of Beachy Head. Locke: *Civil Government* French take Mons.
Beauvillier a minister Bayle: *Dictionnaire Critique*	1692	Treaty of Limerick French take Namur. Battle of Steenkirk. Battle of La Hogue
Famine and economic crisis. King disavows Four Articles. Enlarged edition of Quesnel: *Réflexions*	1693	Battle of Neerwinden. French naval victory off Cape St Vincent
Academy's French Dictionary	1694	Bank of England founded
Noailles Archbishop of Paris. Quietism and Mme Guyon condemned. La Fontaine dies	1695	William regains Namur
Torcy Foreign Secretary	1696	Peace between France and Savoy. Russians take Azov
Duc de Bourgogne marries Marie Adelaide of Savoy	1697	Treaty of Ryswick. Charles XII King of Sweden
Danycan founds St Malo Co	1698	1st Spanish Partition Treaty
Torcy a minister. Fénelon: *Télémaque*. Racine dies. D'Iberville founds Louisiana	1699	Peace of Karlowitz: defeat of Turks. Outbreak of Great Northern War
Chamillart C-G of Finance and War Secretary. Council of Commerce	1700	2nd Spanish Partition Treaty. Charles II of Spain dies. Philip V succeeds. Prussia a kingdom. Battle of Narva
Fort Detroit founded	1701	Emperor at war with France. Grand Alliance formed

FRANCE AND COLONIES		EUROPE AND OVERSEAS
	1702	Anne Queen of England. War of Spanish Succession. Marlborough Commander-in-Chief
Huguenot revolt in Cévennes	1703	Savoy and Portugal desert France.
		St Petersburg founded
	1704	Battle of Blenheim. English take Gibraltar
Bull *Vineam Domini* against Jansenists	1705	French ships in Pacific. Joseph I Emperor
Vauban: *Dixme Royale*	1706	Battle of Ramillies. Peace negotiations begin
	1707	Union of Great Britain
Desmaretz C-G of Finance. Voysin War Secretary	1708	Battle of Oudenarde
Great famine and disturbances. Port Royal suppressed Dixième tax. Acadia (Nova Scotia) lost to British	1709	Battle of Malplaquet. Battle of Poltava. Charles XII in Turkey
	1710	Breakdown of peace negotiations. Tories in power in Britain. French victory in Spain
Grand Dauphin dies. *Grand Dauphin* of St Malo sails round world (1711–13)	1711	Dismissal of Marlborough. Charles VI Emperor. Turkey defeats Russia
Duc and Duchesse de Bourgogne die.	1712	Battle of Denain
Bull *Unigenitus:* final condemnation of Jansenists	1713	Peace of Utrecht
Duc de Berri dies	1714	Treaty of Rastatt. Philip V marries Elizabeth Farnese Charles XII returns to Sweden. George I King of Great Britain
Protestant Church reborn. Louis XIV dies. Orléans Regent	1715	Jacobite rebellion in Britain

PART VII
Conclusion

[30]

France and England

It would be difficult to find any political parallel in European
history – the Tudors might be the nearest – to the sequence of
remarkable rulers who ruled France between 1589 and 1715 –
Henry IV, Louis XIII and Richelieu, Mazarin, and Louis XIV.
Their rule greatly strengthened the concept of the unity of France
and, amid all the crises and struggles of the period, and even
during the Fronde, the acceptance of a French state governed by
a monarch ruling by divine hereditary right was almost universal.
The Midi and Brittany were again and again the scenes of trouble
and the King's authority in these regions was maintained with
difficulty, but they were never separatist or republican. Distant
provinces, and most notably the newly annexed territories,
accepted the Bourbon monarchy and were steadily assimilated.

At the beginning of the period government was centralized but
administration was local, in the hands of powerful governors
and venal office-holders, both virtually hereditary. The Kings
destroyed the power of the governors and established intendants
superimposed on the old order, appointed from the venal official
order but never escaping from the ultimate control of the central
government. France was the largest territory in Europe controlled
fairly effectively from one centre, and had by 1715 the most
developed bureaucracy. Judged by seventeenth-century standards a fair degree of order was maintained except during the
Fronde. At all other times risings and disorders had always

been nipped in the bud and had never spread far beyond the boundaries of one province.

Was France an absolute monarchy? In theory, very nearly. There were few checks on the authority of the King in Louis XIV's reign. The succession to the throne, governed by the Salic Law of inheritance of the eldest sons in a purely male line, was accepted as sacrosanct, and Louis's attempt to make his illegitimate sons eligible was disliked, and ignored after his death. Frenchmen believed they had rights, but they were not well secured, and the Parlements as their protectors were broken reeds on which to rely. The Catholic Church was never brought entirely under the King's power, and its independence was never more clearly seen than in the last months of Louis XIV's reign. Government was also limited in practice by its dependence on an order of officials who had built up a great and unassailable power, nearly as formidable as that of the feudal lords whom they had displaced. The central government was never sure that its decrees would be strictly obeyed by the officials who had to administer them locally. Geographical difficulties were still very great and communications were slow. Turenne's attitude to central control of the generals might well be that of many a distant official about the attempt to guide his own arbitrary government made by an arbitrary regime in Paris. He would at least decide which of the innumerable decrees he would enforce, for he could not enforce them all. Frenchmen liked to think that their government was absolute but not arbitrary; often it was the reverse.

The complete political unification of large areas is a difficult feat, and France in the seventeenth century was possibly too big for this to be practicable. It remained a conglomeration of diversely ruled and taxed regions, and the Bourbons were never able to draw on the full resources of the richest state in Europe. Consequently the results of their almost incessant wars were disappointing. Mazarin and Louis XIV secured very important gains to the north and east, but the failure to annex Lorraine, although it had been occupied by the French for over sixty years, left the frontier problem still without a satisfactory solution. As a consequence of the struggle France had the largest and best army in Europe, one of the main achievements of the regime. The destruction of German power by France was a dubious gain; it precipitated the rapid development of an Austrian Empire and the ultimate growth of Prussia. If Britain emerged as the chief beneficiary of the French wars, this was largely due to the neglect by France of Richelieu's and Colbert's vision of overseas greatness. Even so, the establishment of an overseas empire, due to ministers, merchants, and sailors rather than monarchs, was an outstanding French achievement in this century.

The monarchy provided enough social stability for the growth of a high civilization and a fine culture in the upper and middle classes of French society. The French language was perfected as an instrument of expression of unequalled clarity. French literature, above all the drama, reached heights which it has never surpassed. Paris became the best planned and most finely built city in Europe. All Europe looked to France by the end of the century for leadership in culture, and French became the international language replacing Latin. Versailles set the tone of manners and social intercourse. The dévots contributed remarkably to the deepening and enriching of the spiritual life of France.

Louis XIV fostered many aspects of this development, but in the end it was an added embarrassment; ultimately this vigorous society was not to be contained in the strait waistcoat of the great king's policy of personal glory. The Bourbon repression held French thought back from taking its rightful place in Europe – Descartes in the earlier period, Pascal in the middle years, and many of the precursors of the Enlightenment at the end, felt the pressure of official persecution.

Some of the difficulties and defects of the Bourbon monarchy may be brought out by comparing France with England, a smaller state with fewer external problems, progressing in spite of appearances to a more satisfactory development. Both countries were emerging from feudalism in the seventeenth century. Both were still predominantly rural societies in which a landed aristocracy was dominant, but in each a vigorous middle class, accumulating capital in industry and trade, buying estates, aspiring to aristocratic status, ever pushing upwards, was transforming the social scene. But the politically active elements in these societies operated in very different ways.

In France the monarchs had had a hard struggle to gain and hold control of a large territory and to deal with a succession of internal and external crises. They triumphed with the help of an early systematization of taxation, a paid army, and a body of venal officials drawn out of the middle class, and used the resources of the monarchy to make dependents of more and more of the potentially dangerous. The noble clients of Versailles were largely parasitic unless they served in the army. The privileged noblesse de robe and other tax-exempt officials regarded their position as a hereditary freehold, and this made basic financial reform impossible under the ancien régime

In England the monarch had been too poor to possess a standing army or a paid administration. Recognizing this, the Tudors had developed the medieval institutions of the state, and secured the participation of the nobility and gentry in the work of government. The class structure was more flexible because there was no closed noble class; peers and gentry had differing interests, and younger sons of both became commoners – social mobility operated in both directions. Instead of a hereditary Parlement of lawyers forming the core of a new noblesse, in England Parliament was a legislature consisting of hereditary peers and an elected House of Commons, mainly of gentry. The local administration remained largely in the hands of the gentry; it was cheap and reasonably efficient, though it strengthened the feudal elements in society. Offices were rarely sold. Inheritance of political power was assured only to peers; others might expect it but had to compete for it; even those families which had gained virtual control of a seat in Parliament for a shire or a borough had seldom absolute security, and must usually interest themselves in the electors.

The weakness of the Stuart kings strengthened the aristocratic tendencies of English society. There is no parallel in France to the rise of vigorous new families of landowners such as the Russells, Cavendishes, and Cecils to social and political greatness; instead of Versailles, the great Whig country houses. But it was an open-ended aristocracy, and entry into it was not confined to officials and government financiers. Capitalist interests were very strong. London had greatly increased its commercial dominance in the sixteenth century. Unlike Paris it was the chief port and centre of overseas trade, and the English companies for controlling this trade, unlike the French, developed naturally and vigorously. The City of London was a great political power, and the voice of merchants in affairs became continually greater. The Civil War, if by no means the bourgeois revolution of the Marxist imagination, enormously increased the City's influence. Henceforth government in England had to be such that the merchants and bankers of London had confidence in it, and this necessitated a less arbitrary regime, financially reliable, alive to mercantile interests and overseas trade.

Such a regime was provided by William III after the Revolution of 1688. Already the great rebels Pym and Cromwell had provided a foretaste. Pym had given the government much greater resources than ever before by basic reforms in taxation, and Cromwell as a result had been able to possess armed forces which, in proportion to the population, were equal to anything that Louis XIV was able to develop until almost the end of the reign. Cromwell also produced the first national colonial policy, and Charles II maintained this interest. William III's triumph was a triumph for aristocratic rule through Parliament and the J.P.s, which he had to accept even though he resented it. But in one respect he had little to complain about. This Parliament of landowners increased the tax yield to over three times that of Charles II's reign, and the main new direct tax was a land tax which fell most heavily on themselves. Thanks to the genius of the Chancellor of the Exchequer Montagu, City finance was mobilized for the war by the creation of the Bank of England and the institution of a funded national debt.

Mousnier (in an article in the *Revue Historique*, Vol. 205) has contrasted the finances of England and France during the wars. He estimates the population of England in 1698 as 29 per cent that of France, but the revenue from taxes at 52–55 per cent. Direct taxes brought in a sum almost equal to those levied in

France. The disparity lessened during the later years of the Spanish Succession War, but eventually England had raised a far bigger proportion of the costs of the wars by taxation. According to Mousnier England's national debt at the end of the wars was only one-seventh of that of France.

Englishmen already believed, as both Hobbes and Locke emphasized, that government was made for man and not man for government, and they were proud of the demonstration of the rule of law in the trial of the Seven Bishops. The much freer English society with a weaker government apparatus was not only more progressive but in some surprising ways more efficient than the French. Unpaid commissioners organized the assessment and collection of the land tax at least as well as their official counterparts in France. Farming of customs and excise had been abandoned, and a department for direct collection worked much more efficiently than the tax-farmers in France, and incomparably better than the system of direct collection set up by Desmaretz. Great Britain, established by the English and Scottish Parliaments in 1707, was the largest free trade area in Europe.

It is extraordinary that the political disorder of Stuart times should have left Britain more strongly placed than France for the commercial and political conflicts of the eighteenth century. The more flexible society in which political debate had been continuous produced the outstanding works of political theory of Hobbes and Locke; Newton and Boyle with no help from the government placed English science in the forefront. Dissenters from the Established Church helped colonial development and played a big part in industry and commerce. Parliamentary monarchy and the rule of law fostered credit and stimulated progress more than the arbitrary bureaucracy of the Bourbons.

GLOSSARY OF FRENCH TERMS USED IN TEXT

ancien régime: form of government and society before the Revolution, particularly in the seventeenth and eighteenth centuries.

avocat-général: an official barrister representing the king's interest in the Parlement of Paris.

bailli: chief magistrate of a *bailliage* – purely nominal office by end of sixteenth century.

bailliage: unit of local government for justice and police, a section of a province.

bon français: in Louis XIII's reign an advocate of a strongly anti-Habsburg policy in Europe, making use of Protestant allies.

capitation: a graduated poll tax, the amount depending on the rank, not the wealth, of the taxpayer.

Cinq Grosses Fermes: an area of central and northern France made free of internal tariffs by Louis XIV.

Conseil d'en Haut: from 1643 the name of the small inner governing council, formerly sometimes called the *Conseil des Affaires*.

curé: parish priest.

dévot: a devout Catholic who applied religious criteria to political life.

dixième: the first French income tax based on a return by the taxpayer.

don gratuit: a grant to the king in lieu of tax (a) made by the clergy in their quinquennial assemblies, or (b) made by provincial Estates in order to retain the privilege of assessing their own direct taxes.

dragonnades: billeting of soldiers on Huguenots.

duc-et-paire: highest rank of nobility in France outside royal family.

écu: a silver coin of varying value in livres.

élu: an official appointed by the king to assess and collect the *taille* in one district (*élection*) of a *généralité*.

enclave: an isolated possession entirely surrounded by foreign territory.

gabelle: government salt monopoly, yielding a large revenue.

généralité: unit for financial administration, and later, under Louis XIV, for all local government.

gens de robe: a member of the legal profession.

grands jours: occasional assizes held in provinces by a commission of magistrates from the Parlement of Paris.

hôtel: large town house.

intendant: at first an itinerant inspector (formerly known as a *commissaire*) acting for the central government; later in the period of Richelieu often settled in one centre for a considerable period; during the reign of Louis XIV became the director of local administration in a *généralité,* with wide powers of control of finance, justice and police.

lettre de cachet: a sealed private order from the King, often used to imprison without trial.

lit de justice: a special session of the Parlement of Paris, presided over by the King, where he could order the registration of edicts.

livre (livre tournois): the monetary unit in France, but never a coin. Variable in value, but very roughly worth one fifteenth of the pound sterling of the period.

louis d'or: a gold coin first minted by Louis XIII, originally worth ten livres, but revalued at intervals.

maîtres des requêtes: high judicial officials attached to the King's Council, primarily to deal with petitions and to conduct inquiries.

Midi: The south of France.

ministériat: system of government with king and prime minister.

noblesse d'épée: the old feudal landowning nobility and gentry.

noblesse de robe: privileged order of officials of bourgeois origin established in seventeenth century. By acquiring landed estates and titles which went with them they gradually merged with *noblesse d'épée,* but had not yet been completely accepted as their equals in 1715.

nouveaux convertis: Protestants who became Catholics under the pressure of persecution, often only nominally.

officier: any office-holder under the government.

Parlement: the Parlement of Paris was a venerable supreme law court with some legislative and administrative functions, consisting of over two hundred magistrates split up into various bodies for its judicial work. Augmented on critical occasions by royal princes, *ducs-et-paires,* great ecclesiastics, and high officers of state to form a supreme assembly. With the extension of the French king's power, outlying regions had been given provincial Parlements.

parlementaire: a magistrate of a Parlement.

partisan: a member of a *parti,* or company of tax-farmers.

paulette: a tax of one sixtieth of the annual value of an office, in return for which it became saleable and hereditary.

pays d'élection: provinces where the *taille*, imposed as a round sum by the government, was assessed on parishes and individuals by the *élus*.

pays d'états: provinces with their own Estates, which paid a lump sum to the Treasury and assessed their own *taille* as a land tax.

philosophe: a thinker of the Age of Enlightenment in France.

politiques: Catholics who during the Wars of Religion in France worked for compromise in the national interest.

préciosité: tortuous style of writing and bizarre vocabulary affected by some salons and authors in the mid-seventeenth century.

procureur-général: the chief representative of the King in the Parlement of Paris, and the public prosecutor.

raison d'état: phrase first used by Richelieu to denote the doctrine that the interests of the state should come first.

régale: right of French king to administer bishoprics during vacancies and (a) enjoy the income – *régale temporelle*; (b) appoint to certain bishoprics within the gift of the bishop – *régale spirituelle*.

Religion Prétendue Reformée (R.P.R.): official title given by French government to Protestant Church in France.

rentes: investments in government stock disguised as shares in mortgages on official property such as the Hôtel de Ville in Paris.

rentier: a holder of *rentes* (today anyone who enjoys an unearned income).

robin: a member of the legal profession.

Roi Très Chrétien: a title of the King of France.

salon: a regular assemblage of intellectuals in the drawing-room of their hostess, for the discussion of ideas.

sénéchaussée: an alternative term in the Midi for the area elsewhere called a *bailliage*.

sub-délégué: a subordinate of the *intendant* in charge of a section of a *généralité*.

taille (tallage): the original French direct tax, from which those who owed military service – the nobles – were exempt, and also those who served by prayer – the clergy.

traitant: a tax-farmer.

trésoriers de France: financial officials in a *généralité* who had the tasks of allocating the *taille* among *élections* and supervising the work of the *élus*, the collection and the dispatch to Paris of the balance after local needs had been met. The *intendants* eventually took over their duties.

Index